Digital Games and Learning

Also available from Continuum

Homo Zappiens, Wim Veen & Ben Vrakking
Education and Technology, Neil Selwyn
Educational Potential of Computer Games, Simon Egenfeldt-Nielsen
New Technology and Education, Anthony Edwards

Digital Games and Learning

Edited by

Sara de Freitas and Paul Maharg

A companion website to accompany this book is available online at:
http://education.defreitas.continuumbooks.com

Please visit the link and register with us to receive your password and access these downloadable resources.

If you experience any problems accessing the resources, please contact Continuum at: info@continuumbooks.com

continuum

Continuum International Publishing Group

The Tower Building	80 Maiden Lane
11 York Road	Suite 704
London SE1 7NX	New York, NY 10038

www.continuumbooks.com

British Library Cataloguing-in-Publication Data
A catalogue record for this book is available from the British Library.

ISBN: 978-1-4411-9870-9 (paperback)
        978-0-8264-2137-1 (hardcover)

Library of Congress Cataloging-in-Publication Data
  Digital games and learning / edited by Sara de Freitas and Paul Maharg.
    p. cm.
  Includes bibliographical references.
  ISBN: 978-0-8264-2137-1 (hardback)
  ISBN: 978-1-4411-9870-9 (pbk.)
  1. Education–Computer-assisted instruction. 2. Computer games.
  3. Educational games. I. Freitas, Sara de. II. Maharg, Paul. III. Title.

LB1029.G3D535 2010
371.33'70285–dc22

                                                        2010023569

Typeset by Newgen Imaging Systems Pvt Ltd, Chennai, India
Printed and bound in India by Replika Press Pvt Ltd

This book is dedicated to our parents –
Mary Loretta and Charles William de Freitas,
Maureen and William Maharg.

Contents

Acknowledgements

All edited books owe their existence to a great number of people. While authors' debts are acknowledged at the end of individual chapters, the editors would like to acknowledge the kindnesses of those who helped to bring this text into being.

Many thanks for the inputs and support of the whole team at the Serious Games Institute at the University of Coventry. Special thanks to the Research Team for their inspiration and motivation throughout the writing of the book, in particular Dr Ian Dunwell for his comments and to Dr David Panzoli for crystallizing ideas in the book into graphical format. We are also grateful to the Universities of Strathclyde and Northumbria, who gave Paul time and freedom to work on the book. Various aspects of Chapter 1 were discussed by Paul in conversations and emails with Elisabeth Mertz, John Mayer and Richard Susskind, and he pestered members of the Learning Technologies Development Unit at Strathclyde Law School (Scott Walker and Michael Hughes in particular) – thanks to all for their time in the midst of very busy lives. Ideas were discussed at various conferences, particularly State of Play, ALT-C, IEEE and Virtual Worlds Conferences – our thanks to participants whose discussions helped to refine our ideas . . .

Our thanks to Emma Nicol, our research assistant in the early stages of the book, whose work on the book wiki was invaluable. To the reviewers of the original book proposal we are grateful for their acute comments, from which we benefitted much. We are most grateful to Jill Jamieson for the introductions to Continuum, and also to our ever-helpful editorial team at Continuum, Alison Clark and Ania Leslie-Wujastyk. Finally our authors from whom we commissioned pieces, who wrote well to deadlines and on topic (what more can editors ask) – to them our grateful thanks for their patience in seeing through the project to its conclusion.

The editors owe a more personal debt to our families, for the time we have spent working on this book that ought to have been spent with them. Finally we both dedicate the book to our parents, living and dead – the example of their lives and works have been patterns for us in our own lives.

Notes on Contributors

Karen Barton is Co-Director of Professional Practice Courses at the Centre for Professional Legal Studies in the University of Strathclyde Law School. She is currently working on a number of innovative teaching and learning projects involving transactional, web-based simulations as well as multimedia and webcast environments. Her more general interest in professional education and training is reflected in her involvement in two leading edge projects: *The Standardised Client Project*; and the *e-Portfolio Pilot Project* involving law students, trainees and trainers within a number of Scottish legal firms, and she is author of a number of articles and book chapters in these areas.

Francesco Bellotti received his M.Sc. (summa cum laude) and Ph. D. in Electronics Engineering from the University of Genoa in 1997 and 2001, respectively. He is Assistant Professor at the University of Genova, Dept. of Electronics and Biophysical Engineering (UNIGE), where he teaches Object Oriented Programming and Databases. His research interests include Serious Games, Artificial Intelligence and Human-Computer Interaction. He has authored more than 100 papers on these themes. With the ELIOS Lab, he participated in 11 EU-funded industrial research projects in the fields of new media and Human-Machine interaction. In these projects he was responsible for proposal preparation, design and implementation; and he was also involved in project management.

Riccardo Berta received his M.Sc. and Ph. D. degree in Electronics Engineering from the University of Genoa in 1999 and 2003, respectively. He is a research fellow at the University of Genova, Dept. of Electronics and Biophysical Engineering (UNIGE), where he teaches Multimedia Digital Entertainment. His research interests include Serious Games, Artificial Intelligence for games and Human-Computer Interaction with mobile devices. He has authored more than 50 papers on these themes. With the ELIOS Lab, he participated in several EU-funded industrial research projects in the fields of Cultural Heritage, Serious Games and Human-Machine interaction, where he was responsible for project proposals, design and implementation.

Sara de Freitas is Director of Research at the Serious Games Institute at the University of Coventry where she leads an applied research team working closely with industry. Recently appointed Professor of Virtual Environments she holds a visiting senior research fellowship at the London Knowledge Lab, London, and is a Fellow of the Royal Society of Arts.

In 2003 Sara founded (and continues to Chair) the UK Lab Group, which brings the research and development community together to create stronger links between industrial and academic research through supporting collaborative programmes and for showcasing innovative R&D solutions for the knowledge economy. Voted the Most Influential Woman in Technology 2009 by US Fast Company, Sara chaired the IEEE Serious Games and Virtual Worlds conference in 2009, and is a regular speaker at international conferences. Sara currently holds funding from the Advantage West Midlands, Erasmus Scheme, European Regional Development Fund, European Union and the Technology Strategy Board. Her current lines of research are examining multimodal interfaces, experience design and perceptual modelling in games and virtual worlds. Sara publishes widely in the areas of: pedagogy and e-learning; change management and strategy development for implementing e-learning systems and serious games and virtual worlds for supporting training and learning.

Alessandro De Gloria has, since 2000, been Academic Director of the Bachelors and the Masters degrees in Electronic Engineering at the University of Genoa. He is one of the founders of the University of Genoa's new (2009) interdisciplinary People Inspired Technologies (PIT) Center, which aims to fuse competences and skills from multiple fields in order to put the human person at the centre of the design and development of new products and services. His main research interests are in the field of Computer Graphics, Computing Technologies for the Cultural Heritage, Virtual Reality, Serious Games and Virtual Worlds. He has been responsible for more than 30 research projects in the last 10 years. He is the coordinator of the GaLA EU Network of Excellence on Serious Games in Technology Enhanced learning, that will start in September 2010. He has authored more than 150 papers in international journals and conferences. He has organized the Workshop on Serious Games and Cultural Heritage (SeGaCH), Virtual Reality Archeology and Cultural Heritage (VAST 2008, Braga), Virtual Systems and Multimedia (VSMM 2009, Vienna) and Web 3D Games, in 2007. He coordinated the realization of three Serious Games for the Regional Government and one Virtual World and a Virtual World Support Platform in the Travel in Europe Project under the Culture Programme EU Project.

Michele Dickey is an associate professor in *Instructional Design & Technology* (IDT) at Miami University. She also holds a joint appointment with the *Armstrong Institute of Interactive Media Studies* (AIMS) at *Miami University*. She currently serves as programme coordinator for the graduate programme in IDT and teaches graduate courses for IDT as well as teaching game design and 3D modelling and animation for AIMS. Her research interests include the design of interactive and game-based virtual learning environments. Much of her research has appeared in such journals, *Educational Technology Research & Development* and the *British Journal of Educational Technology*. Currently her work focuses on how various techniques, conventions and elements in popular computer and video games impact cognition and how these elements can be integrated into instructional design.

Ian Dunwell is a postdoctoral researcher at the Serious Games Institute, currently leading the area of games for health. Having obtained his Ph. D. in Computer Science from the University of Hull, he also holds a degree in Physics from Imperial College London, and is an Associate of the Royal College of Science. His research interests lie primarily in the application of an understanding of cognitive processes within virtual environments as a means for providing optimized and effective learning experiences to users, and the use and evaluation of novel HCI interface technologies (such as the NeuroSky and Emotiv headsets) to enable more meaningful and affect-based interactions between humans and machines. In the domain of serious games, he has consulted with a number of leading serious game companies including Blitz Games and PlayGen to design and develop evaluation strategies for serious games such as Patient Rescue, Ward Off Infection, i-Seed and Parent Know-How, and worked extensively with games aimed at reaching difficult demographics as well as changing the affect and motivation of learners. European-funded project involvement has included defining the overarching pedagogic design for serious games within the European-Union funded e-Vita (European Life Experiences) project, and preliminary design work towards the repurposing of medical learning objects within the mEducator consortium.

Keri Facer is Professor of Education at Manchester Metropolitan University where she leads the Create Research Group specializing in emergent technologies, digital cultures and educational change. From 2007–2009 Keri led the UK Government's Beyond Current Horizons Programme tasked with building a set of long-term scenarios for education in the context of socio-technical change. From 2002–2008 Keri was Research Director at Futurelab and, before that, lecturer and researcher at Bristol University. Her research projects range from leadership of over 30 innovative prototypes for learning environments, to large-scale curriculum change projects (such as Enquiring Minds and Teaching with Games) to ethnographic studies of informal uses of technology (ScreenPlay), to formative evaluations of educational change models (the RSA's Area-Based Curriculum). Keri has published widely in education and digital cultures, and acts as advisor to a diverse range of public, third sector and commercial organizations in order to promote educational change in the interests of social justice.

Russell Francis is a Research Fellow at Oxford University's Department of Education and formerly worked as a visiting colleague and post-doctoral associate at MIT's Comparative Media Studies. As a research student he investigated the relationships between learning, motivation and play in digital subcultures and became involved with the serious games movement before moving on to investigate students' informal use of social and participatory media. His first book, *Decentring the Traditional University: the future of (self) education in virtually figured worlds* (Routledge, 2010) develops insights developed by sociocultural theorists, media theorists and game theorists to explore how advanced students are learning through serious play in quasi-virtual contexts of their own figuration.

David Gibson is Associate Research Professor of Education at Arizona State University and directs the Continuous Improvement efforts of the Equity Alliance (http://www.equityallianceatasu.org/). Dr Gibson's research and publications include work on complex systems analysis and modelling of education, Web applications and the future of learning, the use of technology to personalize education and the potential for games and simulation-based learning. He founded The Global Challenge Award (www.globalchallengeaward.org), a team and project-based learning and scholarship programme for high-school students that engages small teams in studying science, technology, engineering and mathematics in order to solve global problems. He is creator of simSchool (www.simschool.org), a classroom flight simulator for training teachers, currently funded by the US Department of Education FIPSE program and eFolio, an online performance assessment system. His business, CURVESHIFT, is an educational technology company (www.curveshift.com) that assists in the acquisition, implementation and continuing design of games and simulations, e-portfolio systems, data-driven decision-making tools and emerging technologies.

Steve Jarvis is a Learning Consultant for SELEX Systems Integration Limited. He has nearly 20 years' experience of specifying and designing training solutions. He has been involved in innovative solutions involving performance support, mobile learning and serious games. He has had a diverse career that has included roles as software engineer, technical training manager and instructional designer. Steve has recently led research into serious games as part of a £2M project part-funded by the Technology Strategy Board (formally the Department of Trade and Industry), which had the aim of determining how serious games should be used to best satisfy training and learning needs.

Eric Klopfer is Associate Professor and the Director of the MIT Scheller Teacher Education Program (http://education.mit.edu) and the Director of the The Education Arcade (http://educationarcade.org). His research focuses on the development and use of computer games and simulations for building understanding of science and complex systems. His work combines research and development of games and simulations, from initial conceptualization, through implementation, piloting, professional development and end-user research. He is the creator of StarLogo TNG, a platform for helping kids create 3D simulations and games using a graphical programming language, as well as several mobile game platforms including location-based Augmented Reality games, and ubiquitous casual games. He is the author of 'Augmented Learning', a new book on handheld games and learning from MIT Press, and is co-author of the book, 'Adventures in Modeling: Exploring Complex, Dynamic Systems with StarLogo.' He is a founding member of the Learning Games Network (www.learninggamesnetwork.org).

Dr Esther MacCallum-Stewart is an Associate Lecturer at the University of Chichester in the department of Media and Media Production, and a Postgraduate Research Fellow in gaming and interactive media at SMARTlab, the University of East London. Her work examines the relationship between narratives and players in online worlds, in particular in online games and communities. She has published extensively on the ways in which players understand themselves in this context, as well as articles on gender and gaming, the representation of warfare in narrative, and griefing in online communities. She is Vice President of the Digital Games Research Association (DiGRA) and is currently editing a forthcoming book on *Lord of the Rings Online*, with Tanya Kryzwinska and Justin Parsler. Her academic profile and selected publications are available at http://chi.academia.edu/EstherMacCallumStewart

Patricia McKellar is the Senior Learning and Teaching Advisor at the UK Centre for Legal Education (UKCLE), situated within the Higher Education Academy, where she supports and develops teaching and learning projects in legal education across the UK. She identifies, manages, advises on and mentors projects funded by UKCLE and works with colleagues throughout the UK in developing project ideas. She also co-ordinates UKCLE's web-based services and materials on e-learning. Prior to this, as Senior Lecturer in Legal Practice at the Glasgow Graduate School of Law (GGSL) based at the University of Strathclyde, she developed a number of new e-learning initiatives, most notably e-lectures contained in a suite of applications embedded in the VLE and designed innovative learning applications for the simulation learning environment used in the professional legal training course. She has been a key member of the teams that created SIMPLE (www.simplecommunity.org) and Simshare (www.simshare.org.uk). She is a member of the executive committee of BILETA (http://www.bileta.ac.uk) and the steering group of the Blended Learning Unit, University of Hertfordshire. She has published widely in the area of legal education and legal practice and regularly gives papers at conferences, workshops and seminars.

Paul Maharg is Professor of Legal Education in the School of Law, University of Northumbria and director of a legal educational centre there. Prior to this he was a Professor of Law in the Glasgow Graduate School (GGSL), University of Strathclyde where he was Director of the innovative Learning Technologies Development Unit at the GGSL, as well as Director of the two-year, JISC/UKCLE-funded project, SIMPLE (SIMulated Professional Learning Environment (http://simplecommunity.org). He is the author of *Transforming Legal Education: Learning and Teaching the Law in the Early Twenty-first Century* (2007, Ashgate Publishing, www.transforming.org.uk), and has published widely in the fields of legal education and professional learning design (http://ssrn.com/author=272987). His specialisms include interdisciplinary educational design, and the use of digital simulations. He was recently appointed a Senior Fellow of the Higher Education Academy, and a Fellow of the RSA (www.thersa.org). He blogs at http://zeugma.typepad.com.

Scot Osterweil is the Creative Director of the Education Arcade (www.educationarcade.org), and a research director in the MIT Comparative Media Studies Program. He is a designer of educational games, working in both academic and commercial environments, and his work has focused on what is authentically playful in challenging academic subjects. He has designed games for computers, handheld devices, and multi-player on-line environments. He is a creator of the acclaimed *Zoombinis* series of math and logic games, and leads a number of projects in the Education Arcade, including *The MIT/Smithsonian Curated Game* (environmental science), *Labyrinth* (math), *Kids Survey Network* (data and statistics), *Caduceus* (medical science), *iCue* (history and civics) and the Hewlett Foundation's *Open Language Learning Initiative* (ESL). He is a founding member of the Learning Games Network (www.learninggamesnetwork.org).

Giulia Panizza received her Master in Humanities from the University of Genoa. Her research interests include Art history and industrial archaeology, where she also studied the German masterpiece Langer Heinrich giant maritime crane. She participated in the Travel in Europe project (Serious Games for Cultural Heritage) as the co-coordinator of the cultural content collection team involving partners from 15 countries.

Nathan J. Patterson is a Research Associate with the Education Research and Development Group (ERDG) at the Morgridge Institute for Research, a group that is focusing on creating engaging and entertaining educational games that utilize the expertise and scientific models from researchers at the Morgridge Institute and the University of Wisconsin – Madison. He is the lead game designer and developer for the ERDG and is working on interfacing agent-based modelling techniques, high-throughput computing resources and complex player behavioural analyses with game design. Dr Patterson received his Ph. D. in Mechanical Engineering from Purdue University, where he became an expert user of Condor, the world's leading high-throughput computing platform, a certified Radio Frequency Identification technician, and received a specialization in Computational Engineering. He used a combination of systems modelling, agent-based modelling and programming, machine learning techniques and nonlinear dynamics analyses to draw conclusions, within his dissertation, on a high-order nonlinear socio-technical system, the Beer Distribution Game.

Matteo Pellegrino received his M.Sc. in Computer Engineering and Ph. D. in Electronics Engineering from the University of Genoa in 2010. He currently works in the Testaluna game software house. He has been software designer and developer in the Travel in Europe and Enhanced Learning Unlimited EU projects, co-authoring several papers on peer-reviewed scientific journals and conferences.

Ludovica Primavera received her Master in Psychology from the University of Padua in 2004 and Ph. D. in Electronics Engineering from the University of Genoa in 2009. Her interests mainly concern cognitive psychology and personal development. She participated in the Travel in Europe project (Serious Game for the cultural heritage) as the co-coordinator of the cultural content collection team involving partners from 15 countries. She also participated in the design and user testing and evaluation of several Serious Game projects. She has co-authored more than a dozen papers in peer-reviewed scientific journals and conferences.

Richard Sandford is a Senior Researcher at Futurelab, an independent not-for-profit organization dedicated to transforming teaching and learning. He is currently based in Singapore, working with the Media Development Authority and Republic Polytechnic to develop and evaluate computer games to support learning. Previously, he led the research scenario development phases of the Beyond Current Horizons programme, a DCSF-funded foresight programme investigating possible educational futures and their implications for current policy and practice. His research focuses on mobility, play and digital games and how these relate to learning.

Kurt Squire is an Associate Professor in the Department of Curriculum & Instruction within the School of Education at the University of Wisconsin – Madison and is an Associate Director of the Education Research and Development Group at the Wisconsin Institutes for Discovery. He co-founded the Games, Learning, and Society (GLS) Initiative at the University and the Games, Learning, and Society Conference. Prior to his position at the UW-Madison, Dr Squire was a research manager and visiting scholar in the Department of

Comparative Media Studies at the Massachusetts Institute of Technology, an associate instructor at Indiana University – Bloomington, and a teacher at the McGuffey Foundation School in Oxford, OH. Dr Squire has also received a National Science Foundation CAREER grant on scientific civic literacy, assessment, and games, is a developer of an augmented reality game engine, and is the vice president of the Learning Games Network.

Ben Williamson is a Senior Researcher at Futurelab and a Research Fellow at the University of Exeter. His research focuses on curriculum innovation related to ICT in schools, on the role of videogames and creative software in young people's social and educational experiences, and on the development of young people's digital media literacy. Ben's recent publications have focused on the use of videogames in school, curriculum innovation, teacher professional development and children's science-fiction literature. Ben also has a Ph. D. in American literature, critical theory and pragmatist philosophy.

Foreword

Henry Jenkins

Several years ago, I attended a conference in Shanghai that brought together leading American and Chinese thinkers about games and learning. The event's organizers asked us to share what we saw as best practices from our respective countries. The Chinese game designers proudly displayed games that included historically accurate and precisely realized recreations of historical villages and cities from pre-twentieth-century China. They have filled these historical recreations with artefacts replicated from cultural museums or used them as settings to re-enact cultural rituals, such as wedding ceremonies. Many of the games were based on classical Chinese literature, especially Three Kingdoms. When asked about what players did in those games, they shrugged. The player was an observer, not a participant. The games were elaborate field trips.

By contrast, the games Americans shared were much more stylized, either because they consciously embraced strategies of abstraction or because they lacked the budget available to industrial titles or the government funding of our Chinese counterparts. The American games, on the other hand, emphasized the learning process as shaped far more by the game mechanics than by what was represented on the screen. Americans were embracing play as experimentation and improvisation: students learn by doing.

As someone who has been part of the push for games and learning from early on, through the work that I did with Kurt Squire, Eric Klopfer, Alex Chisholm and others on MIT's Game to Teach and Education Arcade initiatives, this conference was transformative for me. Early on, we were doing thought experiments, mocking up demos, modding existing games, doing anything we could to try to demonstrate to funding sources that games could be used to enable learning.

Now, we were at an international conference where we could see a range of different models of how games were being used to teach inside and outside of the classroom. Yet, it was also clear that literally and figuratively we were not speaking the same language. The models which we were embracing suggested the cultural specificity of those conversations, the degree to which the question of what makes a good educational game can not be separated from the larger question of what does learning look like, what kinds of pedagogical and social models are we bringing to the conversation, or for that matter, what we see as valuable to pass along across generations. We could spend a long time dissecting why the Chinese participants saw learning games as elaborate representations to be evaluated on the basis of their content's accuracy and detail, while the Americans saw learning games as stylized simulations to be evaluated on the learning activities they enabled. Somewhere, we would boil down to notions of education inspired by Confucious or Dewey.

The gap between the Chinese and American designers, though, simply represents an extreme version of the debates that occur whenever people gather to discuss serious and educational games research. The battle lines get drawn around different issues. One axis would certainly deal with a split between the game designer's focus on play, performance, design, as processes of thought and social interaction vs. the educator's concern with simulation and visualization as means of representing content. For one group, the focus is on making meaning, while for the second, the focus is often on conveying information. Of course, to be fair, we might also see splits between educators in terms of the reliance on what Paulo Freire called a 'banking model' of learning based on the deposit of content and a model of learning based on open-ended inquiry. At one time, games were only capable of drill and practice and educators wanted them to do more. Now games can do much much more but schools are caught in regimes that emphasize drill and practice for standardized testing.

But, the divides don't stop there. Games and learning are bound to larger debates about learning ecologies. Most of us who have had a learning experience with games that was meaningful encountered the game outside the classroom, often as part of our recreational life, and we were struck by how much more fun it was to learn through a game than through a homework assignment. Yet, we are discovering it is far from simple to move games from the realm of informal learning into the formal classroom since the institutional practices of schools impose their own constraints on these activities and in some cases, crush the play out of the game.

The cynic wants to ask whether games stop being fun when they enter schools. Jerry Farber used to say that if schools taught sex the way they taught literature, the human race would die out in a generation. (For those who doubt, watch *Monty Python's The Meaning of Life* for a vivid illustration of how schooling culture might suck the pleasure and fascination out of human reproductive practice.) Part of this has to do with a perceived tension between work and play, learning and pleasure, which seems a fundamental legacy of the puritan work ethic.

I can't tell you how many times I've heard educators reassert the importance of learning things when they are boring, because life is not always playful. Actually, I've never seen games as easy or purely 'fun' experiences. Games can make learning harder not easier in that they support the mastery of more difficult content; games can and often are boring as we repeat activities in the process of mastering them. But games are engaging in so far as they have clearly defined goals, roles and rules that motivate our action and in so far as they encourage us to apply what we know to solve specific immediate problems and challenges. And when I am learning something to me that matters, I am also engaged.

The educators, who defend the importance of boring classes, are policing the boundaries between games and schooling from one side, while gamers are often hostile to bringing games into schools because they object to the potential threat that schools may operationalize or police pleasure. In this view, games are fun precisely because they are not work, not assigned responsibilities, but freely chosen irresponsibilities. These two attitudes are simply two sides of the same coin. Work and play shouldn't be mixed, both sides are arguing, one protecting work from being contaminated by play, the other protecting play from being infected with work.

All of this, of course, builds into another core issue – whether we should bring games produced for entertainment purposes into the classroom and build the education around them or whether we should create games specifically to serve educational purposes. Will Wright, the designer behind *Sim City*, *The Sims*, and *Spore*, once told me that his games support a diverse range of different kinds of learning because they are by design multidisciplinary and allow each player to pursue their own interests as deep as they want to go. By contrast, he said, the first thing schools would do with games was to match them to specific school disciplines and learning goals in ways that would constrain the range of possible learning outcomes. So, the question of commercial games or educational games for learning purposes circles back to the question of specified vs. open-ended outcomes, of disciplined and undisciplined approaches to knowledge.

Each of these debates is worth having – not once but many times – because they speak to the core issues about the unstable and contradictory relationship between games and learning. In this book, you will see smart, caring, engaged, researchers who come at these questions – and many others – from different perspectives. This reflects the healthy status of this field of investigation. We have moved decisively from the original question of can games teach to a richer set of questions about what kinds of games and gaming culture will support particular kinds of learning best under particular circumstances. These questions need to be asked across a range of contexts – across different game genres, across different subject domains, across different grade levels, across different parts of the learning ecology and across different national contexts. *Digital Games and Learning* represents a valuable snapshot of the current state of the field, one which builds on more than a decade of research on games-based learning, one which brings together both veterans and newcomers, one which is sure to spark more debates. And so it goes.

Introduction: Digital Games and Learning

Sara de Freitas and Paul Maharg

Chapter Outline

Background to the book

The rapid emergence of game-based learning over the last ten years has been stimulated at least in part by the emergence and pervasiveness of entertainment gaming. Since the earliest digital entertainment games such as *Pong* and *Space Invaders*, many children and adults have been captivated by gaming genres from puzzle games to driving and flying games to first-person shooters. More recently, the pervasiveness of broadband and the modern PC have led to multiplayer games, such as *World of Warcraft*, attracting 11.5 million players globally to date (November 2009), and where players inhabit complex and engaging immersive worlds. The opportunities for social games through *Facebook* and casual games, such as the *Wii Fit* have opened up gaming to new markets, and today women and girls as well as older gamers pervade the online games forums and contribute to the substantial revenues of entertainment gaming.

This phenomenon has more recently sparked interest in harnessing the power of gaming for non-entertainment purposes, such as training and business support. The emergence of the serious games movement in the USA and later in the UK has capitalized on this interest in leisure gaming and helped to spread applications from the home into schools, colleges, universities and out into professional training and continuing professional development. Many questions arise from this use of gaming technologies in new learning contexts, such as how can gaming technologies be used to engage learners? How can games be used to motivate and accelerate learning? What are the main strengths of games for learning?

A number of these questions are similar to those that drove the use of simulations in training over the last thirty to forty years, and unsurprisingly many of the questions around how to use games have been already considered in that context. However, simulations and games, while having much in common, developed using divergent technologies. An additional divergent issue was the requirement for simulations to have some referent to reality. By contrast, games can be entirely fantasy, or they can be grounded in real-world performance. The two forms have evolved separately, and as such have different design parameters and pedagogic purposes. It is not surprising therefore that games present educators and learners with a different set of constraints and opportunities. Games have certain strengths: they have been associated with increased motivation, engagement, accelerated learning, targeting of specific groups and in particular the targeting of otherwise hard-to-reach social groupings. But games are also more inherently rule-based and structured, where by contrast simulations can be much more free-form and exploratory. For example, feedback in games tends to be instant, while in simulations feedback can be deliberately delayed or dealt with in debrief.

However the comparison of games vs. simulations can never be neat and clear, and with the emergence of virtual worlds the re-convergence of games and simulations is possible, and in many ways desirable, if more effective learning results. Immersive environments and worlds, such as *Second Life* and *Active Worlds*, can be more open-ended than games traditionally are, although developed using the same underlying technologies, for example games engines. This book therefore includes discussions and examples of both games and simulations.

If definitions of digital games present the avid researcher and couch-bound game players with quite a few headaches, the research domain of the newly emerging field has greater challenges when we take into account the actual digital games for learning that have emerged already in nearly every sector and almost every disciplinal area. Reflecting this, the research literature is spread across all sectors, including business, military, medical and education sectors. Many disciplines, including, health, psychology, educational research, computer science and art and design have explored the use of educational games as solutions to their particular training problems and challenges.

To address these challenges, conferences dedicated to games and learning have emerged, communities have developed over the last five years in the USA and Europe, as well as research institutes, all dedicated to exploring the use of the games technologies in different areas of activity. Companies developing serious games content have been started and publishers and e-learning content producers have developed innovative new content. Although uncertain of markets and routes to markets, these content producers are generally experiencing more demand than they can supply.

In addition, the social impact of gaming and in particular the putative benefits of serious and educational games pose interesting questions for society, policy-makers, further and higher education and parents and teachers. How can these forms be harnessed for educational purposes? Will game-based learning replace traditional learning? How can we better design educational games? Will games for learning become as pervasive as games for entertainment?

While we do not aim to answer all of these questions in one volume, this book does attempt to bring together some of the range of leading edge knowledge currently available in the USA and Europe, in terms of selected theories, practice and applications of game-based learning. No single volume can be completely comprehensive in the field, due to its wide inter- and cross-disciplinary engagement, so we have brought together some of the leading researchers in the field to address some of the many unresolved research and practice-based questions as a starting point for future investigations. The volume therefore provides a state-of-the-art contribution, in terms of leading-edge thinking in the field, and is a step towards bringing together some of the diverse voices reflecting different sectors, disciplines and approaches to the concepts and applications of games and simulations for learning.

Structure and outline of the book

The structure of the book centres upon a key claim that games and simulations have the potential to have a significant impact upon learning in our societies. In considering this claim, and with a view to bringing together the diverse voices in the field, the book is divided into three main sections: theoretical positions upon games (*theoria*), cultural perspectives upon games (*cultura*) and theory into practice approaches (*praxis*). Reflecting some of the key challenges of designing, implementing and analysing effective game-based learning approaches, theoretical positions will provide a bedrock for the analysis and evaluation of games, inform the design parameters of games design and highlight the critical challenges for game-based and simulation-based approaches. In this way, the book begins by first presenting some of the theoretical bases for the efficacy of game-based learning approaches, also borrowing from existing theory that supports simulations. Cultural perspectives upon games will provide scope for considering individual case studies in relation to cultural shifts and changes in the wider context of the institutions and places of learning. The second section then explores the cultural perspectives upon games with case studies exemplifying how games are being used in schools and to support informal learning. Practice-centred approaches include case studies in relation to the implications for the practices of learning and teaching that exhibit greater sensitivity to the impact of game-based learning upon learning communities and teaching practitioners more directly. The third section then provides examples from practice to illustrate how all areas of formal and informal learning can utilize elements of game-based and simulation approaches.

The three-section division is an integral part of our argument in this volume. Games and simulations, when taken seriously by educators, nearly always involve a re-appraisal of the elements of theory, culture and practice; and we would argue that successful implementations nearly always involve re-considerations of the three domains. The extent of this re-appraisal depends, of course, on a number of pre-existing factors – teachers' and students' openness to change, the extent of the game implementation, the extent to which the contextual curriculum and its physical environment can be altered and so forth. It also depends on the extent of the implementation under consideration. Small-scale games and simulations (i.e. small in terms of time, effort to construct and play) can be easily accommodated within other more conventional pedagogic approaches. But like other forms of pedagogic innovation such as problem-based learning, when games and simulations are implemented on a significant scale they often challenge accepted theories of learning, institutional cultures of learning, teaching and assessment, and even the physical practices of teaching and learning in classrooms, lecture-halls, labs, seminar rooms, examination halls and libraries. In this context they can become disruptive learning technologies.

Theoria

In the theoretical section, the authors explore varied considerations upon the central claim that games and simulations have the potential to substantially alter learning. The first chapter by Sara de Freitas and Paul Maharg outlines a vision of the use of games for learning as an opportunity to revisit core thinking around 'learning as experience'. Learning in this reading is no longer considered as knowledge acquisition-centred but rather as centred upon social interactions, active engagement and knowledge construction. Building upon this notion, the chapter considers learning as transactions and tutoring as being centred rather upon 'choreography' or orchestration of immersive experiences, providing greater scope for *social interactive learning*. The chapter outlines a vision and an approach to achieving the vision via combining different theoretical work, including 'play as *diegesis*', learning as transaction and signature pedagogies. Bringing these notions together, the chapter provides an interplay of some of the core aspects in need of integration: play, immersive experiences, pedagogy and social interactions.

Building upon these concepts, the second chapter by Ian Dunwell, Sara de Freitas and Steve Jarvis explores one of the core strengths of game-based learning according to new research that outlines the importance and centrality of feedback. Based upon the four dimensional framework, the authors posit a new approach for understanding facilitative feedback in relation to specified game design parameters and game principles. Research arising from recent studies indicates how central feedback is for the efficacy of game-based learning approaches, and as such how important it is to the educational game design process. The chapter indicates how feedback can be integrated and designed into the learning game, and sets out a new approach to considering how feedback can be designed and evaluated.

In Chapter 3, the theoretical ground for simulations is considered through the development of a complex systems model. Here, David Gibson explores the extent to which classroom teaching can be taught using simulations underpinned by the generics of a complex systems model sensitive to the complexities inherent in learning and teaching. *simSchool*, a network-based training and assessment application for teachers, offers a game-like computational framework that represents the actions and dynamics of classroom teaching and learning. The online simulator offers teachers transferable practice in key instructional planning, diagnostic and interpersonal communication activities involved in teaching in a classroom environment. Gibson generalizes the *simSchool* framework into concepts needed for a complex systems model of teaching and learning, providing initial answers to key questions about simulating the complex process of teaching and learning.

These first three chapters provide a theoretical context for exploring the deeper considerations of how learning pedagogies and learning design can be most readily integrated with games and simulation-based metaphors and approaches. The conceptual work provides a basis for building a more inter- and cross-disciplinary approach to game-based learning within which learning design with games can be considered, building also upon insights from simulation design and opening up new scope for improved learning design with games and games metaphors.

Cultura

Cultural perspectives upon digital games and learning are well represented in the book, with four chapters that provide an overview of how games and simulations can affect the culture of learning across a range of situations and applications.

Russell Francis' study, undertaken while he was based at MIT's Comparative Media Studies Lab, documents the power of role play and social interactive learning, providing a unique opportunity to assess the real strengths of gameplay in the context of formal and home-schooled learning. This work, in Chapter 4, outlines an experiment of using games with school children in the USA using a 'mod' or modified version of another game, *Neverwinter Nights*. For the study, researchers created a multiplayer history game called *Revolution*, and used it to explore the children's identification with 'real-life' figures from late-eighteenth-century Williamsburg just prior to the outbreak of the American War of Independence. The main cultural perspectives from the study highlighted lessons for tutors using games, emphasizing how important the role of storytelling is in terms of identification and learning. Through the shared storytelling exercises, young people gained valuable and personalized insights into the experiences of others. The player here is positioned as an actor and a spectator in an interactive cyber-drama, providing new scope and opportunities for supporting collaborative learning and teaching in the Humanities classroom.

The social interactions of learning are also highlighted in Chapter 5, where Esther MacCallum-Stewart documents sets of interactions through an analysis of multiplayer learning, in three separate case studies. The chapter makes the case for the concept of 'stealth learning' in entertainment rather than specific educational games, arguing that we need to understand better how these approaches may and can be fit into game-design for serious games. The chapter provides an interesting cultural approach to research, for the concept opens up perspectives on how some aspects of social learning take place in such games. MacCallum-Stewart's work here takes forward prior research in the forms that learning can take in online communities, for instance Bandura's concept of vicarious learning, as adapted by Lee et al. (1999) and others. She concludes that entertainment games can improve learning capabilities and suggests utilizing these defined benefits and strengths for creating more engaging learning in formal and curriculum-based contexts.

Focusing again on the design of games, Michele Dickey suggests in Chapter 6, a more structured approach to serious games design through her case study on *Murder on Grimm Isle*. The game-based learning environment allows Dickey to trace how research from game design, literature, behavioural psychology and animation studies can be brought together to better inform this design. Building in inter- and cross-disciplinary approaches within the design approach, sets a different agenda perhaps for future development, and begins an interesting debate perhaps upon how design strategies themselves could provide a touch point for greater cross-disciplinarity in learning. Building upon a significant body of previous work in this field, Dickey argues that a design culture composed of narrative, environmental design and interactive design strategies can facilitate learning, in this case supporting the development of better argumentation skills for grades 9–14 in language. Targeted learning in a game-based environment, as Chapters 4 and 5 also attest, is a successful strategy for learning, enriching the learning process and creating opportunities for new approaches to be developed.

The final chapter of this section, written by Scot Osterweil and Eric Klopfer from MIT, explores how games can engage players in learning that is specifically applicable to formal curriculum-based learning. It also considers how teachers can use game-based learning in such a way that formal learning and informal play outside of school are not affected adversely. In some ways,

Osterweil and Klopfer are arguing powerfully for using games in schools but do not think that this will necessarily create a paradigmatic shift of learning culture in schools. They argue for the role of play in learning and explain this power, embedded in four main freedoms, as the freedom to fail, the freedom to experiment, the freedom to fashion identities and the freedom of effort. Together, these freedoms connect to empower the learner. According to the authors the freedoms cross the cultural boundaries of formal and informal learning, free play and formalized learning. Their discussion of games, in particular how at first glance games seem at odds with the freedom of play vis-à-vis their rule-based constraints, is a subtle argument, highlighting as it does the paradox that within the structured game, players 'regularly exhibit all of the freedoms of unstructured play'.

Praxis

The third section contains more experiments and examples of practice than the other two; but what is intriguing about this section is the extent to which the examples themselves generate research. Nor is this research 'action research' alone, deriving from the practice of games. The relationship between action and theory is much more subtle. Squire and Shaffer have investigated this relation with regard to the work of Louis Pasteur, adducing Latour and actor-network-theory, and describing Pasteur's own practice as

> a series of levers by which problems and contexts were more deeply understood, tools and techniques were developed, and systems of practices were reorganized in light of the resulting process of inquiry. (Shaffer and Squire, 2006: 49)

From the editors' experiences of working with games and simulations and their practitioners, the concept of high theory handing down lessons to praxis to enact in the world is simply not what happens in actuality. Educational praxis itself is full of theory and to deny this is to shrink ever further the possible meanings of education. However, in this section we aim to explore the more practical applications of games and their impact upon learning communities and practitioners; and to explore case studies and examples that allow learners' voices to emerge from the research and design experiments.

Richard Sandford, Keri Facer and Ben Williamson present two recent survey studies that focus upon the educational praxis around using games in schools. Their chapter explores the ways in which teachers work to re-construct their professional identities in the light of a model; where tutors are largely 'invisible' in relation to usual gaming practices which often take place in informal settings, and where 'adult/teacher identity' is absent from the dominant accounts. In these informal gaming settings, there is no traditional 'pedagogue' and no formal curriculum that a teacher is responsible for delivering. Researchers, designers and enthusiastic teachers interested in bringing games into school are therefore, to some degree, attempting to bring into a teacher-centred setting a set of practices developed outside education in which the teacher has no role. This has real challenges for improving game-based learning and teaching practices, and to address this, the authors propose the adoption of a new set of professional identities for constructing more effective game-based approaches to be transferred into formal settings. They propose the 'teacher-as-designer' as one new identity used for recognizing the importance of the teacher in creating the environments in which students learn, thereby affirming their new visibilities in the complex exchanges of formal educational practices.

The voices of the learners are filtered in the chapter by Kurt Squire and Nathan Patterson where the authors consider the efficacy of game-based approaches, this time in the context of informal science education. Squire and Patterson outline a brief introduction of simulations and games in informal science education, which attempts to connect the research, theory and practical wisdom from education and entertainment games across a variety of contexts. Helpfully, the book chapter seeks to clarify some of the ambiguities between games and simulations; and with reference to games, including *Resilient Planet*, the chapter examines the research and theory on learning in structured informal learning environments, such as workshops and after-school programmes. The chapter also provides a framework for contrasting these structured informal learning environments with more formalized learning environments, such as school. As part of a comprehensive overview on learning with games, the chapter also reviews research on relatively unstructured learning environments, such as learning in the home or online, highlighting the opportunities and challenges for informal science education with games.

The chapter by Karen Barton and Patricia McKellar looks forward to a moment described by Gee where the 'line between education and entertainment is truly erased'. While the authors argue that this vision of the future has yet to be realized, in their chapter the authors consider what promise this prospect might hold for students, teachers and educational developers.

Building upon ten years of experience with designing and using computer-based simulations to help law students learn how to practise law in authentic situations, the team in Scotland has been able to extend the simulation duration and complexity, improve the interface and integrate the simulation within a blended learning environment. Some design principles and technologies that were initially applied have been adapted or abandoned while others have been reconstructed. The chapter provides evidence from this long experience and the chapter also presents a context of theoretical models from a range of fields, such as situated learning and constructivism that enabled them to create games and simulations as effective learning tools. As such, the simulations they describe are good examples of what Shaffer and colleagues have called 'epistemic games' (2005). The chapter also explores the culture of implementation of the simulation-based approaches, discussing the changed academic and training practices needed to support these new models and forms of learning and the use of these models in the teaching and learning of professionalism.

Finally, the chapter by Francesco Bellotti and colleagues based at the University of Genova in Italy focuses upon the widespread use of online virtual environments and related technologies for supporting game-based cultural heritage learning experiences. In particular, they survey the area of serious games arguing that the related technologies and applications are likely to open important new opportunities to enhance modalities of knowledge and interaction with virtual representations of cultural heritage. In particular they argue, given the possibility of creating compelling virtual adventures set in the context of artistic and natural places of interest, that the player and learner can now explore faithfully reconstructed places and live information-rich, contextualized experiences.

Bellotti and colleagues envisage a future where serious games represent a significant opportunity for learning, allowing for embedding high-quality contextualized information so that the players/learners can explore the virtual environment. The research team is developing new methodologies and tools for effective production, including developing a conceptual framework based upon task-based learning theory and authoring tools that allow users to interface with the virtual world and task-based content. The tools have so far been applied in cultural heritage contexts for supporting and enriching museum visits and trips to places of interest, and their game-based activities include a treasure hunt around art objects in some European cities.

Transformational possibility

The book's three sections therefore present a series of apparent paradoxes – theory-based chapters that draw on practice, practice-based chapters that create theory, culture-based chapters that explore theory and practice. How do they cohere as a whole? As we state above, our general argument is that games and simulations have the potential to improve not just learning but society also. For this to happen, successful implementations need to re-consider the three domains of theory, culture and praxis. But the three can rarely be treated in isolation: we need to examine how they interplay, one with the other. This problem is not new. Dewey and many others after him have advocated this approach. In 1970, the educationalist Joseph Schwab, for instance, warned against seeking foundational theories of education, instead advocating a 'polyfocal conspectus' that is a sophisticated convergence of theories and experience (Schwab, 1970, p. 4).

This has been the approach of the editors in the book. As a result, readers will find touch points, issues and controversies that are threaded through chapters in the different sections and upon which different chapters have different insights. An example of one such issue is the transfer of learning from one domain to the next and which, in one form or another, is touched on by almost every chapter – how does it happen? How can we best facilitate it? Another is the role of teachers in classes and teaching moments where games and sims are used. How do teachers teach differently in such contexts? How do games and sims change their roles? Gibson tackles this issue with the analysis of classroom dynamics embedded in *simSchool*; de Freitas and Maharg describe and analyse a mentoring moment in a simulation; Barton and McKellar discuss how a simulation can change the conventional role of a tutor, and the consequences that has for the rest of the curriculum, and Sandford, Facer and Williamson discuss two studies of teachers within the context of teachers' sense of identity and professional role.

Yet another issue common to most chapters is the concept of immersion – the extent to which game- and simulation-players are engaged in their play. Salen and Zimmerman (2004) describe this as an 'immersive fallacy' – 'the idea that the pleasure of a media experience lies in its ability to sensually transport the participant into an illusory, simulated reality' (2004, 450) – and as an extreme example of it they cite the Star Trek 'holodeck', an immersive reality experience involving matter and energy that is indistinguishable from reality. They critique the idea, following Bateson's concept of metacommunication (Bateson, 2000). They elaborate on Bolter and Grusin's fusion of immediacy (the representation of an alternate reality) and hypermediacy (the constructed technical environment of that representation) as *remediation*, where a form of immersive experience can occur, but where it is a much more complex and multi-layered experience than the directly immersive concept would imply.

The nature of that experience, the effect of context upon it, the way that the frame of game or simulation can powerfully mediate the experience of players – all these are issues that are explored in a number of chapters – MacCallum-Stewart for instance discusses how it affects 'stealth learning' in multiplayer online games; Francis describes the relations between player and adopted character in *Revolution,* and Barton and McKellar describe how the experience can be used in the play of professional identities and professionalism in SIMPLE simulations. The discussions raise intriguing questions about immersion that go beyond the simplistic idea of the holodeck. None in this book describe games or sims merely as simulacra, nor do they hold immersion as such a total experience that the frame of the game or simulation vanishes. For many, it is the tension between game/sim frame and experience that provides the real ground of learning.

Together the three sections highlight many themes, opportunities and challenges. For the editors the core arguments centre upon the efficacy of game-based learning, the authors' positions as advocates and early adopters of the new technologies and the position of learners in the new domain. Design of serious games and learning has been a central theme throughout the book, and approaches to design in Dickey's chapter, in Dunwell and colleagues' work, and indeed in most chapters provide a useful spine to the debate about game-based learning efficacy. Interestingly the agenda for games in schools has not suppressed the learners' own voices from emerging throughout the text. In particular in Part 2 the design approaches seem to centre much more upon the needs of learners than we have perhaps seen in other areas of e-learning development. What those needs are, and how the introduction of games can serve them in schools, colleges and universities is a hotly debated issue in the education sector as a whole. While the use of simulations in professional development contexts is well established and to some extent (in some professions more than others) it is embedded in practice, there are nonetheless many lessons to be learned in education. However, the imperative of engaging new learners and their use of new technologies is driving the implementation of games into everyday teaching practices.

This book has provided a chance to reflect upon the key challenges and opportunities of game-based learning, and has provided a great opportunity for assessing how effective game-based learning can be in the future. The authors collectively have spent many years assessing the impact of this approach to learning and it seems that at least from their perspectives that the benefits significantly outweigh the disadvantages. Game- and simulation-based learning will, we believe, shape and re-shape the education landscape over the next five to ten years, and it is hoped that some of the lessons and observations in this book will help to stimulate others to join all of us in this book in our exploration not just of the scholarship of conventional teaching and learning, but in the scholarship of transformational possibility that is represented by games and simulations.

How to use the book

While the three sections of the book are designed to complement one another, they are also designed to interest three main groups of readers. Researchers, policy-makers and managers may have more interest in the first section, which provides a theoretical basis for game-based learning. The second section may have more appeal for tutors and teachers who are looking to find case studies and examples where games have been designed and used with specific users, such as school children. The third section, containing more discussion of practical examples, may be useful for practitioners eager to use games in their disciplinary areas.

References

Bateson, G. (1972/2000). *Steps to an Ecology of Mind: Collected Essays in Anthropology, Psychiatry, Evolution and Epistemology.* Chicago: Chicago University Press.

Bolter, J. D. and Grusin, R. (1999). *Remediation: Understanding New Media.* Cambridge: MIT Press.

Lee, J., McKendree, J., Dineen, F. and Mayes, J. T. (1999). Learning vicariously in a distributed environment. *Active Learning,* Vol. 10, pp. 4–9.

Schwab, J. (1970). *The Practical: A Language for Curriculum.* Washington, DC: National Education Association.

Shaffer, D. W. and Squire, K. D. (2006). The pasteurization of education. In S. Y. Tettegah and R. C. Hunter, eds. *Technology and Education: Issues in Administration, Policy, and Application in K12 Schools,* Vol. 8, pp. 43–55. London: Elsevier.

Part 1
Theoria
Theoretical Positions

Digital Games and Learning: Modelling Learning Experiences in the Digital Age

1

Sara de Freitas and Paul Maharg

Chapter Outline

Introduction

The wide uptake and pervasiveness of leisure games, which over the last ten or so years has permeated all areas of society, has resulted in the emergence of a new paradigm whereby gaming and gaming technologies are having greater possible applications in non-entertainment contexts of use. A general tendency of games being used in non-entertainment contexts harks back to its earliest uses as war simulations, where military groups used games to mock up real battles thereby allowing them to prepare and rehearse skills in advance of active combat. Games and simulations for training even in these earliest instances offered real potential for rehearsal of skills of individuals and broader practice for coordinated actions in groups which, in more recent times, has given rise to initiatives such as Montessori games that have been described by at least part of the educational community as a highly effective form of learning. However, in the past these opportunities for learning through games were relatively rarefied and modern advances in technology and network connectivity are opening up more pervasive opportunities for using games for learning, to the extent that today game-based learning and simulation approaches can be used to re-organize the basic critical categories of learning in formal learning and professional training contexts.

The extent of this transformation might be considered, not just as tools for glossing conventional training and learning, but for setting up a substantially new paradigm, one where games for learning re-organize the critical constructs of learning from information and knowledge units that are sequenced for learners in curriculum formats, to *learning as experiences* and apprenticeships. This allows learning to be choreographed and re-sequenced according to the personalized and specified requirements of the learner. In this way, peer learning, self-assessment and game-based approaches can support social interactive learning opportunities, greater learner empowerment and user-generated content (de Freitas and Conole, 2010). If game-based learning does provide a real transition for learning in formal and professional learning contexts, what conceptual work can this be based upon, and how can this existing work be extended and developed? Towards understanding and building upon this shift, our chapter therefore explores and analyses some of the supporting conceptual work around game-based learning with respect to its application in formal and professional learning contexts. In other work, the locus of the posited transition seems to be the notion of a *learning experience*, rather than the creation and use of a set of linear texts. While the learning experience can encapsulate and include textual components, and can be linear in presentation, the critical construct of learning is rather about the learning experience *per se* (e.g. Kolb, 1984; de Freitas and Neumann, 2009).

More recently with the emergence of computers and internet technologies, new gaming and simulation formats, for example serious games, are transforming the potential of learning by providing scope for learning in different contexts, over great distances or for supplementing conventional teaching techniques. In addition, the wider availability of broadband has created new opportunities for online collaboration and social interactive learning, as well as supporting more media-rich content for streaming and interaction. Building upon more constructivist approaches, for example Kolb, 1984, one of us has elsewhere put forward the notion of learning components as changing towards a critical construct of 'learning as experience' (de Freitas and Neumann, 2009). The recasting of 'learning as experience' foregrounds two major areas for consideration: the role of social interactive learning (learning in groups) and the role of learning design (designing experiences rather than content).

These two areas present two major challenges: how do we support better opportunities for team learning and how do we provide and develop tools for facilitating tutor authoring of experience-based and exploratory learning scenarios and quests?

Many of the recent responses to these two challenges have come from what might be regarded as the training side of learning and education, especially in military training applications, such as *America's Army*, where game elements have been integrated into simulation-like formats for supporting deeper learning in particular of tasks and skills, and often consistent with more 'associative' modes of learning (Mayes and de Freitas, 2007). The success of these approaches has led to greater involvement of users, particularly in the social groupings so typical of multi-user virtual environments – MUVEs, and in parallel with larger numbers of learners playing games in their spare time, the appeal of game-based approaches in non-entertainment contexts has broadly increased.

The uptake of these approaches in training situations has been stimulated, at least partly, due to the imperative of effective training, but the expense of using these tools has led to its use in areas with larger user cohorts, for example the military. Larger numbers of learners have balanced the higher costs and technical knowledge previously required for running more complex simulations and game-based approaches. Thus in these contexts, training needs are matched by economic viability and rationalized due to the urgency of training needs. For example, medical training and surgical training are complex and are so critical that lives can be saved or lost on the basis of correct training. This necessitates the highest quality of training and simulations in this area. Indeed so sophisticated have the simulations become, in the field of pilot training for example, that simulations here are also used in post-incident analysis to investigate the probabilities of pilot decisions in particular situations. The classic case was the investigation of the ditching of US Airways Flight 1549 into the river Hudson in January 2009. Four simulated flights by experienced pilots of the exact conditions of the flight, with its complete loss of thrust soon after leaving La Guardia airport, confirmed that the pilot, Chesley Sullenberger, had indeed made the only choice of the three open to him at the time that would have saved all 155 passengers (Greenspun, 2010).

Sectorally then, the adoption of game-based technologies, and latterly virtual world technologies, has broadly followed similar uptake curves, often associated with higher imperatives for efficacy: military, medical, business and then later on education. The slowness of uptake of these approaches in primary, secondary and tertiary education is also partly due to the fragmental nature of education, training needs of teachers and tutors and a disconnect between research and teaching. Political aspects have also provided a general resistance to uptake of new technologies in formal learning environments, as several chapters in this book attest.

The use of games and especially simulations in high critical training contexts has provided an implicit endorsement of the innovative training techniques. However, these have not gone unchallenged and in the past the absence of empirical evidence to support the efficacy of game-based learning that is not close to real life, and more simulation-based approaches, has held up development and diffusion of the tools. What the development curve has indicated, though, is a predominance of usage in critical training areas and this has at least provided anecdotal evidence of the effectiveness of multimodal approaches to learning – that is, learning that appeals to more than one sense. Furthermore, the areas of motivation, engagement and empowerment of learners through feedback mechanisms indicate the power of immersive experiences for supporting accelerated learning and supporting ease of learning transfer (e.g. Griffiths and Guile, 1999; Jarvis and de Freitas, 2009). One of the reasons for this success may well be the proximity of training to the live application of that training, for example in emergency response, surgical training etc. Where training is closer to live practice then generally learning transfer tends to be smoother. Immersive learning techniques, including simulations and game-based approaches then have had more success in permeating professional learning, aiding with pre-work and with particular strengths for rehearsal and role plays (e.g. Haskell, 2001; Parush, Hamm and Shtub, 2002; Kato et al., 2008).

While the lack of empirical evidence and the cost of game-based approaches have in the past slowed the uptake of the technologies, more recently studies such as Jarvis and de Freitas, 2009 and Kato et al., 2008 have proven empirically the efficacy of game-based learning over conventional methods. This work has set new agendas for game-based learning and opened up new methods for assessing and evaluating games for learning (e.g. four-dimensional framework, de Freitas and Oliver, 2006; RETAIN framework, Gunter et al., 2008).

In summary, then, several aspects of the complex learning and training context are stimulating a wider uptake of game-based approaches: the reducing costs of developing game content, proof of efficacy of game-based learning for providing significant improvements over conventional learning methods, wider social use of games for entertainment and the wider deployment of the immersive learning techniques in critical training contexts. Together these factors lend support to the premise that game-based learning is a valid and tested approach for supporting formal learning approaches. However if we are to embed game-based learning into formal contexts of learning and into professional learning, two main challenges need to be considered. We need to investigate the role of social interactive learning and further analyze learning design in games. These two research directions can provide a broad research framework for exploring the main strengths of game-based learning and may help to overcome some of the residual impediments to uptake, particularly in mainstream formal learning contexts, such as school and university.

Despite the pervasiveness of entertainment games among young people, broadly speaking, it would probably be fair to say that academic institutions have been reluctant to take up the new tools due to the reasons outlined above. Furthermore, where game-based approaches have been adopted, expectations for all learning to be game-based, immersive, fun and engaging provides a real challenge for learning practitioners because of the low amounts of available serious game content. With increased demand, this may lead in time to the repurposing of existing game content, and to the growth of the games content markets, leading to the growth of middleware tools for scenario authoring and editing and to the expansion of user-generated content that focuses upon mash-up applications and technologies (Protopsaltis et al., 2010).

Following this tendency, our chapter sets out to explore two issues in the design and implementation of digital games and learning in professional learning contexts:

1. why is it so difficult to implement play learning and simulations within formal institutional and disciplinary cultures?
2. how can games be used more effectively to facilitate professional learning?

While there remains much research to be carried out at a fairly basic level on how play and learning inter-relate, it is clear that the relationship is a complex one (Oliver and Pelletier, 2004). In immersive 3D contexts, learning more closely resembles play whereby engagement and motivation support more exploratory and unstructured play, rather than traditional approaches to learning, which usually focus on formal provision and accumulation of data. The transition here is predicated upon the notion of 'learning as activity', constructing experiences that are more immersive and engaging, leading to greater ease of recollection. Like memory palaces used to remember large amounts of data, spatial engagement and multisensory interaction replicate lived experiences and therefore become powerful learning and teaching tools. To recreate these activities and exploratory modes involves a different way of thinking about learning where learning design is centred upon designing *experiences*. This approach to designing learning experiences leads in turn to the definition of the experience *per se*, and to the representation of the learning environment, or *diegesis*. This is the story world of the game or immersive experience, which then becomes a key critical construct, mediating the processes of learning through play and providing an environment for social interactions to take place. The process by which learning can be designed in this context then is one of 'choreography', creating activities and tie-ins between the world inside the game and the world without (de Freitas and Neumann, 2009).

When considering the implications of play as learning in formal educational contexts, there are substantial barriers to uptake of games technologies that stem from the identification of learning with sets of specific pre-organized structures and relationships. Traditionally, our conception of learning has been associated with formal curricular structures, information dissemination and retrieval, formal and regular time patterns and formalized relationships of teacher and pupil, where a hierarchy of power relations is implicit in the sets of learning processes and relationships. A choreographic approach demands a reworking of how we think of learning. It needs conceptual shifts as well as praxis shifts to the infrastructure and practices of learning. We argue that this requires a substantial revision of aspects of our current education system such as types of teaching sessions, curriculum structures and formal educational structures – even departments and disciplinary boundaries need to be revised and re-considered. This shift is an easy one to resist in organizations that are more conventional in outlook, in part at least explaining the reticence of staff and organizations to adopt game-based or immersive learning approaches. Learners however are not so reticent and are adopting the social technologies at least in their spare time – one of the main drivers for this transition is generated by students and their interest in different social forms of interaction (de Freitas and Conole, 2010).

The socially driven changing relationship between the praxis of teaching and learning and disciplinary structures is particularly pressing for those fields where academic knowledge requires to be transmuted into professional knowledge. A significant proportion of the games and simulation literature has proved how second-order symbolic thinking typical of academic learning can be facilitated by simulated activities based upon professional practice. In Law, for instance, the debate is part of the larger question about the identity of the modern liberal law school, with its emphasis on conventional teaching and learning, on the predominance of research over teaching, the hegemony of liberal attitudes to disciplinary content, the separation of academic from professional learning and a cautious attitude towards engagement with society at large (Bradney, 2008; Burridge and Webb, 2008). Contrasting with this are models of Law School development that foreground relationships between students and society, that promote forms of pedagogic intervention which derive from the practice of the profession in society, while providing a critique of that professional practice. Above all, such Law Schools lead the way in the development of new forms of teaching and learning, including problem-based learning, simulations, games and clinics (Maharg, 2007).

The debate that exists in the discipline of Law has its analogue in many other disciplines and the place that student voice has in the debate is increasing through platforms such as the National Student Survey. Eraut has commented on what universities and colleges, for their part, need to do:

> The barriers to practice-centred knowledge creation and development identified . . . are most likely to be overcome if higher education is prepared to extend its role from that of creator and transmitter of generalizable knowledge to that of *enhancing the knowledge creation capacities* of individuals and professional communities. This would involve recognizing that much knowledge creation takes place outside the higher education system, but is nevertheless limited by the absence of appropriate support structures and the prevailing action-orientation of practical contexts. (Eraut, 1994, 57)

Eraut's conclusion stems from the analysis of the academic and professional traditions of dealing with knowledge production and acquisition. He points out how the context of learning profoundly affects what is learned, to what purpose and the effect of context on knowledge transfer:

> . . . the context of use also affects the learning of theoretical knowledge, and . . . it is misleading to think of knowledge as first being acquired and then later put to use. Not only does an idea get reinterpreted during use, but it may even need to be used before it can acquire any significant meaning for the user. Thus its meaning is likely to have been strongly influenced by previous contexts of use; and the idea will not be transferable to a new context without further intellectual effort. (Eraut, 1994, 51)

Context, in fact, affects knowledge to such an extent that it may be said to fundamentally alter the epistemological features of learning. Eraut observed as much in commenting upon the learning of professional knowledge:

> [P]rofessional knowledge cannot be characterized in a manner that is independent of how it is learned and how it is used. It is through looking at the contexts of its acquisition and its use that its essential nature is revealed. (Eraut, 1994, 19)

This perceptive comment leads Eraut shrewdly to suggest that educators 'should treat the compendia of standards resulting from functional analysis as foundations for course design rather than substitutes for it' (ibid., 213). Standards, in other words, should be the springboard for imaginative and innovative learning design.

More widely, Eraut's observation regarding the inextricable links between action, context and knowledge is supported by much of the findings from the literature on situated learning, as well as the literature on professional learning (Brown, Collins and Duguid, 1989). The powerful conservativism of dominant professional modes of learning, in which one may include most universities, has been analysed in some depth by Lee Shulman in his concept of the 'signature pedagogy'. Shulman recently applied this concept to legal education in the Carnegie Report (Sullivan et al., 2007). The signature pedagogy has four features: a *surface structure* with observable, behavioural features; a *deep structure* with underlying intentions, rationale or theory that the behaviour models; a *tacit structure*, with values and dispositions that the behaviour implicitly models, and a *shadow structure* – the absent pedagogy that is, or is only weakly, engaged in the current pedagogy (Sullivan et al., 2007).

It might be easy to misunderstand Shulman's descriptions of these characteristics as static pedagogical qualities. But as he has described a number of times elsewhere, the four qualities are in dynamic tension with each other, constantly interrogated, constantly morphing. Also, as he points out in a keynote address,

> the 'signature pedagogies of the professions,' are not eternal and unchanging. Even though they seem remarkably stable at any one point in time, they are always subject to change as conditions in the practice of the profession itself and in the institutions that provide professional service or can undergo larger societal change. (Shulman, 2005)

The surface structure is thus in tension with the deep structure, because if underlying intentions change, then this can affect surface behaviour.

Surface structure, though is often the only observable way of understanding the deep structure – it is certainly so for students working through a curriculum, and for educational researchers it is indicative of deep structure. Tacit and deep structures seem to be the same, but are not: tacit refers to values that feed into surface behaviour, but which can alter surface behaviour as well; and the reverse is true, in that reflection on surface behaviour can lead to recognition of and possibly a change to aspects of deep structure – for example, teachers realizing that certain forms of teaching are having certain value effects on students. And of course the shadow structure is in constant tension with the hegemonic dominance of all other three. Seen like this, a 'signature pedagogy' is less a stable landscape and more of a seismic region, always threatening to fissure, under cultural, economic and educational pressures, one of which is created by its own modal dominance as signature.

What is interesting about Shulman's subtle construct, then, is that it explains the general features of pedagogies, both as they are and as they change in society. Nor are signature pedagogies limited to the professions, though often the professions provide the clearest examples of methodologies mature enough to be called 'signature' – for example, problem-based learning in medical education, or the case-method in US legal education (other examples are outlined in Woeste and Barham, 2006; Bryant and Milstein, 2007). A 'signature pedagogy' can form in any discipline and in any type of learning encounter. Shulman's model also accounts for the tensions of competing discourses in pedagogical theory and practice: the established pedagogy in opposition to its shadow. It therefore accounts for the micro-shifts within a hegemonic pedagogy and the power and effects of that pedagogy.

Shulman's model, being largely descriptive and analytic, gives us the tools to understand the process by which signature pedagogy comes to dominate a discipline. However it does not indicate what might be required to effect transformative change within a pedagogy. This area of research is highly complex, but there is general agreement that change will be effected less as yet another list of values or competences rather than the negotiation of values and the management of that conflict. Two issues arise from such negotiation.

First, interdisciplinary educational research is important to the change process, as is the way in which the results of such research are implemented in curricula and institutions. The research literature on play and learning has yet to grow into a mature research domain: of its nature, it will be interdisciplinary, and the domain, as with all such laminated research communities, will need to give careful thought to the conditions under which its research is produced and applied (Shaffer and Squire, 2006; Maharg 2007). Some areas of research are obvious candidates for development. The substantial research on cognition in learning, for instance, is being developed in the field of MUVEs – see for instance Ang, Mahmood and Panayiotis (2007); Nelson and Erlandson (2008). A good example of such interdisciplinary research is the work of Shaffer and colleagues (2005, 2006) who have developed 'epistemic games' that allow learners to experience ways of knowing, doing and being (an 'epistemic frame') that approximate the ways professionals learn through reflective practice (Schön, 1983).

Others in the past have shown how this can be done. In the domain of legal education, for instance, there has been a consistent critique of the dominant signature pedagogy in US legal education, namely the case-method. Part of that critique has emerged from research into composition and legal writing. Stratman, following classic lines of research mapped out by Linda Flower and others involved in the New Rhetoric, examined how students actually read legal cases. Did problems in reading arise from readers' cognitive strategies, or from the structure and content of the genre or from the encounter between the two? To research this problematic Stratman constructed professional roles for students – an advisory, a policy and an advocacy role – as well as asking some of his subjects to read as if they were students preparing for a Law class. His findings were significant. The assignation of role affected understanding arising out of the reading task. Higher-level reading strategies such as problem-recognition and resolution were more apparent and were higher when students assumed one of the three professional roles, rather than the role of student preparing for class (Stratman, 2002). These findings were confirmed by other studies – for example Deegan (1995) – and evince the mediational role that professional identity can have in fundamental learning strategies (see also Flower, Long and Higgins, 2000; Maharg 2007). Research such as this can be drawn upon and co-opted by those who advocate games and simulations, not to normalize the position of play strategies within a discipline, but to extend and radicalize the pre-existing research bases, enabling research to effect transformation of disciplinary and professional teaching and learning strategies.

Second, the relationship between play cultures of learning on Shulman's tacit and deep structures of a curriculum need to be analysed and theorized. Examples will be given later in this chapter, but it is relatively easy to alter the surface attributes of a curriculum – for example, to embed a pilot project or design new assessments. It is much more difficult to change the deep and tacit structures. As with the deep grammatical structures of language, these undergo structural change only rarely and under significant pressure. The deep structure of a signature pedagogy is composed of the theory or intention underlying the *explicit* behaviours of teachers and learners, while the tacit structure comprises underlying values and dispositions.

How might the 'shadow pedagogy' of play transform deep and tacit structures of signature pedagogies and conventional curricula? It may do so in two ways. First, it can enable new theoretical positions on learning to be developed, tested and implemented. We shall give examples of such theory in *diegesis* and Transactional Learning. Second, it can enable the development of values that are, or ought to be, important to a pedagogy or curriculum. An example of such a value or quality might be judgement, which as a focus for learning and teaching has always been problematic for formal education. Indeed, in one form or another the debates around qualities such as passion, virtue, wisdom, patience, foresight and humility are evidence of a profound debate about the nature of ethics and the place of moral philosophy within society's higher educational structures stretching back through the nineteenth century, through Enlightenment and Renaissance discourse to the Aristotelian distinction between *sophia* and *phronesis*. We would argue that games and simulations can play a key role in the revival and transformation of this discourse for our own times.

To summarize, then, in order to change tacit values and deep structures we require significant theoretical, cultural and economic pressures equivalent to those that created signature pedagogies in the first place. We can contribute to that, in the domain of play and simulation, in our theory and practice, and this chapter, is an attempt to outline that process.

Transformational theory sets for games and professional learning

So far we have been discussing why it is difficult to implement play learning and simulations within formal institutional and disciplinary cultures. The second question, how games can be used to facilitate professional learning, can be discussed in the context of two theory-sets. The first theory set creates a new representation of the inner life of a game, a diegetic model of play experience; while the second uses the construct of activity theory and Transactional Learning to build a model of context and engagement. They are each discussed below.

Theory set 1: play as diegesis

We have touched upon definitions of play and learning, and their similarities and dissonances above. While there can be no definitive conclusions here, the idea of centring learning upon experience rather than shared curricula focuses perhaps upon the key relationships between play and learning, social interactions and social drivers. For animal play, the intensive periods of play lead to accelerated maturation (Bekoff and Byers, 1998). Studies have shown that no play in childhood and sociopathy may be linked (Bekoff and Byers, 1998). Undoubtedly, thinkers from Plato to Piaget have acknowledged the importance of child play in development cycles. Illustrating this perhaps, the neuroscientist Gerald Edelman has pointed to a 'cartography' of knowledge that is developed and tested during play time (Edelman, 1992) and through rehearsal and role play can be accelerated and improved. For humans, then, broadly play is associated closely with human development. When we consider how play works it becomes an elusive concept, however, and trying to distinguish between learning and play can be difficult even for philosophers (e.g. Wittgenstein, 1972). However, from studies with games and gameplay we can begin to analyse the processes of play-based learning and begin to consider how these processes can best be 'scaffolded' for individuals and groups of learners (Vygotsky, 1978).

The concept of *diegesis* comes from the Greek word for narrative or plot, used in film studies to depict the world inside the film. The word is used here to depict the story world or immersive world within the game rather than in the film. The act of immersion or imagination exerted by the player (or reader or viewer) creates a believability that allows for 'flow' or imagination to cocoon the player and allow them to pass many hours without an awareness of what is happening around them. Narrative is a major aspect of this, as it supports a deeper engagement through the story, the identification with the protagonist and within an activity, such as a quest or mission. Play in this context becomes an inner world, with believable social interactions and activities, vested interests and a physiological 'flow' designed specifically for engaging and maintaining the interest of the player (Csikszentmihalyi, 1991).

Further to this, play is, as it were, an inner world. *Diegesis* in particular, and play in general, opens up a new way of thinking about learning – that is, thinking about learning as activities and experiences – designed to inform our life activities and professional experiences. Thinking about learning in this way, opens up a new way to connect with our cultural and historical life, but we still need tools to allow us to approach learning design in a way that is sensitive to this approach. One of the methods for achieving this practically is emerging from the work of the authors.

In previous work, de Freitas and Oliver (2006) outlined an evaluative framework for the selection, use and evaluation of games in formal learning situations. The work was based upon studies with tutors and learners identifying particular issues associated with the selection, use and evaluation of games. The framework, which was being mapped onto activity theory, focuses upon four main dimensions: the context, the learner, the representation of the game (*diegesis*) and the pedagogies used. The framework is based upon the notion that learning activities are the central construct of learning interactively with games and that these activities need to be considered in relation to experiential or exploratory models of learning, whereby the learner becomes an active participant in the learning processes, for example producing content, sharing content working collaboratively and socially and having significant learner control. See Figure 1.1.

The framework includes a dimension that focuses upon the representational dimension of learning and in the context of game-based learning this necessitates a consideration of the world within the game or simulation (or role play). In the context of the game then, the representational dimension

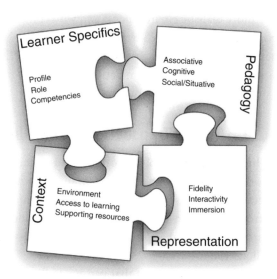

Figure 1.1 Four Dimensional Framework

focuses upon the internal representational world of the game or simulation. The *diegesis* means the presentation of objects and environments, the interactivity of the player within the game and the levels of immersion and fidelity used in the game or simulation. In further work, de Freitas and Neumann (2009) have been developing an exploratory learning model whereby the efficacy of the game or immersive experience is predicated upon the levels of immersion, interactivity, liminality and fidelity of the game.

The diegetic play of the game then relies upon specific levels of immersion within the representational dimension. How high does the level of fidelity need to be? How interactive should it need to be to convey a realistic experience, what is the role in the role play and how accurate does that need to be? What narrative structures need to be used? An element of repetition, quizzes and quests are just a few devices that can be threaded together in the game design to ensure engagement and motivation of the students playing the game. *Diegesis* then becomes the gameplay, how the environment and narrative is structured then supports the immersion and flow. All support a designed experience that is addictive and engaging. Whether painting a picture of a historical period or learning to pilot aircraft, learning and rehearsing skills in an immersive environment relies upon the learning design, and importantly the fidelity and believability of the environment, the actions within the environment and the social interactions between the characters, whether they are player or machine driven. The drive for diegetic cohesiveness then leads in tandem to the drive for ever more realistic environments and with computing processing improving exponentially this is an achievable goal.

Through these kinds of interchanges, play becomes the active diagram of learning in the world of the game or simulation, indeed play becomes a supporting aspect of the *diegesis* of the virtual experience.

Theory set 2: CHAT and Transactional Learning

Activity theory's basic mediational triangle can be used in order to understand the complex factors affecting the embedding of simulation within professional education. That triangle consists of dynamic movement from subject, via tool, to object. Engeström (1999) developed this model to include the social and cultural context in what he called a cultural historical activity theory (CHAT) framework, as follows (Figure 1.2).

Engeström's model is a generic tool that can be applied to most areas of professional learning. The approach has been further developed by Barton, McKellar and Maharg (2007) in the context of simulation learning within a

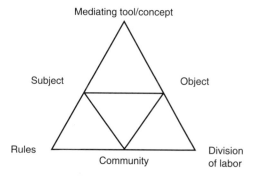

Figure 1.2 Engestrom's mode of mediational activity

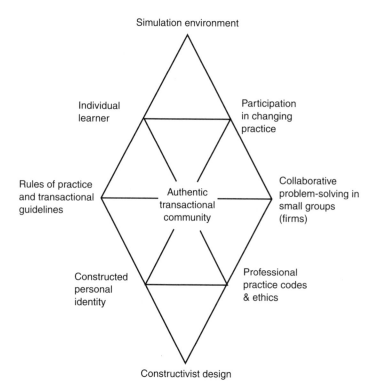

Figure 1.3 Barton, McKellar, Maharg (2007) – mediation activity in transactional learning

professional practice programme in Law. Using the dialectical movement of Engeström's triangle as their basic unit of analysis, Barton and colleagues analysed their educational practice and its effects; and Figure 1.3 describes their model.

The diagram applies to any professional learning context. In the basic mediational triangle at the top, we move from subject, through mediational tool or concept use, to object, namely participation in changing professional practice. Practice refers not just to the quotidian reality of professional trans-actions, but to those practices and personal understandings that students, trainees and newly qualifieds require to change if they are to enter the world of practice. The rules (mid-left in the diagram) are those of the practice commu-nity, together with the resource-base and guidelines given to students as part of their learning environment. The community (centre-diagram) is that of Transactional Learning. The division of labour by which such change is achieved is through collaborative problem-solving in small groups – a feature of the transactional environment that we shall describe in more detail below.

Underlying this structure is the critical element of personal identity con-struction and change that takes place when a student participates in a profes-sional course. It is essential that any constructivist design enables such change, and therefore it is appropriate that the learning design is seen as a mediational element in the process. But mediation is also the role played by the authentic transactional community – the community that willingly suspends its disbelief, enters the transactions and performs them as if they are actual transactions. The community, too, plays an important role in mediating the understanding of professional ethics.

The diagram can be seen as a version or adaptation of the classic CHAT framework and describes many of the contextual features that affect the implementation of play or simulation within situated learning activities (Lave and Wenger, 1991). But in addition it can be seen as a mirroring of the CHAT isosceles triangle, where learners, by constructing personal identity through the medium of the transactional community, learn the effect and consequences of enacting professional practice codes and ethics. Constructivist design is also essential to this mediation. Indeed, a vertical line can be drawn through the CHAT framework from constructivist design through a transactional com-munity to the simulation environment: all three are essential to simulation activity.

Moving up to the central horizontal line of the diagram, the rules of prac-tice and transactional guidelines, mediated by individual students' constructed personal identities, make up the transactional community. The community, mediated by professional practice codes and ethics, manifests itself in collabo-rative problem-solving in small groups.

In addition to the mediatory movement of the dialectical triangle there is also a circular movement around the inner rectangle that describes the process of identity-formation within a structure of professional practice ethics. In the example of professional ethics, then, the individual learner constructs personal identity through the process of entering practice codes and values, and understands professional ethics through participation in changing practice. Through both the rectangle and the triangle, the model places emphasis upon the social interactions of learning that take place within professional cultures and, we would claim, supports greater learning transfer and also accelerated learning within the stages of that culture.

The last claim is an ambitious one, but as the recent report on the SIMPLE project makes clear, there is an evidence base to support it (Gould et al., 2008). A re-interpretation of Engeström's activity theory such as we have above has profound implications for the shape of professional curricula. But if a diagram such as this represents the cultural and historical framework of simulation learning, we also need to consider its practical implementation within a curriculum. It is here that the concept of Transactional Learning can be useful.

Transactional Learning, as defined by Maharg and others, involves simulations and games, and has seven characteristics (Maharg, 2007; Barton and McKellar, this volume):

1. *active learning,*
2. through *performance in authentic transactions,*
3. involving *reflection in and on learning,*
4. deep *collaborative learning,* and
5. holistic or *process learning,*
6. with *relevant professional assessment,*
7. that includes *ethical standards.*

The concepts work best when they interlock within the curriculum. Authenticity is central. Transactional Learning cannot of course be a *mimesis* of real professional life but it can reconstruct aspects of it to enable immersive gaming and simulation to take place. Performance within the game is part of what creates active learning, but professional performance is rarely a singleton activity: it nearly always involves others, either as actor participants or as audience. Extensive collaborative learning (point 4) and active learning (point 1) are therefore complementary activities, as is the concept of process learning – point 5, learning how to carry out aspects of a transaction – with reflective learning. Point 3 involves stepping back from the transaction to think about relationship processes and affect as well as professional projection in the world of the transaction. If Transactional Learning depends upon professional activities to provide the ground upon which learning takes place, then learning is reinforced when its assessment also takes place upon this ground (point 6). Finally, no substantial transactional activity in the professional world takes place unless within an ethical context. Transactional Learning emphasizes the ethical underpinning not just of transactional activity, but also of the relational ethics underpinning all prior six points. Learning, in Transactional Learning, thus becomes acknowledged as an essential component of professional activity.

Transactional Learning, in this way, provides a blueprint for the design of learning and assessment within the broader framework of CHAT theory. It sets out the qualities that such design aims to bring about in games and simulations in professional learning. Moreover, it enhances the qualities of diegetic learning through the emphasis upon social interactions, constructed environments and active learning strategies. The design of learning in this way allows for a scaffolding not just for learning construction but for a more socially driven set of determinants such as interaction, immersion and ease of learning transfer through close to reality representations, activities, role play and rehearsal.

Diegesis and CHAT / Transactional Learning are two theory sets that are complementary in their emphasis on immersive action, action learning and their applicability to professional learning. There are at least five points of contact that could be further explored:

1. Play learning is social. Much of the literature into online multi-user virtual environments (MUVEs), for instance, supports this (Taylor, 2006; Salen and Zimmerman, 2004; Steinkuhler, 2006);
2. The theories are representational in character. That is to say, they describe how learning happens within games, and how it can be recovered, re-used and transferred;
3. They give designers generic guidance on game and learning design processes and procedures;
4. They focus on the convergence of play-representation and reality-representation;
5. They emphasize transformation of curricular practices. Play offers the opportunity to rethink curricular practices, learning resources, assessment practices and even employment hierarchies within institutions.

In the introduction to this chapter we exposed the recasting of 'learning as experience' as foregrounding two major areas for consideration: the role of social interactive learning (learning in groups) and the role of learning design (designing experiences rather than content). In the final part of this chapter we shall briefly describe a case study that exemplifies the convergence of the two theory sets in relation to social interactive learning through the lens of Transactional Learning, and in relation to learning design through the lens of *diegesis*.

Diegetic and transactional dimensions in the SIMPLE case study

One example from practice will give an indication of what we mean. This case study comes from a postgraduate programme in professional legal education, the Diploma in Legal Practice, at the University of Strathclyde's Law School. One of the transactions that is the core of the curriculum is a Personal Injury Negotiation Project which is run using the SIMPLE (SIMulated Professional Learning Environment) where students, working collaboratively in virtual law firms, represent either an employee injured at work, or the insurer for the University of Ardcalloch, where the accident occurs (Barton and Maharg, 2006; Maharg and Owen, 2007). The firms, consisting of four students per firm, are asked to reach a negotiated settlement of the claim. One year, two firms had difficulty completing the transaction. At the point of closing negotiations, one of the firms introduced another very substantial head of damages to be considered. The other side was, not surprisingly, vexed by this. They contacted one of the PI transaction mentors as follows:

> We agreed to negotiate on 6 heads and are now being asked to negotiate on 7, the 7th being the most substantial. This is an underhand tactic by the pursuers and to act in the best interests of our client we would need to investigate this head [. . .]

The tutor responded:

> Well, it might be underhand or it might be just incompetence – hard to tell at the moment. It certainly poses a dilemma for you. But actually, it poses a dilemma for the other side even more. Read [another tutor's] recent postings on the discussion forum: this situation can be turned to your advantage. They [the other firm] have put you in a situation where you are under pressure, for if you are to act professionally you need time (for client instruction, new investigation). You have a range of options – for instance: (1) do what they want, research and obtain instructions

frantically in the time that is left to you; (2) refuse to give in to such pressure, while remaining co-operative and prepared to negotiate the point, for example either they accept a greatly reduced figure, or nothing at all, given the circs [circumstances]; (3) show them how angry you are, send accusatory letters, refuse to negotiate under such conditions. What will be your choice? Or rather – since it is so easy to get caught up in your own personal feelings at this point – what would be best for your client?

After a pause the firm responded that they decided to choose the second option and had agreed to a face-to-face meeting to negotiate. In the same email they went on to relate the difficulty of finding space in diaries with upcoming assessments, ongoing difficulties with the other firm, and then asked,

What sanctions can we impose if there is no settlement on Friday and negotiations continue into next week? In real life we would have additional clients and may in fact need to turn down fee earning work to deal with this situation. In addition, our client would not be pleased about the additional expense. [. . .] Can we agree to Friday, that is if the pursuers ever get round to arranging it, and tell them should the negotiations continue into next week that we will reduce any agreed settlement by say 10% in addition to contributory negligence for the inconvenience and additional expense to our client?

The tutor responded:

You choose whatever you want to do. And this is where things become, from the point of view of professional actings, quite difficult. Because if you are going to go down route 2, it is probably fair to say that if you insist on sanctions and punishment, you may scupper any deal-making activity you are engaging in. You're edging into route 3. You are perfectly right about the extra time you are spending on this. But in the interests of getting the best deal done for your client, you will need to ask yourselves whether this really will be to their advantage.

And yet, when all is said and done, the settlement document signed and the file submitted you will probably still be feeling raw about this, as you are at the moment. Perhaps then would be the time to have a 'debrief' with the other side – to find out why this has happened – how they felt about it (did they do it deliberately? Are they embarrassed, but keeping a poker face on the issue? Totally unaware of any inconvenience?), and what could have happened differently. That debrief outside the bounds of the simulation can be quite a powerful learning moment. Tricky meeting to handle but it gives you good experience for handling such matters in the world of future employment . . .

This excerpt from student/tutor dialogue has many interesting features. First, note that it is saturated in the issues that arise from the simulation. Professional practice thus becomes the ground upon which powerful learning takes place. Second, the main issue at stake is what one firm construes as unethical behaviour on the part of the other firm and the firm members' anger at being treated in this way. The tutor outlines possible courses of action and in this sense is debriefing with the firm before its members return to the simulation to enact solutions on behalf of their client. There is active learning within the performance of the transaction. The whole exchange is an exploration of issues and possible actions that at times approaches Schön's reflection-*in*-action. Above all the firm is concerned with the ethics of the situation: what is ethically possible, feasible, how it will affect the outcome of the negotiation.

There is so much more that can be said about these and many other such exchanges. The emotional commitment to the play, the heartfelt exploration of alternatives that can be undertaken, the true difficulty of choice, the dealing with complex emotions, a deep understanding of what it is to represent a client professionally, sometimes in the face of unprofessional conduct – all this and much more can be learned powerfully through the play of professional activity within a simulation. Through such diegetic interplay, through immersion and dialogue about the transaction, students come to an experiential understanding of what professional culture is, and how its ethics and values play out in transactions. In this way, students learn through activities the culture and history of their profession.

Conclusion

If a socially driven paradigm shift in learning and training is to be argued for then certainly the recasting of 'learning as experience' is at its centre. While in the past teachers were restricted to the classroom and field trip, today with more advanced visualization tools, the internet with its capabilities for social networks and increased broadband connectivity for media-rich environments, immersive learning has become a necessity for critical training, and more recently for professional learning, allowing as it does the use of role play and rehearsal, formative assessment and collaborative learning communities.

While the new tools are still relatively recent, the potential for learning in this way is gathering momentum. As games and simulations become cheaper to produce, and as more and more people are playing in the home, the use of these tools in places of work and education becomes less controversial.

We have two areas worth consideration in the chapter: social interactive learning and how it can be supported through Transactional Learning, and *diegesis* that supports the role of learning design, allowing tutors and students to design experiences rather than content. The experiential route is one way that we can resist the hegemonic dominance of conventional academic pedagogies and signature pedagogies, bringing out of the shadows the pedagogies of clinic, simulations and games that have, to date, had only a minority existence in our learning institutions.

If experience is core to this approach, what are the qualities that are required in order to transform education in Higher Education, and can we use games and simulations to achieve this ambitious aim? Cultural and historical context, as represented in a mapping of the field, is a helpful tool to understand how play learning might be embedded in professional learning. A representation of the life world of the game or simulation – its diegetic nature – is also useful. By using representation as a core construct of learning, as we outline in this chapter, we are asking tutors to consider the potential of the 3D world around them as well as the virtual immersive spaces accessed via the web. While imaginings, text and information were the critical constructs of traditional learning, we ask that imaginings, visual / information spaces and social interactions become the critical constructs of new learning. This is based upon a true transformation of learning from learning as information provision and access, towards learning as play and exploration. The transformation may not be an immediate one for all tutors or learners, but the advantages surely open up a new frame of reference for learning and teaching practices and offer scope for real creativity and interactivity. In many ways, this new learning opens up a more dialogic basis that in some ways better reflects the experiences (both formal and informal) of life and living. When we think back to our childhood days what we remember is rarely the pages of text but more often the experiences of learning.

Looking at the wider context, this chapter has opened up a debate about how games, simulations and immersive learning can inform and shape a new mode of learning, whereby learning is conceived of as activities and play, exploration and social interaction. The chapter has posed some of the key challenges for its wider adoption in formal learning contexts, but equally regards this new learning as a blend of mixed reality, with elements of real and virtual embedded and contextualized experiences. While experience refers not just to the Deweyan construct of experiential learning, but more generally a recasting of the relationship between learning within the academy and learning beyond it, this necessarily implies a transformation of the processes of learning and the educational infrastructure that underpins these processes. This chapter argues that it is through re-conceptualizing these core processes that we will be able to adapt to the challenges of immersive learning.

References

Ang, C. S., Mahmood, S. and Panayiotis, Z. (2007). A model of cognitive loads in massively multiplayer online role playing games. *Interacting with Computers*, 19, 2, 167–79.

Barton, K. and Maharg, P. (2006). Simulations in the wild: interdisciplinary research, design and implementation. In C. Aldrich, D. Gibson, M. Prensky, eds. *Games and Simulations in Online Learning*. Part 2, chapter 6, 170–218, Hershey: Idea Group Ltd, pp. 115–48.

Barton, K., McKellar, P. and Maharg, P. (2007). Authentic fictions: simulation, professionalism and legal learning. *Clinical Law Review*, Vol. 14, pp. 143–93.

Bekoff, M. and Byers, J. A. (1998). *Animal Play: Evolutionary, Comparative and Ecological Perspectives*. Cambridge: Cambridge University Press.

Bradney, A. (2008). Elite values in twenty-first century, United Kingdom law schools, *Law Teacher*. Vol. 42, No 3, pp. 291–302.

Brown, J. S., Collins, A. and Duguid, P. (1989). Situated cognition and the culture of learning. *Educational Researcher*, Vol. 18, No 1, pp. 34–41.

Bryant, S. and Milstein, E. (2007). Rounds: a 'signature pedagogy' for clinical education? *NYLS Clinical Research Institute*, Paper No. 07/08–5, http://papers.ssrn.com/sol3/papers.cfm?abstract_id=1007504. Last accessed 20.4.10.

Burridge, R. and Webb, J. (2008). On liberal neutrality, the value of experience and the loneliness of the long-distance academic: further reflections on the values of a common law legal education. *The Law Teacher*, Vol. 42, No. 3, 339–54.

de Freitas, S. and Conole, G. (2010). The influence of pervasive and integrative tools on learners' experiences and expectations of study. In R. Sharpe, H. Beetham and S. de Freitas, eds. *Rethinking Learning in the Digital Age*. London and New York: Routledge.

de Freitas, S. and Neumann, T. (2009). The use of 'exploratory learning' for supporting immersive learning in virtual environments. *Computers and Education*, Vol. 52, No. 2, pp. 343–52.

de Freitas, S. and Oliver, M. (2006). How can exploratory learning with games and simulations within the curriculum be most effectively evaluated? *Computers and Education*. Special Issue, Vol. 46, pp. 249–64.

Deegan, D. (1995). Exploring individual differences among novices reading in a specific domain: the case of law. *Reading Research Quarterly,* Vol. 30, No. 2, pp. 154–70.

Edelman, G. (1992). *Bright Air and Brilliant Fire: On the Matter of the Mind.* New York: Basic Books.

Engeström, Y. (1999). Activity theory and individual and social transformation. In *Perspectives on Activity Theory,* Y. Engeström , R. Miettinen , R-L. Punamaki, eds. Cambridge: Cambridge University Press, pp. 19–38.

Eraut, M. (1994). *Developing Professional Knowledge and Competence.* Falmouth: The Falmer Press.

Flower, L., Long, E. and Higgins, L. (2000). *Learning to Rival. A Literature Practice for Intercultural Inquiry.* Mahwah, NJ: Lawrence Erlbaum Associates.

Gould, H., Hughes, M., McKellar, P., Maharg, P. and Nicol, E. (2008). SIMulated Professional Learning Environment (SIMPLE). Final Programme Report.

Greenspun, P. (2010). Fly by Wire. Review of Langewiesche, W., *Fly By Wire: The Geese, the Glide, the Miracle on the Hudson,* New York: Farrar, Strauss & Giroud. http://philip.greenspun.com/book-reviews/fly-by-wire

Griffiths, T. and Guile, D. (1999). Pedagogy in work-based contexts. In O. Mortimore, ed., *Understanding Pedagogy and Its Impact on Learning,* London: Paul Chapman Publishing.

Gunter, G. A., Kenny, R. F. and Vick, E. H. (2008). Taking educational games seriously: using the RETAIN model to design endogenous fantasy into standalone educational games. *Education Technology Research Development,* Vol. 56, pp. 511– 37.

Haskell, R. (2001). *Transfer of Learning: Cognition, Instruction and Reasoning,* London: Academic Press.

Jarvis, S. and de Freitas, S. (2009). Evaluation of an Immersive Learning Programme to support Triage Training. *Proceedings of the 1st IEEE International Conference in Games and Virtual Worlds for Serious Applications,* IEEE Computer Society, Coventry, UK, 23–24 March, pp. 117–22.

Kato, P. M., Cole, S. W., Bradlyn, A. S. and Pollock, B. H. (2008). A video game improves behavioural outcomes in adolescents and young adults with cancer: a randomized trial. *Pediatrics,* Vol. 122, No. 2, pp. 305–17.

Lave, J. and Wenger, E. (1991). *Situated Learning: Legitimate Peripheral Participation,* Cambridge: Cambridge University Press.

Maharg, P. (2007). *Transforming Legal Education. Learning and Teaching the Law in the Early Twenty-first Century.* Aldershot: Ashgate Publishing.

Maharg, P. and Owen, M. (2007). Simulations, learning and the metaverse: changing cultures in legal education, *Journal of Information, Law, Technology.* Special Issue on law, education, technology, No. 1. Available at: *http://www2.warwick.ac.uk/fac/soc/law/elj/jilt/2007_1/maharg_owen.* Last accessed 25.4.10.

Mayes, T. and de Freitas, S. (2007). Learning and e-Learning: the role of theory. In H. Beetham and R. Sharpe, eds. *Rethinking Pedagogy in the Digital Age.* London: Routledge.

Nelson, B. C. and Erlandson, B. E. (2008). Managing cognitive load in educational multi-user virtual environments: reflection on design in practice. *Educational Technology Research & Development,* Vol. 56, Nos. 5–6, pp. 619–41.

Oliver, M. and Pelletier, C. (2004). Activity theory and learning from digital games: implications for game design. In paper presented at: Digital Generations: Children, Young People and New Media, London.

Parush, A., Hamm, H. and Shtub, A. (2002). Learning histories in simulation-based teaching: the effects on self-learning and transfer. *Computers and Education,* Vol. 39, No 4, pp. 319–32.

Protopsaltis, A., Panzoli, D., Dunwell, I. and de Freitas, S. (2010). Repurposing Serious Games in Health Care Education. The 12th Mediterranean Conference on Medical and Biological Engineering and Computing – MEDICON 2010. 27–30 May, Chalkidiki, Greece.

Salen, K. and Zimmerman, E. (2006). *Rules of Play. Game Design Fundamentals.* Cambridge, MA: MIT Press.

Shaffer, D. W. (2005). Epistemic games. *Innovate,* Vol. 1, No 6, http://www.innovateonline.info/index. php?view=article&id=79. Last accessed 20.4.10.

Shaffer, D. W. and Squire, K. D. (2006). The pasteurization of education. ACM Portal, http://portal. acm.org/citation.cfm?id=1150034.1150134. Last accessed 20.5.10.

Shulman, L. (2005). The signature pedagogies of the professions of law, medicine, engineering, and the clergy: potential lessons for the education of teachers, Math Science Partnerships (MSP) Workshop, National Research Council Centre for Education, Irvine, CA. Available at: http://www. taylorprograms.com/images/Shulman_Signature_Pedagogies.pdf. Last accessed 20.5.10.

Steinkuehler, C. and Williams, D. (2006). Where everybody knows your (screen) name: online games as 'third spaces'. *Journal of Computer-Mediated Communication,* Vol. 11, No 4, *http://jcmc.indiana. edu/vol11/issue4/steinkuehler.html.* Last accessed 21.4.10.

Stratman, J. F. (2002). When law students read cases: exploring relations between professional legal reasoning roles and problem detection. *Discourse Processes,* Vol. 34, No. 1, pp. 57–90.

Sullivan, W. M., Colby, A., Wegner, J. W., Bond, L. and Shulman, L. S. (2007). *Educating Lawyers. Preparation for the Profession of Law,* San Franciso: Jossey-Bass.

Taylor, T. L. (2006). *Play Between Worlds. Exploring Online Game Culture.* Cambridge, MA: MIT Press.

Vygotsky, L. S. (1978). *Mind in Society: The Development of Higher Order Psychological Processes.* Cambridge and London: Harvard University Press.

Webb, J. (2008). On liberal neutrality, the value of experience and the loneliness of the long-distance academic: further reflections on the values of a common law legal education. *Law Teacher,* Vol. 42, No 3, pp. 339–54.

Wittgenstein, L. (1972). *The Blue and Brown Books: Preliminary Studies for the* Philosophical Investigations. Oxford: Basil Blackwell.

Woeste, L. A. and Barham, B. J. (2006). The signature pedagogy of clinical laboratory science education: the professional practice experience. *Laboratory Medicine,* Vol. 37, No 10, pp. 591–92.

2 Four-dimensional Consideration of Feedback in Serious Games

Ian Dunwell, Sara de Freitas and Steve Jarvis

Chapter Outline

Introduction

Feedback is a central consideration in effective serious game design. Besides the authors' own evidence and experience supporting this (e.g. Jarvis and de Freitas, 2009), of which a case study is presented later in this chapter, many other studies have suggested that feedback is central to sound pedagogic design (e.g. Shute, 2008) and that serious games are no exception to the general rule. This chapter aims to further consolidate our understanding of the characteristics of feedback most relevant to serious games, and analyse the impact that the use of a game-based medium has on established feedback principles and mechanisms.

While identifiable on a high level in terms of concepts such as flow (Cziksentmihalyi, 1991), motivation (Gobet et al., 2004) and reflection (Kolb, 1981; de Freitas and Neumann, 2009), the key influencing factors in effective game-based learning still remain elusive in terms that would allow for pre-scriptive and empirically grounded game designs. While the introduction of game elements into simulations has been shown to increase learning transfer, little conclusive evidence exists to explain either *how* or *why* this increase in learning transfer occurs (Mautone et al., 2008). In an attempt to identify the characteristics of a successful serious game, the four-dimensional framework of de Freitas and Oliver (2005) suggests serious games are defined in terms of four discrete dimensions of pedagogy, context, learner and representational medium, and hence consideration of the individual characteristics of each dimension can be each seen to contribute towards the creation of a successful game-based learning experience. However, in practice, developers are typically able to modify only one or two of these dimensions. Often, the learner, context and representational medium are selected in advance, and therefore the designer must work to evolve and adapt their pedagogic approach alongside already specified game design. With respect to this pedagogic dimension the form, content and frequency of feedback are frequently cited in the literature as essential components of a more general and well-established facilitative approach (Rogers, 1951).

Furthermore, Kolb's (1981) experiential learning model is readily observable as integrating and including feedback as part of the experiential learning cycle. An example given in Kolb's model is that of a child burning their hand; the action, in this case, is touching the stove, the event the burning of the hand and the reflection occurs when the child asks 'why did my hand hurt', reaching the conclusion it was 'because I touched the stove'. In this case the feedback mechanism is a fundamental biological sensation. However if, for a serious game, we virtualize or otherwise abstract this process, while the action and event can be mirrored precisely in a virtual world, a layer of abstraction is introduced between event and reflection. This is an interpretation layer in which the user must identify the real-world implication of the virtual event. This is analogous to the model of 'exploratory' learning defined by de Freitas and Neumann (2009): while the exploratory model considers the impact virtual worlds may have on the link between experience and reflection, our interpretation also considers the effect interactive technology may have on the relationship between intended action and consequential virtual event.

In essence, the critical components of interaction with a virtual learning environment must describe how transitions are handled between, first the boundaries interfacing concept formation and testing, which we term the *input* boundary; and second the relationship between experience, exploration and reflection, termed the *output* boundary. The reader may have observed that this separation, in Figure 2.1, is deliberately ambiguous with respect to exploration: this is to reflect the fact that exploration can occur in virtual space, or real space, for example in the case of blended learning approaches. In either situation, the reflective process can benefit substantially from scaffolding (Gick and Holyoak, 1980) and such scaffolding often forms the basis for feedback approaches.

Building further on Kolb's model, the reflective process can be seen as progressing through three levels: *What?* in terms of identifying the event accurately, to *So what?* e.g. why is the event significant, to *Now what?* (Gass and Gillis, 2000) such as, what action must be taken to avoid or cause the event in future. Reflective exercises frequently encourage this progression through

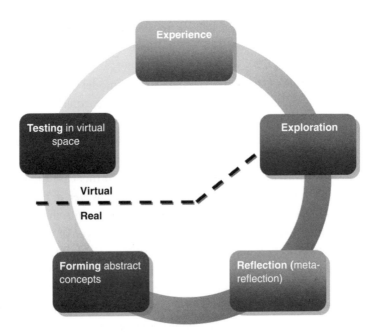

Figure 2.1 Experiential learning in virtual space

stages. Transposing the model once again into a virtual context, the strengths and challenges of the medium become apparent: event significance can in some ways be strengthened through virtual simulation which would otherwise be impossible in the real world, for example in the case of an infection control game through the spread of infection and resulting deaths, but simultaneously the virtualization of the event inherently reduces its significance. Similarly, cause-and-effect can be demonstrated effectively through simulation, but the temptation exists in game and simulation design to deviate from evolutionary cause-and-effect chains in order to produce computationally simpler scripts with fixed outcomes.

With regard to the purpose of feedback, motivation is often seen to be a principal targeted outcome of many serious games, since the inherent motivational appeal of electronic gaming is often a major influencing factor in the selection of a serious game as an educational medium (Gobet et al., 2004). Wright (2001) refers to a study in which games were used in an attempt to address attention-deficit disorder (ADHD), comparing a game-based approach to traditional biofeedback approaches. The study suggested that the key advantage of the game-based approach in this case lay in its motivational character, with the experimental group using game-based approaches that demonstrated increased attendance and retention rates over the control group.

A common classification of motivation is into *intrinsic* and *extrinsic* types (Reynolds, 2002). Intrinsic motivation is commonly described as self-motivation or internal drive to complete a task, whereas external motivation comes from interactions with other individuals such as tutors, as well as the constructs and structures in place to scaffold the learning experience. The benefits of favouring approaches which foster intrinsic motivation over extrinsic pressures in technology-assisted learning are well-documented. Şimşek and Barto (2006), for instance, explore the benefits of an intrinsic reward mechanism for an agent-based reinforcement learning approach. While intrinsic motivation is typically assumed to be endemic to the 'fun' element of gaming, the need to couple instructional design to gameplay infers a need to be aware of the role that instructional design may play in enhancing (or obstructing) the innate motivational characteristics of a game-based approach. Hence extrinsic motivation may also play a factor through the integration of the game into a course or in a blended learning solution, wherein traditional extrinsic approaches may also be applied.

Feedback in Serious Games

It may be beneficial at this stage to narrow and clarify the description of what constitutes a serious game and feedback within it. Since games themselves often facilitate complex interactive processes, feedback can occur not only in an educational context but also in a cognitive dimension, such as the feedback loop between pressing a key and an avatar moving in a virtual space. Therefore, additional simultaneous considerations present themselves that lie in the remit of research into immersion and virtual spaces. For example, the metrics of immersion in a virtual world described by Pausch (1997) consider low-level tactile, auditory and visual feedback as integral components. While it would be an oversimplification to imply these can be easily separated from a more pedagogically driven consideration of feedback, this chapter does, for the sake of scope, consider feedback from the high-level perspective of a pedagogic designer rather than the low-level viewpoint of a virtual world creator. We also consider primarily serious games that are set in virtual worlds, and therefore tend to favour interactive simulation as a means of ensuring learning transfer, as is the case with *Triage Trainer* discussed later, although many principles discussed hold true for more symbolic types of disciplinary learning, such as mathematical reasoning (Bearman, 1997).

In this context, literature reviews of feedback (Shute, 2008; Mory, 2004) suggest the importance of formative models yet provide little conclusive evidence of how these models are best implemented. However, a recurrent distinction exists between the content and format of feedback and the timing with which it is delivered. In the next sections, we decompose feedback into two distinct elements: *timing* and *content*. It should be noted that these are not wholly independent of one another – for example, increasing the frequency of feedback frequently implies it be delivered in a less detailed or concise form to avoid cognitive overload (Warburton, 2008). The subsequent two sections, therefore, expand on these concepts in more detail.

Timing of feedback

Some empirical evidence suggests delayed feedback is situationally advantageous – see for example, Schroth (1992) who focused on the problem of concept-formation transfer tasks – although more ubiquitous models remain elusive.

The results of Schroth suggest within this given context that, while delayed feedback reduced initial learning transfer, it facilitated increased transfer after the delay. Some evidence suggests that whether delay is desirable and the subsequent frequency with which feedback is conveyed is influenced primarily by the nature of the task and capability of the learner (Mathan and Koedinger, 2002). A parallel can be drawn to Cziksentmihalyi's (1991) *flow*, which suggests an optimal flow experience is achieved by careful matching of task difficulty to learner ability.

One perspective is that feedback should endeavour to synergize with a flow experience. Any delays or interruptions to a flow experience induced by feedback are undesirable and therefore feedback should aim to be as unobtrusive as possible. That said, feedback could also be interpreted as fundamental to providing the *perceived* level of challenge – if a learner struggles at a task, then providing constant positive feedback may alter the perception of challenge and thus induce flow more readily. Similarly, feedback that fails to achieve this objective and instills feelings of excessive or insufficient challenge will, in the context of Cziksentmihalyi's model, induce anxiety, boredom or apathy in the learner. Interestingly, when considering the gameplay aspect of serious games, several of the interim characteristics within this model are those often attributed to entertainment gaming, such as relaxation. While entertainment games often induce flow-behaviour and observed traits, such as reduced awareness of stimuli non-relevant to the flow task, the challenge serious game developers face is aligning this to learning requirements. Unlike entertainment game developers, serious game designers seldom have the luxury of defining task difficulty in player-centric fashion and must rather achieve pre-specified learning objectives through constructing or adapting a game to make this learning content as engaging and flow-like as possible.

Shute (2008) cites the many examples of studies examining the impact of feedback frequency on learning transfer, including the works of Surber and Anderson (1975) and Newman and colleagues (1974), which suggest delayed feedback can be as efficient as immediate feedback. If this is the case, then delayed feedback may prove a more optimal paradigm for serious games due to its aforementioned ability to integrate with rather than disrupt flow experiences. The question in the context of serious games is therefore predominantly centred upon how frequently feedback should be conveyed rather than a more general decision between instant and delayed mechanisms and the answer must balance game design and flow with the need for effective learning transfer.

Content of feedback

Building on Shute's (2008) argument that facilitative feedback is an effective paradigm when building on existing knowledge, and given the fact that serious games, including *Triage Trainer*, typically seek to adapt behaviours through the application of this knowledge rather than convey cognitively simple fact-based content, it is important to consider the diverse ways that feedback can be presented in serious games. The framework this section explores is based upon Rogers' (1951) established definitions of such feedback as falling principally into the categories of *evaluative, interpretive, supportive, probing* and *understanding*. Rogers argues that the levels identified are discrete and lists them in order of most common use. Importantly, this does not reflect or presuppose their efficacy, since this is highly dependent on the context in which this feedback is conveyed, as well as the nature of the learner and instructor. However, it can be inferred that a learning intervention or programme that realizes and refers to all levels is described by Rogers as highly likely to be effective, though not necessarily efficient.

The general principles of content design typically hold true for serious games: information overload has been identified as an issue as relevant to virtual contexts as real ones (Warburton, 2008). Similarly principles such as avoidance of feedback perceived as overly critical (Baron, 1993) and that excessive or irrelevant feedback is likely to impede rather than facilitate learning (Bangert-Drowns et al., 1991), are as applicable to serious games as other forms of learning or training media. Furthermore, Shute (2008) notes that effective feedback commonly includes elements of verification and elaboration. Relating this to Rogers' model, verification can be seen as akin to the evaluative type of feedback, also the concept of summative feedback, while elaborative covers several of the higher levels due to its interpretive nature. In the next section, we describe our case study, which uses a secondary analysis of the data collected in the evaluation of the *Triage Trainer* serious game (Jarvis and de Freitas, 2009) to explore how adjustments to the timing and content of feedback impact on the efficacy of learning.

Case study: investigating the impact of feedback content and timing

The comparison of different training media has been criticized by some researchers. Studies have shown that it is not the training medium, for example its delivery method, that impacts learning but rather the training method or instructional strategy (Clark, 1983; Hays, 2005). Some researchers describe a more complex relationship between training media and training method and their impact on learning (Kozma, 1991). It is difficult to conduct experiments that enable the comparison of only one variable that has an impact on learning, such as formative feedback (Clark, 1983). We were cognizant of these issues when we designed a small training media comparison study to investigate the impact of changing timing and complexity of feedback in a serious game on performance for an emergency response scenario involving the need to triage or sort through in order of priority for treatment of mass casualties at the scene of the emergency.

The aim of the study was to evaluate the effectiveness of a serious game called *Triage Trainer* in supporting the teaching and development of basic major incident triage skills. The objective of the study was to compare triage performance after practising the triage process using *Triage Trainer* with a traditional learning method (Jarvis and de Freitas, 2009). Traditionally, triage processes are taught in small practical workshops. Practical restrictions often limit the degree to which the activities undertaken during training reflect real-world conditions. Large-scale real-world training events can create plausible environments, but these require significant resources and do not allow learners to easily repeat activities. A serious game was proposed because it offered a potential solution to these issues. The game is built around the triage sieve process, whereby first-responders are instructed to perform a series of sequential steps and subsequently assign one of four 'tags' to a casualty indicating the urgency with which they require treatment. *Triage Trainer* supplies feedback to learners explicitly through a designed After Action Review (AAR). The first incarnation of this review involved multiple screens showing a detailed performance breakdown. Structurally, this involved a summary screen that presented information on the percentages of correctly and incorrectly tagged casualties for each of the four priorities. The learner can then select an individual tag priority and view their results for a specific set of casualties. Learners are thus empowered with the ability to review their specific individual areas of weakness at the cost of a more time-consuming and cognitively complex feedback format. Furthermore, this feedback was given after tagging ten casualties, repeated for three scenes. Following qualitative feedback from initial trials, which suggested more streamlined and frequent methods could be beneficial, the AAR was modified to supply less detailed feedback (Figure 2.2) with different frequency, in this case after 3, 4, 5, 8, and 10 casualties. Hence, although the total number of casualties triaged (30) remained constant, feedback was supplied with two more intervals at decreasing frequency within the revised AAR.

The evaluation of these two versions was conducted non-simultaneously across four sites within the UK. At each site the game was integrated in the Major Incident Medical Management and Support (MIMMS) course. MIMMS courses are run by the Advanced Life Support Group. They are aimed at clinicians who may be required to attend the scene of a major incident. Triage is one aspect of the course. Participants typically include doctors, nurses and paramedics with an interest in pre-hospital care. Using a pragmatic controlled-trial approach, a total of 91 participants were split into a control group using a card-sort exercise (n=44), and those playing *Triage Trainer* (n=47). Two sites used the initial version of the AAR and two used the modified version. Following participation in either experiment or control, participants took part in a live-action exercise wherein actors simulated injuries and participants were assessed on their ability both to perform steps in the correct order ('step accuracy') and apply the correct tag ('tagging accuracy'). The overall results of this trial are described in detail elsewhere (Jarvis and de Freitas, 2009; Knight et al., in publication). It can be briefly summarized as evidencing the efficacy of *Triage Trainer* compared to the card sort exercise through a significant increase in the number of participants correctly tagging 8/8 casualties (Chi=7.29, p<0.01). Our analysis of the efficacy of feedback types is hence derived through secondary analysis of the data for the two game groups, with the initial feedback as a control (n=24) and the revised feedback as the experimental group (n=23). In this case while the analysis of the impact of modified AAR on tagging accuracy is inconclusive due to the small sample size (p>0.05), Chi square analysis using likelihood ratio indicates participants who used the revised feedback version performed significantly better (Chi=16.44, p<0.05). This analysis therefore shows that as predicted, frequency (timing) and form (complexity) of feedback have an impact on the achievement of learning outcomes.

Clearly, further research would be needed to determine which factors related to in-game feedback have the greatest influence on triage performance. It is suggested by the study that giving earlier and more frequent feedback should accelerate learning, particularly if time for practice is limited. Displaying the most relevant information for performance and having a layout that enables the learner to identify errors quickly should also support more efficient learning. This research seems to suggest that improved learning transfer may be possible with a simple procedural learning task such as the triage sieve process, when immediate feedback is given at the start of practice, representing the situation of a novice who may lack confidence and need the reassurance given by immediate feedback. An increasing delay in feedback may be preferential for later practice when the learner is close to mastering the procedure. This hypothesis will require further experimentation to determine more precisely which attributes of the in-game feedback have the greatest impact on the learning of the triage process for the given learner group, and whether these findings can be extended to a wider set of learning scenarios.

A framework for the four-dimensional consideration of feedback in Serious Games

The benefit of a structured and considered approach to feedback design is frequently noted. Shute (2008) suggests that systematically designed feedback has positive effects on motivation and learner achievement, and therefore it is relevant to consider how feedback within serious games may be orchestrated in a structured fashion. Adapting Rogers' classification of feedback types to certain game-based elements on a high level presents one potential method for relating an overarching facilitative paradigm to practical features, as shown for the case of a score in Table 2.1. *Facilitative,* in this case, is taken to refer to the notion that the feedback approach should be designed around the learner and therefore aligned closely to their needs. In particular, while the inherent scoring mechanisms common to many entertainment games make their use as a feedback mechanism for serious games an obvious avenue, such usage is grounded more in practicality than learner consideration, and therefore a more facilitative approach may offer benefits in broadening understanding of a serious game as an instructional programme (or component thereof).

A particular advantage, therefore, is relating technical challenges in performance assessment and automation of the feedback process to pedagogic challenges in applying technology appropriately and effectively. As shown in Table 2.1, an increasing level of feedback requires an increasing level of technical development and investment, ranging from the simple measurement of performance-related variables to sophisticated artificial intelligence and virtual agency. An alternative to this is the integration of a human instructor or more capable partner into the learning process to provide higher levels of feedback and hence the serious game becomes an integrative part of a training programme. We can identify the key actors in the feedback process in three categories, described in Table 2.1:

1. *Learners* are capable of self-reflection and intrinsically conducting the five levels of feedback shown in Table 2.1 in an introspective fashion. However, without extrinsic support they are limited by their own 'zone of proximal development' as defined in Vygotsky (1978). That is, they may face challenges they are independently unable (or unwilling) to overcome.

2. *Instructors* are taken very generally to mean any real-world individual supporting the learner and including, with reference to Vygotsky, 'more capable partners'. Their use in a serious gaming context suggests that the game plays a role in a blended learning solution rather than as a standalone learning application and hence there are practical constraints to learning programmes that necessitate or advocate instructor involvement. This can be particularly undesirable in serious game or e-learning development since a key influencer in the use of digital technology is its capacity for large-scale deployment at low cost *per capita*.

3. *Technology* is taken to mean any artificially driven system or character that seeks to take the role of an instructor as defined above. The motivation for its development is to leverage the advantages of e-learning with respect to large-scale deployment and autonomous learning, through the provision of synthetic instructors and more capable partners. While they can convey the more common feedback types – evaluative and interpretive – efficiently, their capacity to provide the higher levels is constrained by the complexity of the activity being assessed and the level of interactivity and dynamism required of the agent. While expert knowledge may be held in a database and conveyed to a learner autonomously, the greater the capacity of learners to diverge and explore a learning environment the more difficult becomes the task of providing effective feedback autonomously (Mott, 2006).

With respect to this final actor, Kort and colleagues (2001) suggest a design approach for this for implementing a learning partner that considers the relationship between emotion, affect and learning. Erfurt (2008) further demonstrates how other dialogic interactions can form a basis for learning environments through a single case study of the *Killer Phrase* game, wherein the learner adopts the role of a mediator between two debating synthetic characters. Finally, the passive use of brain-computer interfaces to drive intelligent agents that respond to inattention (Rebolledo-Mendez et al., 2009) has also been tentatively explored and presents an interesting avenue for future development. Since enacting the highest level of feedback is either expensive in terms of human resources or technical development, key questions are *when* is it beneficial to enact higher levels of feedback and *how* to adapt the model to consider more generally the traits of serious games that also play a role in the feedback process such as impact of feedback frequency, as well as other features indicated to play an important role such as nonlinearity through branching narratives (Mott, 2006). With respect to the first question, general evidence within the background literature is of use, although testing whether many hypotheses remain true when applied to serious games rather than more established training approaches remains a topic of ongoing research.

Table 2.1 Rogers' feedback types in the context of serious gaming

Feedback Type	Example for a score-based element	Technical demands (cumulative)
Evaluative	You got a score of 120/200	Measure variables
Interpretive	You got a score of 120/200 because you failed to respond quickly enough	Measure variables and model their relationships
Supportive	You got a score of 120/200, and need to improve your response times to challenges	Present and format measured data in a form relevant to learner
Probing	You got a score of 120/200, because your response times were too low, was this because the user interface was too complex, or due to the game being too hard, or was it something else?	User interaction model and support for dynamicism and adaptivity in content through intelligent agency
Understanding	You got a score of 120/200, because you found the user interface too complex, and as a result you responded too slowly to the challenges, you should complete the tutorial on the user interface	Link expert knowledge and experience to understanding of root causes of failure

As a result of the initial consideration of a simple element in Table 2.1, we note several high level observations likely to be common to many other elements:

1. Higher levels of feedback require increasing technical ambition to realize using technology as the primary actor;
2. Higher levels may be beyond the zone of proximal development of learners and therefore the involvement of other actors may be necessary to achieve learning outcomes;

3. Higher levels may be realized through experience rather than independent analysis, for example an instructor who has repeatedly observed similar problems among a group of learners may be able to bypass the analysis process;
4. The original supposition of Rogers that the frequency of use decreases with level is qualitatively observable to remain true for serious games, if not more so in light of the previous three points.

An initial inspection of Rogers' established model, therefore, suggests that it retains its relevance when considered in the context of serious games. While games and simulations offer the potential for additional feedback mechanisms which may layer on top of, or be integrated into, Rogers' model, in many cases they realize only evaluative feedback paradigms. Hence in the remainder of this section, we discuss the motivation for more fully addressing the multiple layers of feedback described and introduce a model for their consideration alongside cyclical and user-centric design processes often inherent to serious game development.

Earlier in this chapter, we discussed how serious games, as a consequence of their roots in training simulations, offer an avenue for feedback through evolution of simulation. That is, the learner performs an action, then in an experiential fashion observes the consequences directly rather than being informed by an abstract feedback process that their actions were correct or optimal. It is interesting to consider how this 'fits' Rogers' model. In some ways it can be perceived as a composite of probing and understanding feedback, placing the emphasis on the learner rather than the instructor to self-construct and self-analyse their choices and actions. However, if we take Rogers' model as being purely a guide for instructors, then such feedback mechanisms may indeed be an additional layer which could be described as *evolutionary* feedback: *the learner acts and the world evolves in response* providing feedback indirectly. As an example, in the case of a game intended to teach first-responders, visually demonstrating the impact of their incorrect choices on simulation in the form of patient deaths, using the evolution of the virtual patients, could form a basis for intrinsic feedback. From a critical perspective, this could be seen as a paucity or even absence of feedback, since it relies entirely on the learner being capable of relating their impact on a virtual, abstract space to the real world and unscaffolded attempts to achieve this have been frequently demonstrated to be ineffectual (Gick and Holyoak, 1980). However as fidelity increases, the emotive power of games is becoming easier to realize, with quantitative research already showing that small elements of virtual spaces, such as lighting can change learner affect (Knez and Niedenthal, 2008). Qualitatively, it is frequently reported by observers that the virtual patient technology developed as part of *Triage Trainer* has a powerful emotive component.

Quantifying and understanding in more depth the power this emotive approach has to deliver feedback through simulation of consequence is a topic of future work. It is likely that the power of this approach can only be realized if the learner is engaged and immersed within the virtual space and this engagement and immersion is scaffolding the learning transfer from virtual to real space. Thus, a key motivator for the development of increasingly high-fidelity serious games is the ability to explore ways not only to provide feedback through innovative and powerful mechanisms, but also to close the gap between virtual and real space described earlier in this chapter (see Figure 2.1) and invoke experiential learning processes that place less of a requirement on the learner to interpret abstract virtual events and relate them to real-world scenarios.

With respect to the design and evaluation of *Triage Trainer*, we applied a *four-dimensional* approach (de Freitas and Oliver, 2005) as described earlier within this chapter. Feedback is by no means exempt from such consideration and indeed tailoring feedback to these four dimensions is a critical activity in creating and implementing effective learning processes within a serious game. We describe feedback in serious games as *facilitative* as opposed to *evaluative* in an attempt to emphasize the need for feedback to be considered on multiple levels, as defined by Rogers (1951). While instructors and educators have long been aware of the benefits of such approaches to feedback (Mory 2004), the simplicity of implementing evaluative feedback for many game elements (Table 2.1), coupled with the frequent aim of serious games to provide learning outcomes *in lieu* of a human instructor, often leads to games that implement feedback in a principally or exclusively evaluative form. *Triage Trainer* is principally evaluative in form, although it was integrated into a course to achieve other feedback levels. Previously in this chapter, we described the measurable, positive outcomes of simplifying and increasing the frequency of feedback and this provides some further evidence that complex or voluminous evaluative feedback can disrupt flow.

For each of the three actors defined previously (learner, instructor and technology), our experience suggests initial feedback schemas should be generated from objectives, in the case of the learner and assessment methods and metrics in the case of instructor or technology-driven feedback. This process may then be repeated for each of Rogers' feedback types to establish an initial feasibility assessment for which levels of feedback can be implemented. The rationale for this approach is to perform at the earliest possible stage a review

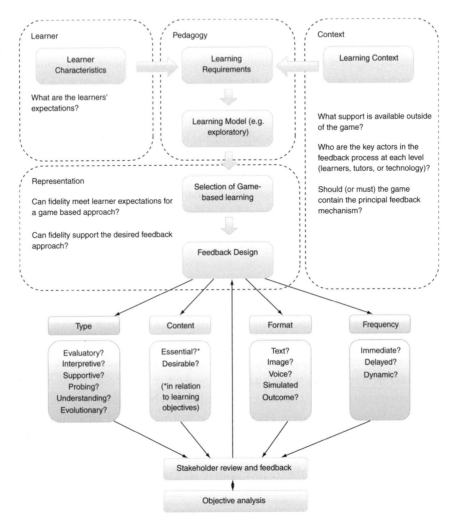

Figure 2.2 A four-dimensional approach to consideration of the feedback process

of which levels of feedback are likely to be problematic and to encourage a broad spectrum approach that considers how automated feedback may be better integrated, with respect to the learner and their context. Furthermore, by suggesting that a minimum of one actor be selected for each of Rogers' feedback types, we are able to advocate the development of serious games that encapsulate a fuller understanding of the different mechanisms through which feedback can be supplied to the learner, enabling a broader spectrum approach. Such an approach also aligns to the participatory and user-centric design processes advocated by the four-dimensional approach. An initial cost/efficacy comparison for each type can be conducted qualitatively with some exclusions mandatory as a result of external constraints, for example in some situations it may not be possible to incorporate face-to-face instruction due to practical considerations. In such a case, the model implies that the learner and available technology are analysed to the fullest possible extent to provide continuous high-level feedback support. Further comparisons of cost/efficacy are made possible by the participatory approach as well as user-centric design and ongoing evaluation. Indeed, cyclical development along spiral models such as that of Boehm (1988) is not only beneficial but, in the absence of existing studies that would allow us to make better decisions on the matter, is essential. This continued participatory design allows for refinement both in terms of the feedback design on each level and also in terms of the actors selected as best positioned to supply this feedback.

With respect to the *context* dimension, we suggest as a central consideration the evaluation and identification of the level of support available outside of the game to scaffold the learning process. A fundamental question in this dimension is whether the game *should* include the principal mechanism of feedback to learners – blended learning solutions have been shown to be effective contexts for serious games and a tutor or learning partner may often be better placed to provide certain types of feedback, such as supportive or probing, than a technological solution. Similarly, the advantages of technology in offering rapid and accurate 'evaluatory' feedback based on actions and behaviours can have merit over 'evaluatory' feedback delivered by instructors, which as noted earlier in the chapter, can be more prone to misinterpretation or be ambiguous, and whether this is likely to have a positive or negative effect on learning outcomes is an important design consideration.

With respect to *learners*, their expectations also play a central role in how feedback should be formulated and delivered. Feeding into a central consideration of *pedagogy*, this should reflect prior consideration of learners and their contexts and be evaluated with respect to the question of whether game-based learning is an appropriate choice of medium either *in lieu* of, or supplementary to, an existing course or course component. We identify also, and with particular regard to a game-based medium, four characteristics of feedback: *type, content, format* and *frequency*. Through *type* we refer to Rogers' established notion of different underlying paradigms: consideration of these paradigms with regard to their three potential providers – instructors, technology and the learner/s – allows a designer to move beyond a simplistic evaluatory approach through looking not only at the potential of technology but also the potential for the integration of serious games into the learning environment. We also suggest the clear identification of content as *essential* or *desirable*, with respect to learning outcomes, and consider also the format (or media) through which it is delivered, as well as considering frequency. Note that *dynamic* in this context refers to the notion that the rate of feedback may be controlled, either via technology or instructor, responding to the performance or other characteristics of the learner. Finally, we promote the notion of participatory design through stakeholder review and feedback, though we also note the importance of objective review of this feedback; stakeholders are not necessarily effective game or instructional designers, and frequently emphasize either game or instruction without sufficient regard to the balance between both, which lies at the core of other effective serious games.

Returning to Table 2.1, it is worth noting that in many cases only the first (Evaluative) level of feedback is often realized in serious games and therefore a case exists for not only research into the means through which the higher levels can be provided autonomously, but also for consideration of how serious games may be integrated and deployed into contexts which enable the higher levels to be fulfilled outside of the game. Encouraging a shift from purely evaluative feedback approaches towards a facilitative approach that considers each level of feedback, this model provides a high-level abstraction of the considerations that should be undertaken to enact effective facilitative feedback. We have neglected to consider the evolutionary feedback described earlier within the chapter since the principal role of the model is to identify the actors best placed to supply each feedback type. In our case here, evolutionary feedback is exclusively achieved through technology and therefore the use of the model in prescribing and analysing this mechanism is limited. It is indeed true, however, that a participatory approach can encompass the analysis of evolutionary mechanisms for feedback and hence support their integration into the learning process. Finally, another relatively untested theory in the case of serious games is that immediate feedback is more effective for the *retention* of procedural or conceptual knowledge (Anderson, 1995), primarily since immediate feedback on instructional outcomes can be difficult to align to game design without becoming obtrusive, an issue which evolutionary feedback may be capable of addressing by allowing the learner to immediately perceive a negative effect without obstructing gameplay.

Summary and conclusions

In this chapter, we have explored the notion of feedback in the context of serious gaming. While many questions remain unanswered, notably through a lack of large-scale empirical study of the situational efficacies of individual pedagogic elements and their resulting gameplay features, we have taken the first steps in linking feedback on a fundamental, biological level, to higher-level constructs and theories. Future work will seek to consolidate, explore and verify these links. The outcomes of this work will hence allow for more prescriptive approaches to serious game design built upon a consolidated base of evidence demonstrating best practices for given learning requirements. Within this model, feedback plays only one role, but an important one in maintaining flow while ensuring effective learning transfer. As a cautionary note, Shute argues that while 'conventional wisdom suggests that facilitative feedback . . . would enhance learning more than directive feedback . . . this is not necessarily the case' (Shute, 2008, p. 163). Shute outlines directive feedback as more effective for learners transitioning into new content areas, scaffolding the early stages of learning. Reapplying this theory to the specific domain of serious games and the four-dimensional approach highlights the need for careful consideration of the learner dimension when developing pedagogic approaches. Typically, while learners may be practitioners and situated in a context that uses other media for core knowledge transfer, and therefore well-positioned to benefit from a facilitative approach, the learning curve associated with the transition to a virtual world or game-based representation may benefit more from a directive approach during early stages as the user becomes familiarized with the capabilities of the representational medium.

Our secondary analysis of data from the evaluation of *Triage Trainer* has provided some insight into, and support for, the notion that feedback is a centrally important part of game-based learning. With reference to the four-dimensional analysis approach (de Freitas and Oliver, 2005), feedback can be seen to be related to all four dimensions: it must be understandable and relevant to learners and their context, it must work within the limitations of the representational medium and it must be underpinned by pedagogy. Moreover, it must do so without affecting flow and engagement within a game, and be closely integrated to gameplay. We have described how this is particularly the case in experiential learning, where feedback consolidates and scaffolds the link between virtual experience and real-world learning, although it should be noted that behaviourist approaches also place feedback as a central concern. Such scaffolding approaches are particularly sensitive to the alignment between positive feedback and successful learning outcomes – a number of well-documented cases exist where failure to create such an alignment has resulted in learners able to 'beat the game' but unable to demonstrate successful learning outcomes (BinSubaih, 2006). Egenfeldt-Nielsen (2005) cites this danger as a key motivator behind the shift from behaviourist to experiential approaches in serious game design, further reinforcing the notion that feedback is a central concern regardless of pedagogic approach.

There are practical as well as conceptual issues to be addressed. Instructors themselves may be reluctant to embrace technology that is perceived as either partially or fully replacing their role and the importance of fostering positive attitudes to serious games at early stages of the design process is worth noting (de Freitas and Jarvis, 2007). This may present a particular challenge when seeking to involve instructors as critical actors in the feedback process, since they may fail to engage with a serious game and therefore this concern is not restricted solely to learners.

In conclusion, this chapter has presented the case for a broader, facilitative view of feedback within serious games. While the example provided in Table 2.1 offers some preliminary insights into how this paradigm can be realized in serious game design, future work is required to test and evaluate the model and assess the efficacy of individual feedback types as well as their translation to technical features of serious games and course designs. Enacted successfully, the combination of learner, instructor and leading-edge technology has the potential to significantly improve learning experiences. Next-generation serious games must offer the potential to seamlessly integrate this feedback and pedagogic approach without compromising gameplay.

Acknowledgements

The authors would like to thank the following individuals and organizations for their contribution to the development and evaluation of *Triage Trainer*: TruSim, a division of Blitz Games, and all their development team involved with the project, SELEX Systems Integration, Bryan Tregunna, Dr. James Knight of the University of Birmingham, the Advanced Life Support Group and in particular Dr. Simon Carley and Professor Kevin Mackway-Jones.

References

Anderson, J. R., Corbett, A. T., Koedinger, K. R., and Pelletier, R. (1995). Cognitive tutors: lessons learned. *Journal of the Learning Sciences*, Vol. 4, pp. 167–207.

Bangert-Drowns, R. L., Kulik, C. C., Kulik, J. A. and Morgan, M. T. (1991). The instructional effect of feedback in test-like events. *Review of Educational Research*, Vol. 61, pp. 213–38.

Baron, R. A. (1988). Negative effects of destructive criticism: Impact on conflict, self-efficacy, and task performance. *Journal of Applied Psychology*, Vol. 73, pp. 199–207.

Bearman, M. (1997). Narratives and cases: implications for Computer-based Education. In *Proceedings of ASCILITE '97 Conference*, Perth, Australia.

BinSubaih, A., Maddock, S. and Romano, D. (2006). A serious game for traffic accident investigators. *International Journal of Interactive Technology and Smart Education*, Vol. 3, No. 4, pp. 329–46.

Boehm, B. (1988). A spiral model of software development and enhancement. *Computer*, Vol. 21, No. 5, pp. 61–72.

Clark, R. E. (1983). Reconsidering research on learning from media. *Review of Educational Research*, Vol. 53, No. 4, pp. 445–59.

Csikszentmihalyi, M. (1991). *Flow: The Psychology of Optimal Experience*. London: Routledge.

de Freitas, S. and Jarvis, S. (2007). Serious Games – Engaging Training Solutions: A research and development project for supporting training needs. *British Journal of Educational Technology*, Vol. 38, No. 3, pp. 523–25.

de Freitas, S. and Jarvis, S. (2009). Towards a development approach to serious games. Games-based learning advancements for multi-sensory human computer interfaces. In T. Connolly, et al., eds. Hershey: IGI Global, pp. 215–31.

de Freitas, S. and Neumann, T. (2009). The use of 'exploratory learning' for supporting immersive learning in virtual environments. *Computers and Education*, Vol. 52, No. 2, pp. 343–52.

de Freitas, S. and Oliver, M. (2005). A four dimensional framework for the evaluation and assessment of educational games. In *Proceedings of the Computer Assisted Learning Conference, 2005*.

Egenfeldt-Nielsen, S. (2005). Beyond edutainment: exploring the educational potential of computer games. Ph. D. thesis. IT-University Copenhagen.

Erfurt, F. (2008). 'Killer phrases': design steps for a game with digital role-playing agents. *Lecture Notes in Computer Science*, Vol. 5080, pp. 150–61.

Gass, M. and Gillis, L. (2000). *The Essential Elements of Facilitation*. Dubuque, IA: Kendall/Hunt.

Gick, M. L. and Holyoak, K. J. (1980). Analogical problem solving. *Cognitive Psychology*, Vol. 12, pp. 306–55.

Gobet, F., de Voogt, A. and Retschitzki, J. (2004). *Moves in Mind: The Psychology of Board Games*. Hove (UK): Psychology Press.

Hays, R. T. (2005). The effectiveness of instructional games: A literature review and discussion. *NAVAIR Technical Report 2005–004*, Naval Air Warfare Center Training Systems Division, 12350 Research Parkway, Orlando Florida 32826–3275.

Jarvis, S. and de Freitas, S. (2009). Evaluation of an immersive learning programme to support triage training: In-game feedback and its effect on learning transfer. In *Proceedings of IEEE Games and Virtual Worlds for Serious Applications (VS-GAMES '09)*, pp. 117–22.

Knez, I. and Niedenthal, S. (2008). Lighting in digital game worlds: Effects on affect and play performance. *Cyberpsychology & Behavior*, Vol. 11, 129–37.

Knight, J., Carley, S., Tregunna, B., Jarvis, S. Smithies, R., de Freitas, S. Dunwell, I. and Mackway-Jones, K. (in publication). Serious gaming technology in major incident triage training: A pragmatic controlled trial. Accepted for publication in *Resuscitation*, the European Journal of Emergency Medicine.

Kort, B., Reilly, R. and Picard R. W. (2001). An affective model of interplay between emotions and learning: Re-engineering educational pedagogy-building a learning companion. In *Proceedings of IEEE International Conference on Advanced Learning Technologies*, pp. 43–48.

Kozma, R. (1991). Learning with media. *Review of Educational Research*, Vol. 61, No. 2, pp. 179–211.

Mathan, S. A. and Koedinger, K. R. (2002). An empirical assessment of comprehension fostering features in an intelligent tutoring system. In *Intelligent Tutoring Systems, 6th International Conference, ITS,* S.A. Cerri, G. Goudarderes and F. Paraguacu, eds. New York: Springer Verlag, Vol. 2363, pp. 330–43.

Mautone, P. D., Spiker, V. A. and Karp, M. R. (2008). Using serious game technology to improve aircrew training. Proceedings of the interservice/industry training. *Simulation and Education Conference (IITSEC),* December 2008, Orlando, Florida.

Mory, E. H. (2004). Feedback research revisited. *Handbook of Research on Educational Communications and Technology,* 2nd Edition, D. H. Jonassen, ed. Mahwah, NJ: Lawrence Erlbaum Associates, pp. 745–83.

Mott, B. W., McQuiggan, S. W., Lee, S., Lee, S. Y. and Lester, J. C. (2006). Narrative-centered environments for guided exploratory learning. In *Proceedings of the Agent Based Systems for Human Learning Workshop,* 5th International Joint Conference on Autonomous Agents and Multiagent Systems (ABSHL-2006), Hakodate, Japan.

Newman, M. I., Williams, R. G. and Hiller, J. H. (1974). Delay of information feedback in an applied setting: effects on initially learned and unlearned items. *The Journal of Experimental Education,* Vol. 42, No. 4, pp. 55–9.

Pausch, R., Proffitt, D. and Williams, G. (1997). Quantifying immersion in virtual reality. In *Proceedings of the 24th Annual Conference on Computer Graphics and Interactive Techniques,* International Conference on Computer Graphics and Interactive Techniques. ACM Press/Addison-Wesley Publishing Co., New York, NY, pp. 13–18.

Pessiglione, M., Seymour, B., Flandin, G., Dolan R. J. and Frith C. D. (2006). Dopamine-dependent prediction errors underpin reward-seeking behaviour in humans. *Nature,* Vol. 442, pp. 1042–045.

Reynolds, J., Caley, L. and Mason, R., (2002). *How Do People Learn?* London: Chartered Institute of Personnel Development.

Rogers, C. (1951). *Client-centered Therapy: Its Current Practice, Implications and Theory.* London: Constable.

Schroth, M. L. (1997). The effects of delay of feedback on a delayed concept formation transfer task. *Contemporary Educational Psychology,* Vol. 17, No. 1, pp. 78–82.

Shute, V. J. (2008). Focus on formative feedback. *Review of Educational Research,* Vol. 78, No. 1, pp. 153–89.

Şimşek, Ö. and Barto, A. G. (2006). An intrinsic reward mechanism for efficient exploration. In *Proceedings of the 23rd International Conference on Machine Learning* (Pittsburgh, Pennsylvania, 25–29 June 2006). ICML '06, Vol. 148, pp. 833–40.

Surber, J. R. and Anderson, R. C. (1975). Delay-retention effect in natural classroom settings. *Journal of Educational Psychology,* Vol. 67, No. 2, pp. 170–3.

Warburton, S. (2008). Defining a framework for teaching practices inside virtual immersive environments: The tension between control and pedagogical approach. In *Proceedings of RELIVE '08 Conference.*

Wright, K. (2001). Can custom-made video games help kids with attention deficit disorder? *Discover,* Vol. 22, No. 3.

Vygotsky, L. S. (1978). *Mind in Society: The Development of Higher Order Psychological Processes.* Cambridge and London: Harvard University Press.

A Complex Systems Framework for Simulating Teaching and Learning

3

David Gibson

Introduction

Using digital games and simulations to help prepare teachers is inspired by the dramatic rise and growing appreciation of the potential for games and simulation-based learning (e.g. Aldrich, 2004; Foreman et al., 2004; Gee, 2004; Prensky, 2001; Squire and Jenkins, 2003). Model applications are needed that computationally represent teaching and learning, in order to apply the potential of simulations to the challenge of training teachers and school leaders. The simulation engines in these new applications will need to be complex enough to allow a user to make subtle decisions and 'play out' an essentially countless number of outcomes of the interaction of a teacher's intention and their impact on different learners in a classroom.

However, since all models have inherent limitations due to their simplification of reality (Holland, 1998), we are naturally led to question and explore the underlying assumptions of such frameworks for their limitations and potentialities in representing the act of teaching and the impacts of a teacher's decision-making on student learning. Thus, several key practical and philosophical questions arise concerning the use of games and simulations in teacher education and educational research. Can there be sufficient verisimilitude to be useful in teacher training? Can the complexities of learning be computationally modelled? What kinds of theories are amenable for representation in games and simulations and how do developers work with those theories? Will games and simulations ever be useful for discovering new knowledge – for example, discovering a cure for a disease – or are they just self-fulfilling prophecies, that is, they merely illustrate the knowledge of their creators?

This chapter offers initial responses to these questions in order to initiate a discussion about complex systems theory and its potential for mapping the reality of classrooms. The chapter begins by presenting an example application, *simSchool*, and uses it to illustrate a complexity framework for computationally representing teaching and learning. Since detailed treatments of the *simSchool* model are available elsewhere (Gibson, 2004, 2006; Gibson and Halverson, 2004), this chapter refers only to its broadest outlines in order to reveal the underlying complex systems model in the hopes of showing how a complexity framework is useful for thinking about computational and representational challenges in learning theory. For this discussion, a complex system model is one that can deal with widely varying yet integrally interconnected factors that integrate very large numbers of variables and represents behaviour that is difficult to predict and control.

Starting with *simSchool*

This section briefly describes the *simSchool* application, addresses some key questions often asked about its underlying theories and connects it to complex systems theory.

The *simSchool* application is an online simulation of a classroom that can model thousands of different kinds of students and allows a teacher to attempt to meet their different learning needs by assigning tasks in sequences and saying things to the students as they work on the tasks (Zibit and Gibson, 2005).

The teacher faces a classroom that can be filled with 1, 5 or 18 students. Interactions with the underlying model of teaching and learning are mediated through mouse and button clicks. Teachers can read about student personalities, learning preferences and past performance, including the traits of custom-designed students created by the teacher or trainer. A set of standardized tasks is available and the teacher or trainer can also make up new tasks in order to better reach and teach the simulated students. The students change body positions and offer comments in cartoon bubbles in response to the tasks and conversational choices of the teacher. A variety of immediate feedback displays are available, including a timeline of all the interactions displayed during and after the session. The teacher can also download data from the session and a coordinating professor or training leader can download and analyse all the sessions of a group of teachers.

In field trials and teacher training programmes that have been researching the use of *simSchool*, three findings have begun to emerge (Kim, Gibson and Baek, 2008; Knezek and Vandersall, 2008; Zibit and Gibson, 2005). First, people who use the simulation develop a significantly stronger sense of readiness to teach, most likely as a result of having many more opportunities to practise and develop skills through trials. This indicates that using the simulation might contribute to the development of a teacher's self-efficacy. Second, beliefs are strengthened concerning the potential for using games and simulations in teaching. This indicates that working with the simulator might influence someone to better appreciate the usefulness of games and simulations in education. Third, even though people have difficulty expressing exactly what they have learned from working with the simulator, different groups of people will rank key teaching skills significantly different across different groups. They will, however, be in strong alignment within their group with the goals of their professors for using the simulation. This might indicate that procedural knowledge is engaged and developed when using the simulation and that the application acts as a non-biased platform for illustrating and offering practice in differing kinds of teaching knowledge and skills.

As *simSchool* has been used in teacher education programmes, played by teachers and studied by researchers, a number of philosophical and practical questions have arisen. The philosophical questions concern matters such as whether and why simulations might be legitimate sources of knowledge that are suitable for use in training and professional development of teachers and administrators, and the practical questions concern matters such as how such simulations are built and how they can be best used to improve education.

Answers to the practical questions, by contrast, primarily require description and explanation of *simSchool*'s sub-models and theories and its implementation details. For example, one question is whether the simulation favours one kind of pedagogy over another. The answer is provisionally 'no' (the question is still being investigated) because the underlying logical engine of *simSchool* was designed with the intention of supporting several models of teaching and learning. The dynamics of the teacher-student relationship are based on a broad integration of foundational psychological and sociological theories that are potentially involved in many pedagogical approaches. For example, the Big Five Model of personality (Digman, 1990; McCrae and Costa, 1996; Raad, 2000; Srivastava, 2006), circumplex theories of personal interactions (Acton, n.d.; Carson, 1969; Cattell, 1957; Digman, 1990; Leary, 1957), the integration of personality theories with intelligence and performance theories (Brooks, 1999; Budaev, 2000; Chamorro-Premuzic and Furnham, 2004; Gardner, 1983; Hawkins and Blakeslee, 2004; Hofstee et al., 1992; Howard and Howard, 2000; Leary, 1957; McGrew, 2003; Pfeifer and Bongard, 2007), social theories of personality (Bandura and Walters, 1963; Hofstee et al., 1992; Moberg, 1999) and computational models of these processes (Busetta et al., 2002; Morris, 2002; Parunak et al., 2006; Rao and Georgeff, 1991, 1992; Silverman, 2001). The integration of these various foundations has been discussed in some depth elsewhere (Gibson 2004, 2006, in press; Gibson and Halverson, 2004; Zibit and Gibson, 2005) but even without reviewing them again, it is hopefully plain to see that there must be some complexity involved when bringing the theories together. The purpose here is not to claim anything specific about how they have been integrated, but to point to the need for an understanding of complex systems in the design of some simulations.

The philosophical questions on the other hand need to be further examined now as part of the rationale for employing the concepts of complex systems in the design of simulations to improve education. Such questions include the following – would a simulation with sufficient realism be useful in teacher training? Can the complexities of learning be computationally modelled? What kind of knowledge is engaged when using such a simulation? To answer these questions requires a brief review and critical examination of scientific modelling in education that point out the conundrums and confines of an overly linear scientific programme, for example typical epistemological and methodological perspectives prior to complex systems theory, for discovering and validating knowledge about teaching and learning.

A new scientific modelling effort is needed for learning theory, one aimed at making operational a collective understanding of the dynamics of teaching and learning – that is, how a teacher influences someone to learn, how that learning builds into a student's evolving structure of knowledge and understanding and how social relationships and feedback play a role in the process. The argument then shows that new dynamic modelling efforts are emerging within games and simulations aimed at improving education, in the sense of both the experience and outcomes for students and the preparation of the adults who work with them. These modelling efforts presuppose a computational form for the complex mixture of theories underlying the logic engines, since their goal is to create digital games and simulations. This is not to say that traditional forms of scientific discovery and modelling are obsolete, but to point out that the tools and methods of computational science offer a unique and rich array of alternatives for creating as well as collecting, analysing and representing knowledge. The new complex system alternatives allow creation of learning theory sub-models situated along a spectrum of scales that range from the microscopic levels of neuroscience to the mesoscopic scale of cognition and creativity and the macroscopic scale of sociocultural theory. These issues will be addressed and illustrated below. To begin, a few questions and responses offer a starting point into the discussion, with links to the main question of why a complex systems framework is needed.

Can a model of a classroom provide a realistic experience for training aspects of teaching?

All models are incomplete representations (Coyle, 1996; Pritsker, 1998), so it is important to emphasize that models are never fully in a one-to-one relationship with reality. Otherwise their efficacy and efficiency characteristics would be the same as in reality, when the purpose is instead to provide a substitute for reality that improves some of those characteristics, for example saving time, increasing rates and scales of expertise development, while lowering dangers, risks and expenses.

A concern for realism arises in many fields where computer-based simulations are used for training and professional development. For example, realism is no less important for training educators than it is for pilots, search and rescue squad members, fire fighters, emergency management team members, doctors and others. In spite of the trade-offs of interaction simplicity versus realism and the possibility of increased cognitive load as realism increases, how individual users construe the cognitive load of a simulation seems largely independent of the level of simulated realism (Stanney, 2002) and may be less important than other variables, such as prior knowledge, training, experience and psychological traits. The concern for realism is thus appropriate, but has to be weighed against other criteria, such as the efficacy of a model's simplification for teaching purposes and its efficiency factors.

Finally, the level of realism available in classroom simulations today is less than it will be in the future, but is adequate to provide practice in many arenas of decision-making. Examples of current teaching simulations illustrate their efficacy for teaching instructional planning, adapting instruction, interpreting student records, managing a range of classroom behaviours, designing tasks that provide learning opportunities, estimating the impact of those tasks on different kinds of learners and building and using assessments and reflecting on teaching (Cheong and Kim, in press; Gibson, 2004; Girod et al., 2006; Kim et al., 2008). In summation, a model of a classroom that is suitably realistic for developing teachers seems to be a reachable goal.

Is learning too subtle a phenomenon for modelling?

Some people may believe that there are parts of teaching and learning that are not amenable to scientific understanding. If so, then those aspects would indeed be too subtle for modelling, perhaps too subtle for academic discussions as well. However, even in the absence of explicit and operational scientific models, interpretation is needed in order to apply theory to reality. For example, even though the 'atom' of Aristotle was not the same model that today's physicists have in mind, the 'charitable interpretation' (Putnam, 1992) is that both words point to a similar subtle phenomenon. In fact, all models rely on interpretation to transform concrete 'stand-ins' into meaningful metaphors of subtle 'real things'. This allows a science teacher, for example, to teach a lesson about the phases of the moon using a lamp, a basketball and a soccer ball. Everyone knows that the lamp model of the sun is less subtle than the real situation, but that does not prevent its meaningful use for teaching and learning about the astronomical positions of earth, sun and moon.

Other people may believe that current modelling methodologies simply do not have the complexity required to adequately represent teaching and learning, but they would allow that future models might be better. Before the age of computational science tools, most branches of knowledge suffered from computationally unsophisticated models. Whatever was taught about 'cell biology' in high school a few years ago, there are now vastly different models that have emerged with the aid of computers. Many of today's mechanisms were unknown and those that were beginning to be understood could not be accurately modelled because important computational tools and capabilities were not available. Such could certainly be the case with theories of teaching and learning. We are fortunate to now have advanced computers and frameworks, such as complex systems and dynamics as modern tools of analysis and modelling.

Finally, developing and testing simulations is an important part of the leading edge of many other scientific pursuits that are challenged by complexity and subtlety, for example an understanding of life on earth, consciousness and universal evolution. It follows that the science of teaching and learning should be able to benefit from a similar approach. Complex systems theory (Bar-Yam, 1997; Sterman, 1994) provides researchers and modellers with tools to deal with the challenging and surprising emergent behaviours that are the consequences of having many variables, relationships and conditions. In the framework outlined below, some key concepts of complexity are briefly presented in the hope of providing signposts to deeper study and reflection that will be required for using the theory to build models capable of showing more of the subtleties of teaching and learning. In summation, teaching and learning contexts are not too complex to model with some degree of fidelity and effectiveness given some "charity of interpretation" (Putnam, 1988).

What kinds of theories of personality, teaching and assessment can be dynamically modelled?

Any theory that can be computationally represented can be dynamically modelled in a computer game or simulation. This statement is both obvious and is at the same time laden with problems and concerns, especially for those who have not encountered the possibility that a theory can produce data as well as analyse and represent it. It is possible that not all theories can be computationally represented to everyone's satisfaction, but it seems reasonable to expect that all theories can be approximated and computationally represented to an arbitrary level of realism suitable for teaching and learning purposes. Discussing this conjecture and methods for 'quantizing' (Coyle, 1998; Miles and Huberman, 1994) qualitative and quantitative data for system dynamics modelling engages us with two issues:

1. simulated theories that produce as well as analyse and represent data;
2. problems and opportunities of self-reference.

Theories that produce data

Traditional theorizing produces static quantitative representations or highly contextualized descriptions and narrative propositions (Creswell, 2003). The two main traditions of educational research – statistics in quantitative methods and narratives in qualitative methods – are by themselves insufficient for directly representing dynamic processes, because the role of time and evolution is often missing or vague and data is primarily treated as an input, not the result of computation. Theories developed from strictly quantitative or qualitative research traditions might be labelled 'non-computational' to help signify that computations (if any) are conducted before but not during the presentation of findings or the re-telling of the narrative. This contrasts with a dynamic and interactive simulation, which computes new data in real-time in conjunction with or in response to someone working with the underlying model. 'Simulable' models of theories (Rosen, 1991) come to life through a process that involves quantifying their elements and putting those elements into mathematical relationships that are computed to interact and behave over time.

The task of dynamically modelling the evolution of elements and relationships requires integrating insights from traditional methods while introducing active models of the forces that cause the system to evolve. Theories developed this way might be labelled 'computational' to help capture the idea of the moment-by-moment unfolding of the relationships and elements and the central role of a computing device in the process. In an interactive simulation the production of data is the centrepiece of gameplay, agent behaviour and the representation of physical processes. Thus, an important and defining new role of an underlying theory in game and simulation-based computational modelling is to provide an operationally defined structure for the production of data. Furthermore, in a teaching and learning simulation, the modelling of important processes extends into psychological and social arenas, including the production and manipulation of hypothetical or conceptually constructed variables and mechanisms, for example motivation to learn, learning preferences, cognitive functions, emotional processing. The need for a complex systems framework is apparent, to integrate the widely differing personal, social, intellectual and physical dimensions of the phenomenon being modelled.

The problems and opportunities of self-reference

If traditional modelling creates, analyses and represents data with the same theory, a tautology or self-fulfilling prophecy is created, 'circular reasoning' in other words, which is to be avoided at all costs within the logical framework. But in models based in complex systems theory, tight logical tautologies are most unlikely, because nonlinearity and sensitivity to initial conditions makes it impossible to predict the exact behaviour of the system. Only a theory that is sufficiently linear, well-behaved and relatively simple can produce data that fulfills its own analytic and representational expectations and thus become useless for discovering new knowledge. Although such a tautological argument would be of little use to research aimed at discovering new knowledge. It might still be useful for training and teaching.

The observer, through both interpretation and error, accounts for most of the uncertainty in the 'simple – linear' circumstance. By contrast, the uncertainty in the 'complex – nonlinear' circumstance is guaranteed to be inherent in the structure of the theory and its computational implementation and this is a good thing because it allows us to model complex behaviour and to search for new discoveries in the data produced by the models. For example, cosmologists may look at results in their modelling to find promising places to look into the heavens for evidence that validates their models. New 3D conformations of chemicals are tested virtually before expensive laboratory methods are developed and deployed. In this light, the tight logical or linear tautology that is usually to be avoided as a self-fulfilling prophecy, becomes a broader concept of richly interwoven multiple nonlinear causes of emergent behaviours and is to be sought for its generative role in advancing knowledge.

The switch from avoiding errors in linear modelling to cherishing them in nonlinear modelling requires a new form of thinking about the epistemology and methodology of educational research. To begin on a path of discovering and developing the new frame of thinking, it helps to have an outline of the framework of a complex system such as those found in serious games and simulations of teaching and learning.

The complex systems framework

A complex system has a large number of distinct interacting parts that are integrally connected and entwined. If the parts are fully separable, then the system is less complex; it may even quit 'working' as a system altogether. The interdependent entwinement of the parts in a complex system is a substrate for whole system behaviour that is not completely explained by understanding the component parts, for example a floating iceberg is made up of water molecules but does not behave on the same scale. We may for example observe emergent behaviours that depend upon many sets of parts or even upon the patterns of relationships among the sets rather than the parts, for example a heartbeat rather than a single firing nerve. If we peer closely at the relationships between the parts, we lose focus on global interactions that emerge when we consider the system as a whole. Conversely, if we view the large, emergent behaviours of the system, we may not pinpoint exactly which parts are responsible for particular aspects of the behaviour. Studying such systems is thus highly inter-disciplinary and requires flexibly changing points of view to encompass the wide variety of scales of the parts and their connections. To use a complex systems framework to model teaching and learning then requires making decisions about the variety of components and which of the many connections and interrelationships are to be considered.

Since the goal is to simulate teaching and learning, the complex systems framework has to represent what a teacher does and what students do in response or what the student initiates and what a teacher does in response. The concepts of the framework will be developed by starting with an unpromising initial simple linear model, the S-R (stimulus-response) model with two 'black boxes' and arrows connecting them to represent the flow of stimuli and responses (Model A in Figure 3.1). Black box systems allow us to concentrate for the time being on just the inputs and outputs flowing on arrows represent-ing relationships between two entities, not the internal structure and dynamics of the entities. This controls the spatial scale of the model. One box represents the teacher and the other the student. As the model is developed, boxes will be added and some turned into 'glass boxes' to look inside, changing the scale and increasing the complexity of the model. At this initial level there are two

Figure 3.1 S-R static models of teaching and learning

practical ideas needed for an abstract model of the dynamic teaching-learning relationship: boxes for the parts of the system or *nodes* and connection relationships or arrows of *influence* linking the nodes.

Almost immediately the incompleteness of the S-R model is evident, with only the teacher and student in a static *hierarchical relationship* represented in Model A (Figure 3.1). Allowing for the signal from the student to the teacher to be either the stimulus or a response and allowing the same for the teacher, expands the model from two paths to four and creates the possibility for mutual *peer-to-peer relationships* represented by the slightly more complex Model T (Figure 3.1). Peer-to-peer relationships will be needed to model more than one student in a classroom as well as the one-on-one relationship of teacher to student. Introducing equality and uncertainty into the *dependencies* introduces a new level of complexity. A teacher stimulus might produce either a student response or a student stimulus, which in turn might produce either a teacher response or stimulus.

Mutuality of peer-to-peer relationships more than doubles the possible outcomes in a multi-step process. Multi-step processes introduce another critical feature of the general framework: *time*, which has to be introduced in order to represent the evolution of the dynamic relationships. Static pictures drawn with boxes and arrows cannot represent evolving relationships. The same can be said for similarly static correlational, multivariate, hierarchical linear models and static 2D graphic representations of teaching and learning. Time, quantified and represented as a succession of states of a system and new attendant *dynamic graphical representations* (e.g. 'movies' of data flows) need to become a common part of learning theory in order to move beyond the limitations of many current research methods.

Consider, for example, a three-step interaction initiated by the teacher in Model A (Figure 3.1). The three steps would be (T>s>T>s), where the large letter 'T' represents a stimulus from the teacher, the small letter 's' stands for a response from the student and the '>' sign stands for 'influences.' Compare that with the possibilities of the slightly expanded S-or-R 'Model T', started by the teacher again, but allowing both the student and teacher to either respond or initiate a new stimulus. The one-path possibility of Model A expands rapidly to eight potential paths in Model T: (T>s>T>s); (T>s>t>s); (T>s>T>S); (T>s>t>S); (T>S>T>s); (T>S>t>s); (T>S>t>S); (T>S>T>S). Those familiar with basic mathematics can see that as the number of steps (i.e. units of time) and the number of possible states for teacher and student action increase, the computational challenge skyrockets.

The results of just twenty minutes of class time (where 1 step = 1 minute) with the expanded but still overly simplified S-or-R Model T, would produce over a million different possible outcome paths. Clearly as more sophisticated ideas are introduced about how teachers and students interact, there will be a very large number of paths available to represent a wide array of teacher and student behaviours.

In addition to the path complexity created by time, the uncertainty of whether the next step will involve a response or stimulus increases complexity. The node, which in the Model A had only one role, in the Model T now has two potential roles that are simultaneously present in instant of time. Each step in a multi-step process (e.g. T>s>T>s) is composed of the current state, the influence and the resulting impact (e.g. T>s) but note that the resulting impact 's' is simultaneously the current state for the next step (e.g. s>T or S>t or S>T). This curious uncertain double meaning that unifies the stimulus and the response into a single multi-casual state is similar to a hyperlink in that it has a surface structure (e.g. the response is like the interpreted text) as well as a pointer to something else (e.g. a stimulus travelling outside itself is like the URL address that is the 'meaning' of the text). To see this, view the student box as a 'glass box' at two points in time (Figure 3.2).

Introducing time and uncertainty transforms the initial context of a response-only node into one with a new state that can potentially signal to an outside context. This multifaceted aspect of a node in the network introduces the possibility of hypermedia effects, such as *feedback*, reflection and by

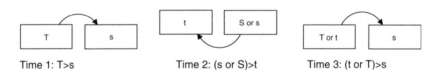

Time 1: T>s   Time 2: (s or S)>t   Time 3: (t or T)>s

Figure 3.2 Mutual peer to peer S or R relationships introduce uncertainty and complexity

extension perhaps, meta-cognition. Most important, it introduces a mechanism for the influence of an action back on itself, which is a fundamental requirement for learning and control of behaviour as well as a sign of a complex system.

Based on the example of *simSchool* (Zibit and Gibson, 2005), the Model T can be expanded with two more concepts: *arrays of factors of a domain* and a *continuum of activity on each factor*. The arrays of factors provide the model with many types of responses and stimuli, and the continuum on each factor provides many levels of intensity. To illustrate, the domains in *simSchool* include physical, emotional and intellectual arenas of experience and cognition. These domains roughly correspond to a well-known taxonomy of educational objectives (Bloom et al., 1964), and in *simSchool* are additionally defined with underlying subcategory factors that reflect modern psychological, cognitive science and neuroscience concepts. For example, the Five Factor Model (McCrae and Costa, 1996) of psychology comprises the emotional domain. A simplified sensation model with auditory, visual and kinesthetic perceptual preferences comprises the physical domain; and a flexible array of factors suitable to each specific academic, intellectual or cognitive domain is used to represent salient factors for classroom teaching and learning. Representing mathematics for example might use an array of factors such as computation, problem-solving and communication.

The initial idea of stimulus is thus expanded to mean a complex mixture (i.e. *a multidimensional surface* or metaphorically, a landscape) of both internal and external conditions that give rise to behaviours. A teacher who notices a raised hand in the classroom and then talks to the student and presents the student with a task is acting on, as well as within, a mixed landscape of responses and stimuli. The complex systems framework allows overlapping conditions, such as these, to influence both the student and teacher simultaneously, as well as in sequence. Complementing the notion of complex stimuli mixtures, the initial simple idea of response is also expanded to mean a mixture or *composition of executable behaviours linked to internal states* of the teacher or student. For example, when the teacher makes a decision about which task to select next, or what to say and how to say it to a student, or when a student slumps in the chair or raises a hand for help, those actions are taken as signs of internal conditions that are both responding to previous and current states as well as signalling intentions about the future.

For each salient factor involved in a given learning situation, *simSchool* represents both the current state of the student and the student's potential actions along a *continuum*. The interpretation of the continuum can be adjusted to the *representational* needs of the factor and domain, for example from too little to too much; under to over-reliance; weak to strong preference; negative to positive influence. For example, one of the factors in the emotional domain is introversion to extroversion. Each student has an initial setting at the beginning of class that lies somewhere between highly introverted and highly extroverted. When faced with a task with a requirement for high extroversion, for example singing a song in front of one's peers, a requirement condition is broadcast into the environment. Given enough time and support, *simSchool* assumes, each student can potentially do this task. But some students may be highly introverted while others may be moderately extroverted. For the introverted students, the task will be harder to face and take longer to master.

To compute how much harder and how long it will take, the setting on the external condition's factor acts like an *attractor* on the matched factor's internal setting in the student. An attractor can be thought of as influencing or indirectly causing complex changes over time, such as the way a heavy object on a bumpy rubber sheet might 'attract' a small marble placed on the sheet; the paths the marble can take are numerous and varied due to the bumps and dips. The context – the set of all conditions that are in place in a given moment in time – has many attractors (dips) and *repellents* (bumps), each of which can pull on several marble-like variables at differing rates and strengths as the system evolves over time. For example, we might imagine the extroversion requirement of a task influencing the student's introversion variable more than other factors present. Bumpiness on the contextual landscape allows minor perturbations and smaller influences to complicate the path of the student's introversion variable. This makes room for simulating the difference between whether the student is agreeable or disagreeable in character, or whether the student prefers repetitive performance to unfamiliar new experiences and how such considerations impact the student's introversion when faced with the task of singing at the front of the class.

It is important to note that both teachers and students have agency in classroom situations and either can perturb the current landscape of dips and bumps, by what they say or do, which is related to how they are experiencing the situation.

The key features of a complex systems framework presented here, and illustrated by current *simSchool* classroom simulation, point to the possibility for suitable models of teaching and learning that reflect a sufficient degree of verisimilitude to be useful in training, as well as researching aspects of teaching, learning and teacher and learner agency.

Conclusion

Elements of a complex system model of teaching and learning have been outlined above and are asserted as a new framework for theorizing, modelling and simulation. This chapter generalized from the example of a classroom simulator – *simSchool* – in order to outline a complex systems framework for simulating teaching and learning. The new way of thinking requires a new vocabulary that includes terms such as: nodes, lines of influence, hyperlinked peer-to-peer and hierarchical structures, interacting representational domains comprised of factors expressed as continua, and dynamics characterized by multidimensional fields with attractors and repellents controlling the evolution of system and subsystem states. The issues represented by these terms are especially salient when creating computational models, simulations and games that are intended to improve teacher or school leadership education, because of the complexity of the many overlapping and interacting systems involved in teaching.

References

Acton, S. (2007). Interpersonal complementarity. Last accessed 7 May 2007 from http://www.personalityresearch.org/interpersonal/comp.html.

Aldrich, C. (2004). *Simulations and the Future of Learning: An Innovative (and Perhaps Revolutionary) Approach to E-Learning.* San Francisco: John Wiley & Sons.

Bandura, A. and Walters, R. (1963). *Social Learning and Personality Development.* New York: Holt, Rinehart, and Winston.

Bar-Yam, Y. (1997). *Dynamics of Complex Systems.* Reading, MA: Addison-Wesley.

Bloom, B., Mesia, B. and Krathwohl, D. (1964). *Taxonomy of Educational Objectives.* New York: David McKay.

Brooks, R. (1999). *Cambrian Intelligence: The Early History of the New AI.* Cambridge, MA: MIT Press.

Budaev, S. (2000). The Dimensions of Personality in Humans and Other Animals: A Comparative and Evolutionary Perspective. Unpublished manuscript, Moscow.

Busetta, P., Bailey, J. and Ramamohanarao, K. (2002). A reliable computational model for BDI agents. 2007. Last accessed 9.4.10 from http://sra.itc.it/people/busetta/papers/safeAgents03.pdf.

Carson, R. C. (1969). *Interaction Concepts of Personality.* Chicago: Aldine.

Cattell, R. (1957). *Personality and Motivation: Structure and Measurement.* New York: Harcourt, Brace & World.

Chamorro-Premuzic, T. and Furnham, A. (2004). A possible model for understanding the personality-intelligence interface. *British Journal of Psychology,* Vol. 95, pp. 249–64.

Cheong, D. and Kim, B. (in press). Design and development of a simulation for improving teachers' motivational skills. In D. G. Y. Baek, ed. *Digital Simulations to Improve Education.* Hershey, PA: IGI Global.

Coyle, R. (1998). The practice of system dynamics: milestones, lessons and ideas from 30 years experience. *System Dynamics Review,* Vol. 14, pp. 343–66.

Coyle, R. G. (1996). *System Dynamics Modelling: A Practical Approach.* London: Chapman & Hall.

Creswell, J. (2003). *Research Design: Qualitative, Quantitative and Mixed Methods Approaches.* Thousand Oaks, CA: Sage Publications.

Digman, J. (1990). Personality structure: emergence of the five-factor model. *Annual Review of Psychology,* Vol. 41, 417–40.

Foreman, J., Gee, J., Herz, J., Hinrichs, R., Prensky, M. and Sawyer, B. (2004). Game-based learning: how to delight and instruct in the 21st century. *EDUCAUSE Review,* Vol. 39, No. 5, pp. 1–66.

Gardner, H. (1983). *Frames of Mind: The Theory of Multiple Intelligences.* New York: Basic Books.

Gee, J. (2004). *What Video Games Have to Teach Us About Learning and Literacy.* New York: Palgrave Macmillan.

Gibson, D. (2004). Simulation as a Framework for Preservice Assessment. Paper presented at the Proceedings of the Society for Information Technology in Teacher Education Conference, Atlanta, GA.

Gibson, D. (2006). *simSchool* and the conceptual assessment framework. In D. Gibson, C. Aldrich and M. Prensky, eds. *Games and Simulations in Online Learning: Research & Development Frameworks.* Hershey, PA: Idea Group.

Gibson, D. (in press). Modelling classroom cognition and teaching behaviours with COVE. In D. G. Y. Baek, ed. *Digital Simulations to Improve Education.* Hershey, PA: IGI Global.

Gibson, D. and Halverson, B. (2004). *SimSchool*: Preparing tomorrow's teachers to improve student results. Paper presented at the Society for Information Technology in Teacher Education Annual Conference, Atlanta, GA.

Girod, G., Girod M. and Denton, J. (2006). Lessons learned modelling 'connecting teaching and learning'. In D. Gibson, C. Aldrich and M. Prensky, eds. *Games and Simulations in Online Learning: Research & Development Frameworks.* Hershey, PA: Idea Group.

Hawkins, J. and Blakeslee, S. (2004). *On Intelligence.* New York: Henry Holt and Company.

Hofstee, W., de Raad, B. and Goldberg, L. (1992). Integration of the Big Five and Circumplex approaches to trait structure. *Journal of Personality and Social Psychology,* Vol. 63, No. 1, pp. 146–63.

Holland, J. (1998). *Emergence: From Chaos to Order.* New York: Perseus Books

Howard, P. J. and Howard, J. M. (2000). *The Owner's Manual For Personality At Work: How The Big Five Personality Traits Affect Performance, Communication, Teamwork, Leadership and Sales.* Atlanta, GA: Bard Press.

Kim, B., Gibson, D. and Baek, Y. (2008). Effects of *simClass* [Electronic Version]. *simZine*, Vol. 3.

Knezek, G. and Vandersall, K. (2008). *simMentoring* Results [Electronic Version]. *simZine, Vol. 3.*

Leary, T. (1957). *Interpersonal Diagnosis of Personality.* New York: Ronald.

McCrae, R. and Costa, P. (1996). Toward a new generation of personality theories: theoretical contexts for the five-factor model. In J. S. Wiggins, ed. *The Five-Factor Model of Personality: Theoretical Perspectives*, New York: Guilford, pp. 51–87.

McGrew, K. (2003). Cattell-Horn-Carroll CHC (Gf-Gc) Theory: Past, Present & Future. Last accessed 8 May 2007, from http://www.iapsych.com/CHCPP/CHCPP.HTML.

Miles, M. and Huberman, A. (1994). *Qualitative Data Analysis: An Expanded Sourcebook.* Thousand Oaks, CA: Sage Publications.

Moberg, D. (1999). The big five and organizational virtue. *Business Ethics Quarterly,* 9(2), 245–72.

Morris, T. (2002). Conversational agents for game-like virtual environments [Electronic Version], from http://tinyurl.com/357ne48

Parunak, H., Bisson, R., Brueckner, S., Matthews, R. and Sauter, J. (2006, 8–12 May). A Model of Emotions for Situated Agents. Paper presented at the Autonomous Agents and Multi-Agent Systems, Hokkaido, Japan: Hakodate.

Pfeifer, R. and Bongard, J. (2007). *How The Body Shapes The Way We Think: A New View of Intelligence.* Cambridge, MA: MIT Press.

Prensky, M. (2001). *Digital Game-Based Learning.* New York: McGraw-Hill.

Pritsker, A. (1998). Principles of simulation modelling. In J. Banks, ed. *Handbook Of Simulation: Principles, Methodology, Advances, Applications and Practice.* NY: John Wiley & Sons.

Putnam, H. (1988). *Representation and Reality.* Cambridge, MA: MIT Press.

Putnam, H. (1992). *Renewing Philosophy.* Harvard, MA: Harvard University Press.

Raad, B. D. (2000). *The Big Five Personality Factors: The Psycholexical Approach to Personality.* Kirkland, WA: Hogrefe & Huber.

Rao, A. and Georgeff, M. (1991). Modelling rational agents within a BDI architecture. Paper presented at the International Conference on Principles of Knowledge Representation and Reasoning.

Rao, A. and Georgeff, M. (1992). An abstract architecture for rational agents. Paper presented at the Third International Conference on Principles of Knowledge Representation and Reasoning (KR'92), San Mateo, CA.

Rosen, R. (1991). *Life Itself.* New York: Columbia University Press.

Silverman, B. (2001). *More Realistic Human Behaviour Models for Agents in Virtual Worlds: Emotion, Stress and Value Ontologies.* Philadelphia, PA: University of Pennsylvania.

Squire, K. and Jenkins, H. (2003). Harnessing the power of games in education. *Insight, 3*(5), 5–33.

Srivastava, S. (2006). Measuring the Big Five Personality Factors. Last accessed from http://www.uoregon.edu/~sanjay/bigfive.html.

Stanney, K. (2002). *Handbook of Virtual Environments: Design, Implementation, and Applications.* Mahwah, NJ: Lawrence Erlbaum Associates.

Sterman, J. D. (1994). Learning in and about complex systems. *System Dynamics Review,* Vol. 10, No. 2 / 3), p. 291.

Zibit, M. and Gibson, D. (2005). *simSchool*: the game of teaching. *Innovate,* Vol. 1, No. 6.

Part 2
Cultura
Cultural Perspectives

Revolution: Experiential Learning through Virtual Role Play

4

Russell Francis

Chapter Outline

Introduction

Story-telling has played an important role in Humanities education since the advent of formal schooling. Stories are fictional constructs. However, stories based on historical events or stories that explore real-world issues allow learners to step out of the immediacy of the present and imagine what it might be like to be someone who lived during different times, places or under different social-historical circumstances. Murray (1997) charts the evolution of the technologies of story-telling from Malory's *Morte d'Arthur*, a hand-written manuscript, to postmodern films like Harold Rami's farcical *Groundhog Day* that, she argues, 'push against the boundaries of linear narrative'. Dungeons and Dragons role-playing games transformed story-telling into a participatory process in which players took an active role in co-constructing an evolving drama within a rule-bound system. Similarly text-based online multi-user dungeons (MUDs) allow players to become actively involved in the production of an interactive drama. Indeed, Murray suggests that the technologies of story-telling are evolving towards the fictional holodeck used for recreation and more serious professional training purposes aboard the *Star Ship Voyager*.

In the early twenty-first century story-telling technologies continue to evolve driven by consumer demand for ever more active and immersive experiences. In the home, massively multiplayer online role-playing games (MMORPGs), such as *EverQuest*, *Lineage II* and *World of Warcraft* have become the entertainment medium of choice for millions of young people (de Freitas and Griffiths, 2007; Steinkuehler, 2004, 2005). This chapter's investigation was motivated by an interest in the potential that MMORPGs have to provide a rich experiential base to support teaching and learning in the Humanities classrooms. Theories of experiential and situated learning from Dewey (1938) to Gee (2004) are central to its line of inquiry.

New media for experiential learning

In 1938, John Dewey wrote *Experience and Education* in an attempt to bring some understanding to the growing conflict between 'traditional' education and his 'progressive approach' (Dewey, 1938; Tanner, 1997). Dewey's work, seen in the context of other progressive educationalists, such as Montessori and Kilpatrick (Montessori, 1912; Kilpatrick, 1997), emphasizes the need for rich and holistic experience in and of the world as a prerequisite for the construction of knowledge. For Dewey, experience involves 'transactions' with designed artefacts, such as a novel and objects of the fancy, as well as lived experience:

> An experience is always what it is because of a transaction taking place between an individual and what, at the time, constitutes his environment, whether the latter consists of persons with whom he is talking about some topic or event, the subject talked about being also a part of the situation; the book he is reading (in which) his environing conditions at the time may be England or ancient Greece or an imaginary region; or the materials of an experiment he is performing. The environment, in other words, is whatever conditions interact with personal needs, desires, purposes and capabilities to create the experience which is had.

Even when a person builds a castle in the air he is interacting with the objects he constructs his fancy. (Dewey, 1938, p. 39)

Kolb (1984) has argued that Dewey's ideas resulted in a renewed interest in non-formal modes of learning that preceded the advent of formal schooling. This movement subsequently led to the integration of apprenticeships, internships, work/study programmes, studio arts, laboratory experiments and field trips into formal curricular structures. In *Experiential Learning* (1984, p. 21), Kolb argues that 'immediate personal experience is the focal point for learning, giving life texture, and subjective personal meaning to abstract concepts and at the same time providing a concrete, publicly shared reference point for testing the implications and validity of ideas created during the learning process'. He goes on to suggest 'when human beings share an experience, they can share it fully, concretely and abstractly' (Kolb, 1984, p. 21).

Similarly, for Bruner (1960, p. 13) intuition, the 'intellectual technique of arriving at plausible but tentative formulations', plays a much neglected but essential role in the learning process. Moreover, Bruner stresses that 'learning must be kept from going passive' and must emerge from 'arousal of interest in what there is to be learned' (p. 80). These insights inform his recommendations for a *spiral curriculum* in which early learning of core concepts grounded in holistic concrete experiences are repeatedly revisited at increasing levels of sophistication and abstraction. Given these conditions, he asserts 'any subject can be taught effectively in some intellectually honest form to any child at any stage of development' (p. 33).

In Maths and Science considerable efforts have been made to translate abstract symbolic principles into modes of representation that could be grasped by people at more concrete stages of cognitive development (Papert, 1993; Resnick, 1994). In the Humanities, teachers traditionally use photographs, film clips or role-playing exercises to simulate topic discussion and help young people grasp abstract concepts and access themes explored in fictional form. The *Humanities Curriculum Project* (Elliot, 1991; Stenhouse, 1975) actively promoted the use of a wide range of materials that helped children draw upon prior experiences and co-construct knowledge through discussion with a teacher or 'lead learner'. The reading materials were not simply regarded as context to be mastered. Rather, they served as the cultural basis of interaction within the learning group (Stenhouse, 1983: xiii). In each of these initiatives rich experience is regarded as the missing component in traditional textbook-based pedagogies.

Immersive game worlds offer teachers new ways to ground and situate learning in a rich, albeit simulated experience. Unlike storybooks that require a passive reader to follow a linear narrative, role-playing games require learners to take an active role as they explore, investigate, formulate hypotheses and attempt to solve problems.

Existing research on the pedagogical possibilities of virtual role play

Research into the educational potential of role-playing games is still in its infancy. Nevertheless, design-based research initiatives have started to advance our understanding of the new pedagogical possibilities. Several educational researchers have started to map out this rapidly emerging field (e.g. Kirriemuir and McFarlane, 2004; de Freitas, 2006). In addition, conceptual tools for understanding how the experience of virtual role play can facilitate learning have emerged from studies of young people's experiences of playing commercially available games. The work of James Paul Gee (2003, 2004, 2005) is particularly significant in this respect. He notes that 'immersion is one of the great powers of video games' and argues that first-person role-playing games allow players to experience a new blended way of being, termed a 'third being' a synthesis between their real-world identities and the virtual personas they develop during gameplay. Further, players develop 'embodied empathy' for the complex systems modelled in the game world as they start to interact with virtual objects and characters (Gee, unpublished manuscript). In *Situated Language and Learning: A Critique of Traditional Schooling*, Gee argues that these 'designed experiences' can help young people from impoverished backgrounds to overcome the socio-linguistic barriers that prevent them from accessing the benefits of formal schooling and gaining access to higher education and the professions (Gee, 2004). In a parallel development, Shaffer (2005, 2006a, 2006b) has developed 'epistemic games' that allow learners to experience ways of knowing, doing and being (an 'epistemic frame') that approximate the ways professionals learn through reflective practice (Schön, 1983). The experience of virtual embodiment within epistemic games facilitates 'thickly authentic' (Shaffer and Resnick, 1999) experiences that approximate the way learning occurs in real-world situated contexts (Brown, Collins and Duguid, 1989; CTGV, 1993; Lave and Wenger, 1991). In this respect, 'epistemic games' provide powerful tools that present new opportunities for vocational training in which players learn the 'epistemic frames' associated with particular professions.

The military have led the way in the development of games for training and recruitment purposes (Li, 2004). However, educationalists are not so well funded. Indeed, initial attempts to use games in classroom settings tended to make use of available commercial off-the-shelf games – or COTS. In 2004, a research team based at Futurelab in the UK set out to explore the viability of using COTS to support teaching and learning in secondary schools (Sandford et al., 2005). The team found that gameplay often simulated engaged students and promoted learning. However, they encountered a number of problems. In particular the fixed length of lessons constrained the kind of open-ended activities promoted by commerical games. Further, the use of 'games as a resource' presented teachers with new challenges. Egenfeldt-Nielsen (2005) and Squire (2005) encountered similar problems when attempting to use *Europa Universalis* and *Civilisation III* as pedagogical tools to teach history. It appears that the open-ended exploratory ways young people are accustomed to playing commercial games remained at odds with the demands of a standardized curriculum. All initiatives pointed to the need for purposefully designed educational games.

The *Games-to-Teach* project (later renamed the *Education Arcade*) based at MIT's Comparative Media Studies set out to develop games that could be used as a pedagogical tool in real classrooms and after-school computer clubs. In the initial stages the team developed dozens of design-concepts for education games that could help student access abstract concepts. The most interesting and viable game concepts were then selected and prototypes were developed using the toolkits made available by an online community of game fans (Jenkins and Squire, 2003). *Revolution* is one of the game concepts that the team developed to an advanced level.

The genesis of *Revolution*

Revolution was designed expressly to help students to learn about aspects of social history. Rather than attempt to build the game from scratch, the game was modified from *Neverwinter Nights*, a commercial available multiplayer online role-playing game. In the process the existing graphical content was replaced by material modelled and developed in collaboration with the Colonial Williamsberg Living Museum. As a result, the game offered students

Figure 4.1 Screenshot from *Revolution* as a crowd gathers outside the courthouse

an opportunity to learn about history through interactive role play in a virtual reconstruction of eighteenth-century Colonial Williamsburg.

The interactive drama is set at a time when tensions between the loyalists and patriots were beginning to mount prior to the outbreak of the American War of Independence. Each character follows a personalized learning path through the controlled emergent narrative that culminates in a meeting outside the courthouse. Figure 4.1 is a screenshot from the game showing the crowd who had gathered outside the Courthouse to discuss the relative merits of taking up arms and storming the Governor's mansion.

A key design objective was to give players a chance to experience a vision of history that was not static or abstract, but one that allowed students to participate in events, see visible repercussions and consider how events at a personal and local level might have implications for events on the wider political and societal level (Weise and Squire, 2004). Moreover, unlike *Civilization III* in which the player adopts the role of a godlike Emperor, *Revolution* was designed to help players experience life in Colonial Williamsburg from a first-person perspective. This approach allowed players to experience a mounting conflict through the perspective of ordinary people, rather than generals and world leaders.

Each player takes on the role of one of the player characters: a blacksmith, a seamstress, an indentured servant, a local lawyer, a gunsmith, a basket-making slave and a virtual house slave. Variables define each character's class, political affiliation, race and gender. In turn, these variables constrain the range of interactions possible between any two players. Players intuitively learn about these invisible constraints as they start to interact and progress through the game. In this respect, *Revolution* models a complex social system governed by a set of social protocols peculiar to eighteenth-century colonial society. In theory, the experience of being immersed within this complex interactive model enables students to become familiar with the social, political and cultural mechanisms that figured within the revolutionary war.

The *Revolution* workshops

During the development phase versions of the game had been played by groups of MIT students. These sessions served to identify bugs in the system and inform ongoing design and development. However, by spring 2005, it was decided to test the game with a small group of school students to explore its potential as pedagogical resource. To this end, the game was installed on twelve networked computers in the MIT Teacher Education Lab, and groups of students, in the 12–15 age range, were invited to participate in a series of workshops. Five workshops were held in total. Each lasted approximately four hours. Four workshops were conducted with small groups (4–7 students) recruited from the Massachusetts home school community. A fifth workshop was then conducted with a group of fifteen students from a local high school accompanied by their regular history teacher.

The workshops were designed to investigate how the game could be used to support teaching and learning about aspects of social history. As a researcher, the author was particularly interested to explore how the experience of virtual role play might support reflective discussion and ground learners' understanding of abstract concepts. In practice, this involved a high degree of innovation, adaptation and experimentation within and between workshops as the research team attempted to understand exactly how, why and under what circumstances the game could be used. In retrospect, the workshops were conceived as a series of design experiments rather than a formative evaluation.

The design experiment paradigm finds its origins in the work of Brown (1992). It is particularly suited to exploratory work in which pedagogical innovation goes hand-in-hand with conceptual development and technological innovation. Advocates of design-based research have argued that design experiments respect the 'messiness' of real-world contexts upon which findings are always dependent (Barab and Squire, 2004; Design Based Research Collective, 2003; Collins et al., 2004; diSessa and Cobb, 2004; Fishman et al., 2004). Cobb and colleagues (2003) note that 'issues that arise in the environment are to be accounted for and integrated into existing theory'. They add that it is through understanding the 'recursive patterns of researchers framing questions, developing goals, implementing interventions and analyzing resultant activity that knowledge is produced' (2003, 10). This position assumes that real-world activity systems cannot be reduced to dependent and independent variables.

Design experiments have been critiqued from positivistic perspectives (Dede, 2004; Gorard et al., 2004). Squire and Barab (2004) concede that, not unlike ethnography, there is a danger that 'hands on' engagement leaves the researcher 'awash in immediacies'. However, to combat this tendency they emphasize that 'design-based research strives to generate and advance a particular set of theoretical constructs that transcends the environmental particulars of the contexts in which they were generated, selected or refined' (2004, p. 5). Furthermore, unlike formative evaluations, advocates of design-based research aim to generate theoretical knowledge that, in turn, might inform further technological and pedagogical innovation.

Designing a scheme of work

A scheme of work designed for the workshops followed a four-stage model summarized below. This model adapted a more abstract schema proposed by the New London Group (1996).

1. Situated learning in a virtual environment
Through situated role play within the virtual world students develop embodied empathy for their virtual persona and gain a deep, but tacit, understanding of a web of social relationships while talking and interacting with dozens of player and non-player characters.

2. Overt instruction and reflective discussion
The teacher leads discussion or devises activities that encourage systematic analytic reflection upon the experience of virtual role play. This stage enables

students to consciously articulate knowledge that might otherwise remain tacit.

3. Practical media production

Students are assigned a production task that requires the reapplication of the knowledge they have acquired in Steps One and Two. In the first three workshops students focused on work diary entries that explored the political conflict from the point of view of their character. In the fourth and fifth workshops students produced a video diary, recycling visual material they have captured during the game using *Windows Movie Maker.*

4. Critical framing

The New London Group (1996) defines critical framing as 'interpreting the social and cultural context of particular designs of meaning' and argues that 'this involves the students standing back from what they are studying and viewing it critically in relation to its context'. Critically framing an interactive game text might require a student to question the representations embedded in the game world and consider how the 'bottom up' model of history implied by the game medium might differ fundamentally from that implied by a textbook or by audio or film media.

   This chapter explores data that sheds light on the first two phases of this strategy: the students' experience of virtual role play and how this experience mediated their capacity to participate in whole group discussion about aspects of social history. A full account of how the pedagogy evolved through iterative design and adaptation is available (Sandford and Francis, 2006). Further, one can view four machinima diaries produced by students during the workshops at http://www.educationarcade.org/.Manuscripts documenting the making of machinima video diaries and the cultural barriers confronting teachers wishing to use *Revolution* in real-world educational contexts remain in progress.

Data collection

The workshops threw up a host of issues and questions, which made it difficult to anticipate, in advance, which data sources would provide the most interesting insights. Given the extensive preparation required to recruit subjects, gain informed consent and set up each workshop, data was captured from all available sources during the workshops. This chapter draws on a subset of the rich data set produced to explore how the experience of virtual role play might provide a rich experience that grounds reflective whole group discussion. Additional insights that have influenced the interpretation of data were gained from in-depth interviews with selected students, parents and teachers participating in the workshops, from analysis of paper-based diaries and multimedia machinima produced by students after playing the game and from digital data capture techniques (using FRAPS) that allowed excerpts of game-play to be recorded and saved to disk. Students also completed a questionnaire started at the outset and completed at the end of the workshop. However, this did not prove a rich source of insight compared to the raw data collected via stimulated responses and recordings of whole group discussion.

Stimulated responses recorded on a digital Dictaphone while students were playing the game provided a raw data source directly related to students' experience of participating in the cyber-drama. Data collected using this method provides the basis of the seven localized insider perspectives presented below. Segments of transcripts made from recordings of whole group discussions that followed periods of gameplay are then used to suggest how this experience prepared students to engage in discussion.

Seven insider perspectives on the experience of virtual role play in the *Revolution* game world

Students participating in the workshops began to make observations from the moment they entered the game world. Simulated responses reveal the diversity of experiences captured, a selection of the responses are re-represented here as condensed narrative accounts. Each suggests the experience of an individual learner as they enacted a role within the game.

Jacob (12 years) playing John Lamb the gunsmith
Jacob was asked what he found out about the geography of the town. He responded, 'it's very flat and rocky, well not many rocks, it's more just flat and green.' When prompted to consider how this compared to a modern day town he commented, 'Well there's no really tall buildings, it's all small houses, dirt roads . . . so now, unlike now in the days when they have cars, they have to walk around on foot with their little lamps.'

Suzanne (13 years), playing William Waddill the Blacksmith
Suzanne had been collecting signatures for a petition but noticed that some characters would not sign it on the grounds that they 'didn't think it was right'.

John (14 years) playing Robert Carter Nicholas the town Magistrate
John had been observing the speech bubbles appear above the heads of the crowd gathered at the courthouse as he prepared for a speech he was about to make. He concluded that the crowd must be 'angry about the Governor's confiscation of the gunpowder from the magazine'. After the speech, he felt indignant that he had been accused of being the Governor's 'lackey' for preaching non-violent protest. A little later, when the crowd started to riot, he expressed shock that the women were bearing firearms and commented that 'it didn't seem right for that time period.' He attempted to talk to a female character about this matter but she rebuffed him saying, 'I'm too common to be of interest to you.'

Ruth (14 years) played Hannah a house slave
Ruth had been sent to the market to buy some fish for her master's supper. She was able to talk to the vendors selling fish at the stalls and purchase the fish. However, after a short period wandering around the Market Square talking to people she complained, 'nobody wanted to talk to me'. On one occasion she attempted to talk to a well-dressed white man on the green but was reprimanded with a curt, 'remember your place, slave.' As a result she chose to switch character.

Ajaree (13 years) also playing Hannah
Ajaree said her job meant that she had to stay in the kitchen and 'cook and clean'. When asked how this compared to the other slave characters she remarked, 'Well I got the easiest job probably, because they are out there working and they get beat more and stuff like that.' Interestingly, she described the slaves in the cotton fields of Steadmond Farm, 'farming and singing'. When asked what they were singing, she replied, 'Spirituals probably, signalling that someone was going to run.'

Ishani (15 years) playing Catherine Grymes a seamstress
Ishani described the process of 'making a fake redcoat uniform for a guy, so he could hack into the armoury'. Talking about her character she stressed: 'She's a daughter of liberty' who 'believed in the cause to be free.' Nevertheless, she added that her character did not want to take up arms and then added: 'but I'm not sure because I haven't read her background yet.'

Huda (12 years) playing Margaret Chadwell an indentured servant
Huda had been serving the customers in Chowning's Tavern. At first she had struggled to remember all the customer's names but was proud of the fact that

she had had 'almost done it'. After a while she grew frustrated and sneaked out to have a look around the market square. When asked what she was doing she hurried back to her job baking bread in the tavern. Describing the kitchen she noted, 'it's not like a modern day kitchen where they have blenders and everything.' She seemed particular interested in the fact that they 'use a fire'. She then decided to make extra bread because everyone 'seemed to like that'. Huda had switched from playing Hannah to Margaret Chadwell after the training sequence. When asked to compare how the experience of playing an indentured servant differed from playing a field slave she commented, 'Well you are more free to go around and you don't have to take orders really – only in the Tavern.'

The pedagogical value of designed experience within the *Revolution* game world

The pedagogical value of the designed experience of a player character within the *Revolution* game depends upon how this experience is used as a resource in various follow-up activities that encourage critical reflection. However, it is important to assess what is distinctive about the designed experience offered. Four features are now abstracted from the localized insider perspectives described above.

1: Learners develop an intuitive understanding of their character's place within a social field

The *Revolution* environment allows players freedom to follow their own curiosities and explore the game world within a loosely structured controlled emergent narrative. The game provided a considerable amount of structure in the form of on-screen directives and prompts from non-player characters. These help to position players in distinctive roles. However, players were free to push against these implicit constraints. This occurs when Ruth (playing a house slave) attempts to speak to a well-dressed white man and is told to remember her place. Similarly, it occurs when a loyalist refuses to sign Suzanne's petition and when John (playing the town magistrate) attempts to talk to a lowly female character and is rebuked with the remark, 'I'm too common to be of interest to you.' These interactions constantly remind players of their characters' race, class and political affiliation. Overtime, each player develops an intuitive understanding of their place within the social field (Bourdieu, 1977) modelled in the game. In a sense, the game embeds each 'third being' in an individuated world of virtual *habitus* that requires them to develop an intuitive understanding of the social protocols of eighteenth-century society.

2: Students develop a holistic understanding of the social system modelled through multiple modes of representation

Players absorb information through multiple modes of representation, for example visual, textual and symbolic interactions, as they explore the game world. In the examples given we see John forming conjectures after observing the speech bubbles rising above the heads of non-player characters gathered at the market, we find Jacob comparing the townscape, rendered in 3D graphics, with his own experience of a contemporary American town and we find Ruth, Suzanne and Ajaree forming conjectures as a result of interactions with non-player characters. Crucially, information generated as a result of symbolic interactions produced rich experiences. In turn, these experiences stimulate the formation of tentative hypotheses.

3: Learning about the game world is a by-product of a personalized quest

All students playing a role in *Revolution* are free to explore the world, go where they like and talk to whomever they please. However, each student also has two or more personal goals that they are directed to achieve during the day. In this respect, the game equips each player with a personal quest that guides and focuses their exploration of the game world. For example, Suzanne refers to the task of collecting signatures for a petition. Similarly, Ruth describes going to the market to buy fish and Huda takes orders from the customers in the Tavern. In these cases, players are pursuing goals assigned to their virtual characters at the start of the game. As a result the process of exploring and learning about the social system modelled is goal-orientated.

The importance of students' intentions in the learning process has been highlighted by Bereiter and Scardamalia (1989) who suggest personal needs, values and priorities affect the degree to which students absorb knowledge.

In *Revolution* each character has an overall goal and an associated set of virtual needs and priorities that motivate their personalized exploration of the game world. In this respect, each character's emerging understanding of the complex social system modelled is individuated and purposeful.

4: Tentative hypotheses are generated through an iterative problem-solving process

Each player's emerging understanding of the social system modelled is constructed as players test out and revise hypotheses in situated practice. For example, Suzanne noted that some of the characters refused to sign the petition because they did not think it was right. Similarly, Huda commented that indentured servants were 'more free to go about' than slave characters and Jacob comments that people had to walk around with their 'little lamps' because of the absence of electric lighting. In this manner, players start to make inferences and form dozens of tentative hypotheses.

Hypotheses formed and subsequently revised as a result of symbolic interactions with non-player characters appear to offer a particular powerful form of designed experience. For example, when Jacob attempts to talk to a non-player character named Carla he is rebuked with the words 'your association has done me enough harm already.' As a consequence he correctly identifies her as a 'loyalist to the King'. However, following this incident he mistakenly assumes that all the people patrolling the streets were loyalists. In particular, Jacob assumed that, Deputy Throgmorton must be a loyal subject to the king. However, when he starts to interact with the Deputy whose appearance symbolizes a man of law and order he is forced to revise this assumption. The following extract suggests this process of hypothesis revision.

Researcher: Do you feel that there are certain people you can speak to and certain people you can't?

Jacob: Yes, there's the patriots, then there's the loyalists and then there's the moderates who are in-between.

[Jacob wanders around the town, approaches Deputy Throgmorton and initiates a conversation.]

Researcher: So you're now talking to Deputy Throgmorton. [pause] What kind of reaction did you get from him?

Jacob: Umm, fairly modest actually. He's just more into regular day-to-day life unlike some people who worry about the war.

The extract suggests that Jacob was expecting to be rebuked by the Deputy as he was previously rebuked by Carla. However, the 'umm' suggests that the interaction forces Jacob to revise his initial hypothesis and entertain the possibility that the Deputy may not have a strong political affiliation despite the fact that his job requires him to act like an authority figure.

In summary it is worth emphasizing four ways in which the *Revolution* game mediated learners' experience and facilitated a shift in the locus of agency towards a more personalized learning experience. First, students followed their own paths through a loosely structured controlled emergent narrative. Second, the personal quest designed into each character's profile focused and guided an individual's exploration of the virtual world without dictating a particular reading path. Third, each player's understanding of the social system modelled was constructed iteratively as players tested out and revised particular hypotheses in situated practice. Finally, symbolic interactions with non-player characters stimulated hypothesis formation and revision as they explored the game world. These features of the interactive game text helped to furnish each player with a distinctive designed experience. In turn, these experiences can be harnessed as a resource to support reflective discussion and practical production activities. The next section explores how and why these experiences informed whole group reflected discussion on a range of topical issues.

From private experience to discursive knowledge

The argument so far has highlighted ways that the experience of virtual role play furnished learners with a rich and holistic experience. Nevertheless, in the workshops, players were not always able to articulate the knowledge they had acquired through virtual role play. These designed experiences must be recruited as resources as part of structured learning activities that encourage learners to articulate and reflect upon the experience (Squire, 2006). The role of the teacher remained critical. Indeed, Sandford and colleagues (2005, 4) have argued:

> Using games in a meaningful way within lessons depended far more on the effective use of existing teaching skills than it did on the development of any new, game-related skills. Far from being sidelined, teachers were required to take a central role in scaffolding and supporting students' learning through games'.

This was self-evident in the *Revolution* workshops. Nevertheless, the data generated suggested that particular questioning strategies were more or less effective than others. In general the discussion that followed game-playing episodes was rich, diverse and multifaceted – if somewhat chaotic. In all cases the experience of immersive role play appeared to furnish students with a rich pre-verbal knowledge-base upon which to draw. Further, the rich holistic experience appeared to empower students to discuss a broad range of topics. At times, rich discussions emerged as successive students contributed, drawing inferences, making comparisons and offered alternative interpretations. Further, discussion ranged across a variety of topics, from the social status of William Waddill, who 'dressed all raggedy' but 'owned his own shop' or what it meant for Robert Carter Nicholas to be a 'conservative patriot', to broader themes such as different forms of non-violent protest, the wisdom of armed struggle and the circulation of information in informal compared to public spaces.

The following two examples chart the way a very private designed experience becomes the object of a whole group discussion. The extracts are taken from workshop five (conducted with a group of 15 students from a local high school) in which the discussion was led jointly by the researcher and the students' regular history teacher. Both examples suggest how players start to map abstract concepts onto their pre-verbal experience of virtual role play. However, the questioning strategy used in the first is less successful than the strategy used in the second.

Kacie playing William Waddill the carpenter

In a discussion about different forms of social protest, Kacie starts to talk about her experience of collecting signatures for a petition.

Kacie:	My character was like a carpenter and I was getting a petition together for my friend who was unjustly charged and so I was mad at the government because my friend was in jail. Yer, because I felt it was unjust.
Researcher:	Why do you think he chose to use a petition? Do you think it was an effective strategy?
Kacie:	Because it was a rational way of going about it. And I went around getting signatures and I got a bunch but I didn't really know what to do with them.
Teacher:	[intervening] Does everyone know what a petition is? [Tom starts to suggest an answer. Teacher tells him to speak up].

Tom:	It's a document that you get people to sign to show that they care about something.
Teacher:	Right, so people are putting their name and reputation on paper to say they have a joint demand and it's a non-violent way of doing this.

Significantly, Kacie's contribution was not explicitly prompted by the researchers' questioning. She realizes that her experience was relevant to the topic under discussion and offered it spontaneously. Interestingly, she begins talking about the experience using the first-person pronoun, 'I'. That is to say, her contribution appears grounded in her immediate experience of playing William Waddill. However, in response to the researcher's question she switches register, 'because it was a more rational way of going about it' and employs the more abstract language of reflective generalization. At this level, her initial insight, grounded in an intuitive private experience, becomes available for whole group discussion. The teacher sees this as an opportunity. He spontaneously intervenes and takes over the role of questioner, 'does everyone know what a petition is?' Another student supplies a definition. The teacher then picks up on this point to stress that petition making is a form of non-violent protest that requires people to stake their reputations to make a joint demand.

Compared to the experience of answering questions by re-working language readily available in a printed textbook this activity appeared to challenge students who did not possess the vocabulary necessary to articulate their experience. In this case the teachers' intervention is not entirely successful. At the point he asks: 'does anyone know what a petition is?' the discussion shifts into a teacher-led mode that shuts down a discussion that was directly related to Kacie's experience. In this instant, the teachers fail to respect the possibility that the student may have acquired conceptual knowledge but simply lacks the vocabulary required to articulate the insights gained. A second example illustrates a line of question that equips a student with the vocabulary he requires to articulate his experience of virtual role play. In this case the discussion remains anchored in this experience.

Tim playing the Town Magistrate

Tim's comments regarding the Governor's confiscation of the gunpowder are interesting precisely because he was the only student interviewed who failed to correctly identify the three political factions present.

Teacher:	So there were a group of people and there seems to be three different kinds of people. Let's focus on these different people. Can you tell me who they were?
Tim:	There were moderates, liberals and I don't know the last one.
Teacher:	The patriots, the loyalists and the moderates. So could you tell me anymore about that? Why would different people want different things?
Tim:	Because of their roles in society, how it affects their lives.

Interestingly, Tim does not accurately identify the three political factions in the game. He misapplies the adjective 'liberal' and forgets the third term he needs to articulate an answer to the question. In response the teacher provides a corrective comment. However, he continues with a follow-up question, 'can you tell me anymore about that?' This comment respects Timothy's existing knowledge. As a result, the discussion that develops remains grounded in his experience of playing a character in the game. Furthermore, Tim's failure to pick up on the correct vocabulary does not prevent him from supplying a confident answer to the follow-up question to which he replies, 'because of their roles in society, how it effects their lives'. In short, the comment suggests that he has developed a pre-verbal understanding of the significance of political partisanship before he had acquired the correct terminology required to identify the three political factions.

How the experience of virtual role play helps students resist reductive interpretations

Existing knowledge and lived experiences were frequently synthesized with the experience of virtual role play as students attempted to make meaning and engage in discussion. In a sense, students were compelled to make meaning out of the designed experience offered. Unlike a story book there is no narrative voice making sense of events. Rather, the onus remains on the player to do the work of interpretation. In this respect, game texts are what McLuhan (1994) described as a *cold* medium because they do not over-determine the meanings available to a reader.

Extracts from a whole group discussion about the predicament of the slaves in the eighteenth-century society suggest some of the ways students started to develop a complex understanding of the divided loyalties of slave characters in the game. Students who played the slave characters all came to a recognition that the political dispute over taxation was of little concern to them. For example, Ajaree argued that 'it didn't really affect them and they probably would have remained slaves anyway'. Indeed she argued that they were more concerned with 'working and trying not to get beat'. Ruth argued that they were going to be 'slaves either way', regardless of who won but added, 'I've read like that Britain would say that if slaves would join them they would give them freedom . . . so I could see why they would, that's what concerns them really'. Ishani develops a slightly more considerate response that takes into account the personal relationship of the slave with her owner.

Researcher: What about the political dispute between the royalists and the patriots. What do you think, Dan and Hannah – thought about that?

Ishani: They wouldn't be able to talk but I think they would be more of a patriot but sometimes, later in the war, the British, they offered freedom to those slaves who helped them so you can't really be sure about a slave's point of view. It's personal.

Researcher: What do you mean by personal?

Ishani: If one slave felt that the owner was nice to him and that owner was a Patriot he would probably be more likely to support that cause. But if their owner was cruel and he was still a Patriot then he would probably support the loyalist cause and also because he might be getting free later on.

Researcher: So what was the primary concern of the slave characters, what would they have been most concerned about?

Ishani: Their own skin.

In her response, Ishani quickly forms two hypotheses. In the first, she considers the possibility that the offer of freedom might be used by opposing powers in an attempt to recruit the loyalties of the African-American peoples. In the second, she suggests that the loyalty of an individual slave might be influenced by the personal relationship she has with their owner. Indeed, in the game, Master Steadmond, Hannah's owner, is kind to her and compliments her on her cooking. However, at the same time she is attempting to help her brother Dan who bears a grudge against Master Steadmond because his wife and daughter were sold off to another farm. Thus she is torn between her conflicting desire to please her master and help her brother. The example suggests she cannot state what the slave characters thought about the political dispute without weighing up conflicting loyalties involved. Consequently she arrives at the conclusion, 'it's personal'. The example suggests that virtual role play can lead to deep intuitive insights into the competing factors that pull on individuals during periods of social upheaval.

Discussion

The insights gained from the *Revolution* workshops move forward the debate about the educational potential of video games. This chapter demonstrates, above all, that virtual role play presents interesting new possibilities for experiential learning in the Humanities classroom. Furthermore, it lends weight to arguments put forward by Gee (2003, 2004, 2005), Shaffer (2005, 2006a, 2006b) and Squire (2004, 2005, 2006) about the potential of virtual role play as a pedagogical resource. In particular it suggests that virtual role play allows students to develop 'embodied empathy' for complex social systems. However, rather than helping students imagine what it might be like to be a professional, here the experience of virtual embodiment helps students empathize with ordinary people who lived in a specific historic juncture during a period of social upheaval. Indeed, the designed experience offered by *Revolution* provides what Kolb (1984) identified as the 'immediate personal experience' that provides a 'focal point for learning' and gives 'subjective personal meaning to abstract concepts' (p. 21). In addition, the activity nurtured what Bruner (1960) described as the 'intellectual technique of arriving at plausible but tentative formulations' (p. 13) and allowed students as young as 12 and 13 years of age to engage in topical discussion. The invisible constraints pertaining to each character's race, gender, class and political affiliation play an important role in this process.

The findings also suggest that virtual role play may provide a more inclusive and arguably a more intrinsically motivating experience than learning supported by paper-based media. However, teachers wishing to mobilize the experience of virtual role play as an experiential resource need to respect the student may not always be able to articulate the tacit knowledge acquired through virtual role play. Consequently, the role of questioning strategies and follow-up activities that encouraged analysis, synthesis, hypothesis formation and abstraction are all important. Without these additional activities intuitive insights acquired through virtual role play might remain tacit. Consequently, serious games should not be thought of as another genre of 'educational' software. Unlike drill-and-test 'edutainment' products the pedagogy is not hard-coded into the game. The designed experience offered is comparable to the experience of reading a storybook, listening to an audio book or watching part of a film. In all cases, the onus remains on the teacher to decide how best to harness this designed experience as a learning resource. In this respect, purpose-built MMORPGs like *Revolution* should be considered as an extension of a tradition of story-telling media that have long since been appropriated by classroom teachers to serve educational agendas in the Humanities classroom. A well-designed MMORPG remains an open-ended resource that can be used in a variety of ways to support learning, not just in history but across the Humanities curriculum and beyond. Indeed, the themes and issues touched upon during the workshops were relevant to a host of subject areas: History, English, Drama, Geography, Sociology, Politics, Citizenship and Media Studies.

Acknowledgements

My involvement with *Revolution* was as a visiting colleague to MIT's Education Arcade Team, led by Philip Tan at the time, with Professor Henry Jenkins as Principal Investigator. My thanks to all those involved in the design, development and testing of *Revolution*: Philip Tan, Nick Hunter, Brett Camper, Ravi Purushotma, Eric Klopfer, Matthew Weise, Kurt Squire and Professor Henry Jenkins (The Education Arcade, MIT Comparative Media Studies). Thanks also to Scot Osterweil for his valuable comments on an earlier draft of this chapter, and continuing assistance since then. Finally I wish to acknowledge MIT Education Arcade as the source of the image in Figure 4.1, and thank them for permission to reproduce here.

References

Barab, S. A. and Squire, K. (2004). 'Design-based research: putting a stake in the ground'. *Journal of the Learning Sciences*, Vol. 13, No. 1, pp. 1–14.

Bereiter, C. and Scardamalia, M. (1989). 'Intentional Learning as a goal of instruction', in L. B. Resnick, ed. *Knowing, Learning, and Instruction: Essays in Honor of Robert Glaser*. Hillsdale, NJ: Lawrence Erlbaum Associates, pp. 361–92.

Bourdieu, P. (1977). *Outline of a Theory of Practice*. Cambridge: Cambridge University Press.

Brown, A. L. (1992). 'Design Experiments: theoretical and methodological challenges in creating complex interventions in classroom settings'. *Journal of the Learning Sciences*, Vol. 2, No. 2, pp. 141–78.

Brown, A. L., Collins, A. and Duguid, P. (1989). 'Situated Cognition and the Culture of Learning'. *Educational Researcher*, Vol. 18, pp. 32–42.

Bruner, J. S. (1960). *The Process of Education*. Cambridge, MA: Harvard University Press.

Cobb, P., Confrey, J., DiSessa, A., Lehrer, R. and Schauble, L. (2003). 'Design Experiments in Educational Research'. *Educational Researcher,* Vol. 60, No. 3, pp. 9–13.

Collins, A., Joseph, D. and Bielaczyc, K. (2004). 'Design research: theoretical and methodological issues'. *Journal of the Learning Sciences,* Vol. 13, No. 1, pp. 15–42.

CTGV (1993). Anchored instruction and situated cognition revisited. *Educational Technology,* Vol. 33, No. 3, pp. 52–70.

Dede, C. (2004). If design-based research is the answer, what is the question? *Journal of the Learning Sciences,* Vol. 13, No. 1, pp. 105–14.

de Freitas, S. (2006). Learning in immersive worlds. Bristol. Joint Information Systems Committee. Online Available w ww.jisc.ac.uk/media/documents/programmes/elearninginnovation/gamingreport_v3.pdf. Last accessed 25.4.10.

de Freitas, S. and Griffiths, M. (2007). Online gaming as an educational tool in learning and training. *British Journal of Educational Technology,* Vol. 38, No. 3, pp. 535–37.

Design Based Research Collective (2003). Design-based research: an emerging paradigm for educational inquiry. *Educational Researcher,* Vol. 32, No. 1, pp. 5–9.

Dewey, J. (1938). *Experience and Education.* New York: The Macmillan Company.

diSessa, A. and Cobb, P. (2004). Ontological innovation and the role of theory in design experiments. *Journal of the Learning Sciences,* Vol. 13, No. 1, pp. 77–103.

Egenfeldt-Nielsen, S. (2005). Beyond edutainment: exploring the educational potential of computer games, Doctoral Thesis, IT-University of Copenhagen. Denmark. Online. Available http://www.itu.dk/people/sen/egenfeldt.pdf.> Last accessed 25.4.10.

Elliot, J. (1991). *Action Research for Educational Change,* Milton Keynes: Open University Press.

Fishman, B., Marx, R. W., Blumenfeld, P., Krajcik, J. and Soloway, E. (2004). Creating a framework for research on systemic technology innovations. *Journal of the Learning Sciences,* Vol. 13, No. 1, pp. 43–76.

Gee, J. P. (2003). *What Video Games Have to Teach us about Learning and Literacy.* New York and Basingstoke: Palgrave Macmillan.

Gee, J. P. (2004). *Situated Language and Learning: A Critique of Traditional Schooling.* New York and London: Routledge.

Gee, J. P. (2005). What would a state of the art instructional game look like? *Innovate,* Vol. 1, No. 6. <http://tinyurl.com/34n2ojl>. Last accessed 25.4.10.

Gee, J. P. (unpublished manuscript). Video games: embodied empathy for complex systems'. <www.labweb.education.wisc.edu/room130/index.htm> Last accessed 25.4.10.

Gee, J. P. (2005). *Why Video Games Are Good for Your Soul: Pleasure and Learning.* ,Melbourne, Victoria: Common Ground Publishing.

Gorard, S., Roberts, K. and Taylor, C. (2004). What kind of creature is a design experiment? *British Educational Research Journal,* Vol. 30, No. 4, pp. 577–90.

Jenkins, H. and Squire, K. (2003). Harnessing the power of games in education. *Insight,* Vol. 3, No.1, pp. 7–33.

Kilpatrick, W. H. (1918). The project method. *Teachers College Record,* Vol. 19, pp. 319–35.

Kirriemuir, J. and McFarlane, A. (2004). *Report 8: Literature Review in Games and Learning.* Bristol: Futurelab.

Kolb, D. A. (1984). *Experiential Learning: Experience as the Source of Learning and Development.* London: Prentice-Hall.

Lave, J. and Wenger, E. (1991). *Situated Learning: Legitimate Peripheral Participation.* Cambridge: Cambridge University Press.

Li, Z. (2004). The Potential of *America's Army:* the Video Game as Civilian-Military Public Sphere, PhD Thesis, Massachusetts Institute of Technology. Available www.gamasutra.com/education/theses/20040725/ZLITHESIS.pdf. Last accessed 25.4.10.

McLuhan, M. and Lapham, L. H. (1994). *Understanding Media: The Extensions of Man.* Cambridge, MA: MIT Press.

Murray, J. H. (1997). *Hamlet on the Holodeck: The Future of Narrative in Cyberspace.* New York: Free Press.

New London Group (1996). A pedagogy of multiliteracies: designing social futures. *Harvard Educational Review,* Vol. 66, No. 1, pp. 60–92.

Papert, S. (1993). *Mindstorms: Children, Computers, and Powerful Ideas* (2nd edn). New York and London: Harvester Wheatsheaf.

Resnick, M. (1994). *Turtles, Termites, and Traffic Jams: Explorations in Massively Parallel Microworlds.* Cambridge, MA: MIT Press.

Sandford, R. and Francis, R. J. (2006). Towards a theory of a games based pedagogy, in G. Minshull and J. Mole, eds. *Discussion Summary of Innovating e-Learning 2006: Transforming Learning Experiences.* JISC Online Conference, UK.: Joint Information Systems Committee (JISC).

Sandford, R., Ulicsak, M., Facer, K. and Rudd, T. (2005). *Teaching with Games: Using Commercial Off-the-Shelf Computer Games in Formal Education.* Bristol: Futurelab.

Schön, D. A. (1983). *The Reflective Practitioner: How Professionals Think in Action.* New York: Basic Books.

Shaffer, D. W. and Resnick, M. (1999). 'Thick' authenticity: new media and authentic learning. *Journal of Interactive Learning Research,* Vol. 10, No. 2, pp. 195–215.

Shaffer, D. W. (2005). Epistemic games. Innovate, 1(6), http://tinyurl.com/2w69tzx Last accessed 25.4.10.

Shaffer, D. W. (2006a). Epistemic frames for epistemic games. *Computers and Education,* Vol. 46, No. 3, pp. 223–34.

Shaffer, D. W. (2006b). *How Computer Games Help Children Learn.* Palgrave: Macmillan.

Squire, K. (2005). Replaying history: learning world history through playing Civilization III. Doctoral Thesis. University of Indiana. USA. <website.education.wisc.edu/kdsquire/REPLAYING_HISTORY.doc.> Last accessed 25.4.10.

Squire. K. (2006). From content to context: digital games as designed experiences, *Educational Researcher,* Vol. 35, No. 8, pp. 19–29.

Steinkuehler, C. A. (2004). Learning in massively multiplayer online games. Paper presented at the International Conference of the Learning Sciences (ICLS), Los Angeles CA.

Steinkuehler, C. A. (2005). The new third space: massively multiplayer online gaming in American youth culture. *Tidskrift Journal of Research in Teacher Education,* Vol. 3, pp. 17–32.

Stenhouse, L. (1975). *An Introduction to Curriculum Research and Development.* London: Heinemann.

Stenhouse, L. (1983). *Authority, Education and Emancipation: A Collection of Papers.* London and Exeter: Heinemann Educational Books.

Tanner, L. (1997). *Dewey's Laboratory School: Lessons for Today.* New York: Teachers College Press.

Weise, M. J. and Squire, K. (2004). Design Document for *Revolution:* A Massively Multiplayer Online RPG of the American Revolutionary War. MIT Games to Teach Project.

Stealth Learning in Online Games 5

Esther MacCallum-Stewart

Chapter Outline

Introduction

This chapter examines how Massively Multiplayer Online Games (MMOR-PGs) commercial gaming, specifically online gaming, have started to promote learning objectives as a naturalized aspect of gameplay. This has given rise to 'Stealth Learning', a phrase that will be defined more clearly in the course of this chapter. In MMORPGs, users gain significant learning during their attempts to interact with and comprehend the game world, and as a result of this, they form social structures that comprise thinking communities. These thinking communities learn collectively, portioning learning between users in order to achieve a cohesive outcome.

In MMORPGs, players meet in an online environment and join together to defeat monsters, to craft objects and to interact socially. These structures make them fertile places for disseminating learning. As part of gameplay, players must pursue a variety of skills encoded within the game dynamic. These skills are broad in nature, often taken for granted by designers, and frequently designed with social and ludic objectives in mind rather than educational ones. Nevertheless, educational activities often underpin social and ludic activities: players reading a quest objective in a different language still need linguistic knowledge in order to comprehend their mission; those who gather gemstones and then sell them on an auction house are still balancing financial and economic concerns, and yet others who make videos explaining how a group should kill a particularly difficult monster and download them to YouTube, are all demonstrating different strata of learning as a by-product of the central gameplay objective (perform the quest, make gold, kill the monster). In part, Stealth Learning consists of the ways in which players gain additional skills to those that appear foremost within the gameplay of an MMORPG. Throughout this chapter, the nuances of how this form of learning plays out within an MMORPG will be explored.

The social networks that players form within MMORPGs are instrumental for developing and refining these learning processes. The advent of games with the capacity for huge 'worldscapes', as well as the collective and often highly communal nature of online gaming, mean that learning narratives can be created both in and out of the game by both player and designer. The complexity and scope of MMORPGs often lead players to regard their existence within worlds as an open-ended journey and this awareness makes them more receptive to discovery. The intensely social aspect of these games also enables peer learning as well as the more subtle forms of educative consumption detailed above (see for example Taylor, 2006; Mortensen, 2007; Klastrup and Tosca, forthcoming 2010).

These emergent issues are examined in the context of existing social structures within online gaming. This chapter considers how players might be aware of, and active in, the propagation of learning objectives, and how they engage with systems that already exist. In doing so, my objective is to demonstrate how pre-existing learning structures might be exploited in more proactive ways within learning specific games, and that gamers are active agents in their own learning processes, even if these might appear obscure to outsiders.

Virtual pioneers, such as Prensky (2001); Gee (2003) and Beck and Wade (2006) are the forerunners of an active movement demonstrating that commercial games can provide learning content. However, all of these earlier authors argue largely for the viability of games as learning tools. The new theoretical frameworks they construct around games are more often used to direct serious games initiatives than they are to investigate how this trend has continued apace within mainstream commercial gaming. More recently, the work of designers such as Jane McGonigal has started to integrate more familiar types of gaming activity into the serious gaming genre, but there is still a divide between games that are intended for learning and those that are released commercially for leisure. However, because of the diffracted way in which skills are interjected into the central gameplay of MMORPGs, and the fact that gain within them is usually measured through more traditional tasks such as finding and killing monsters, these skills are seldom considered collectively as learning criteria.

A MMORPG is a persistent environment. Players log into the world at regular intervals and play characters that perform quests, carry out activities like harvesting or making, venture into harder areas with other players in groups, duel and fight against each other and sell their ill-gotten gains to other players, often through centralized market systems. Crucially, a MMORPG is large enough that every player takes a different route through the game, possesses different skills and abilities (this is often forced by the game itself) and has a different perception of how they relate to this world. There are ludic objectives to an MMORPG: even though it is unusual that the game can be 'won' in any discernable way, the world itself is full of quests, objectives, trials, levels and skills to win, either collectively or alone. Very often, because players have to take their own routes, these obvious criteria are overlaid by personal ludic agendas. These might be for a character to possess the finest equipment, to have killed the strongest monster, to be top of a ratings list, or sometimes, during staged events in the game, to have helped the player to have collected all of a certain item.

MMORPGs are separated by these ludic aims from virtual spaces and worlds such as *Second Life*, *Whyville* or the late *There.com*, which are *not* MMORPGs, and will not be discussed here. Virtual worlds are also being increasingly appropriated for directly educational purposes and do not always encapsulate the inadvertent or hidden learning methods within MMORPG gameplay discussed here.

Game development and their publishing companies need players to play on a regular basis, since most MMORPGs gain revenue through monthly subscription fees. They factor in narrative elements, knowledge components, tasks that require a strong degree of social interaction and skills loops, into the game. It takes time to acquire these skills, and players need sustenance. Armour breaks and must be repaired, potions help players become stronger, status objects like pets or attractive hats can be gained by collecting tokens, spells or powers can be gained as a player gains points rewarded for killing monsters, skills are limited by character so that players must seek the skills of others and so forth. All of these acquisitions require knowledge – the knowledge of where a certain plant can be found, the techniques to kill a certain monster or craft a particular object. These can be viewed in a different way, however – by regarding the player's progression through the game as a learning process in itself.

In addition to these activities players also engage in secondary activities, which also require knowledge and learning in order to produce. They publish their results on external sites such as wikis, demonstrate strategies and successful battles by recording themselves on machinima, and devise programs that aid the game such as macros that allow curses to be lifted quickly or targets to be swapped when needed. *Everquest II* and *Lord of the Rings Online* contain built-in web browsers so that players can access information while in the world, should they need it. On 15 April 2010, Wowwiki, which serves the *World of Warcraft* community, had 81,044 articles (the figure rose by nine as the author was checking it was correct) and 201,499 individual pages describing everything from individual quests and detailed guides about the best places to fish, to lists of role-playing guilds and player-led events, categorized by server. Wowwiki is the second largest wiki on the web, after Wikipedia (Dybwad, 2008). As with most wikis, the content is entirely player-generated and players do not always agree about the best ways to go about things or to describe solutions, resulting in debates and discussions on forums, comparative strategies or arguments and so on. Overall, the collective output for any one game far surpasses the actual content that players see when they log in, and certainly does not exist entirely within the framework of the game world.

It is this type of multidirectional learning that allows players to be more open to educational experiences within online games, as well as enabling the potential to factor learning elements into gameplay. Since players see the game as complex enough to require learning stratagems, they are also open to absorbing content in this manner. Complex MMORPGs factor social, as well as physical or scientific objectives, into a game where players must spend time understanding its intricate aspects in order to progress. Several MMORPGs and virtual spaces have included scientific mini-games as a necessary part of game experience. Crafting systems, which are often central to the internal economies of MMORPGs, employ aspects of basic mathematics as well as requiring players to combine different items together in specific ways. Crafters gain significant rewards – both monetary and personal, usually in the form of better equipment or items they can use or sell and crafting is always a popular secondary activity to the game. *Whyville* awards virtual money (clams) based on a range of activities from the completion of scientific puzzles to the posting of 'good' questions on the forums signifying that knowledge and good social practice obtain more points than simply play. *Runescape* gives more experience points for the 'hunter' ability if a player investigates the museum and learns about the animals, rather than going outside and trapping rabbits. *A Tale in the Desert* is almost wholly geared towards both scientific and mathematical tasks; the creation of gears for mines, glassblowing, breeding beetles and mixing wines being among the many tasks that inhabitants must engage in. *World of Warcraft* and *Lord of the Rings Online* both contain immense crafting systems, which demonstrate how the combination of certain elements (better soil, different types of cloth or reagents and so on) work together to produce a collective end product.

Given the immense capacity to expand these simple aspects of MMORPGs, as well as the player's familiarity of how this resident content functions, there is still little work being done to develop the *existing* aspects of games towards more educational criteria, often from a lack of recognition that these parts of the game convey strong messages to the players. Prensky (2001, 2006) argues that information is assimilated in entirely different ways in games, and that because learning is achieved through many paths at once, it is difficult for users and for those attempting to prove linear objectives to recognize that it has taken place at all.

There is a need to understand the assimilation of details, ideas and communication techniques in digital worlds and games by recognizing that they convey information in different ways. Equally, players often wish to remain as players rather than learners – they often resist the idea that they are digesting learning concepts (Egenfeldt-Nielsen, 2005), even though they are actively consuming them and often produce ones of their own. This new way of absorbing information is termed here, 'Stealth Learning': the phrase describes the ways in which players take, gather and are given learning content.

Stealth Learning

Stealth Learning is a term to describe how players absorb information unintentionally within games. This outcome can be social, psychological, educational or even physical. It is not necessarily a result of the intent of either the interaction or the artefact engaged with. Stealth Learning recognizes that learning may evolve in ways unintended by the designer, and argues that these ways must be capitalized upon, even if they seem counter-intuitive, or even work against the gameplay product. The player who produces a witty machinima such as 'Code Monkey' (Booth, 2007) is a perfect example of a stealth learner – through playing the game the author has then gone on to learn the techniques of recording, editing, uploading and acting in a machinima. He has interacted with *World of Warcraft*, a recording program, an animation program that allowed him to change and edit the footage, sound recording software that overlays music to the video and finally downloaded the final product to YouTube. All this was learned in order to produce a comic video about the game.

The concepts of Stealth Learning provide new ways with which to understand how knowledge is transferred within gaming, recognizing that learning can occur in different ways to those intended, as well as through aspects that may not have been paramount in the original game design. Stealth Learning acknowledges the argument that studies cannot conclusively prove learning takes place within games (Egenfeldt-Nielsen, 2005; Squire, 2002). This is because users gain information, ideas and responses through interaction with an online artefact that are simply not possible to capture and categorize in conventional terms. Furthermore, the outcomes that users produce may be unintended or wildly different from the more obvious 'aims' of the game.

Thus, Stealth Learning consists of the educational gain by players, when either a learning objective is not immediately apparent, where content helps a player to gain information in some way, or where secondary learning objectives are achieved as a result of the content. Stealth Learning also attends to the law of affordances, infiltrating non-learning environments because users may wish to learn something that is not necessarily within the formal domain of learning. Often they do this as a normal part of their interaction with a game or digital artefact, as has already been demonstrated.

Indeed the concept of Stealth Learning is an acknowledgement that games may educate without having the intention of doing so. The domain of learning may not be extensive in terms of knowledge or skills, and the learning experience may not be extensive in time, but nevertheless it can be seen as taking place in an unexpected area. Some games, by their social natures, their diversity and through the range of abilities needed to enact them, have considerable amounts of Stealth Learning embedded into their content as a naturalized part of gameplay. Sometimes, as noted, this learning is a by-product caused entirely by players in their desire to broaden their understanding of a game. Stealth Learning is explicitly not simply applicable to the domain of educational games or Serious Games, although it is vital in appreciating how players wish to learn and how they absorb information.

Seen in this context, games can become enabling devices for learning. Two players sharing tips on gameplay, communicating through textual speech or perhaps even across language barriers, for instance, could be considered to be performing a genuine learning experience. The player who needs to research an artefact in order to better understand it, another who makes a video about the game and learns both production values and cinematographic technique, or the person who writes a detailed, coherent guide to an aspect of a game – are all stealth learners, accessing secondary information about how to enhance their own personal play. Nor are these unusual activities in MMORPGs. Browsing wikis and research sites, making videos, learning to delegate among feuding players, asking what a word in a different language means are all activities that happen on a regular basis among MMORPG players and all involve secondary elements that can be specifically classed as learned activities. Importantly, the game leads participants to direct their energies towards a multitude of tasks that could be seen as directly interacting with aspects of learning. The crafting menu screens in *World of Warcraft*, for example, could be seen to be teaching basic fractions as well as linking imagery, numbers and text together in meaningful ways.

To summarize, there are five major tenets of Stealth Learning in MMORPGs:

1. MMORPGs can be enabling devices for learning.
2. Such games may educate though they may have no explicit intention of doing so.
3. Learning outcomes may be unexpected or different from those that are presented on the surface.
4. Users are often receptive to learning, although they may not recognize they are learning and may actively resist / refute it if this is pointed out to them. Users frequently seek knowledge and learn skills beyond the game in order to teach themselves and others about the object they are interacting with. Such learning complements, but is not identical to, surface objectives.
5. Because Stealth Learning works below the surface, as long as these differences are anticipated and respected, educative agendas can be inserted into existing frameworks by designers (i.e. a secondary objective can be hidden beneath a primary one).

Stealth Learning can increasingly be seen in the ways that players interact socially in MMORPGs, as well as through the content of online worlds, which has the increasing capacity to convey complex ideas and structures. Designers who encode learning agendas into these worlds do so with various degrees of awareness. Three short case studies exemplify how each aspect of Stealth Learning above can take place within MMORPGs.

Case study 1: unexpected outcomes: *A Tale in the Desert*

A Tale in the Desert is an explicitly non-combat MMORPG where players live within an environment based visually on Ancient Egypt. The objective of the game is for the players to win each 'Telling' of the game. Tellings last between one to four years in real time. Beginning with an entirely undeveloped landscape at the beginning of each Telling, players must complete large-scale tasks within the worlds such as creating their own dwelling, from the ground up, discovering all the known abilities from universities and ultimately building a series of pyramids. Additionally, at least seven Oracles must arise. A player becomes an Oracle by succeeding at every Test in a given learning tree and thus perfecting one of 'The Seven Disciplines of Man'. A Test is split into two sections. Passing the Principle of each Test allows the player to gain a level and perhaps access to new skills. If a player wishes to become Oracle, they must pass the Test by winning it outright. Tests become progressively more difficult if more players engage in them as individuals and it is not intended that all players should complete them for the Telling to be 'won'. So, for example, passing the Principle of one of the Tests of Leadership involves standing in an election. Winning the Test means players must win the election.

A Tale in the Desert is heavily based on architectural, scientific and mathematical problem-solving. To achieve the given objectives of the game involves building increasingly complex structures and artefacts, all of which must be discovered in the first instance by players. Although a player starts by learning to combine materials such as straw, water and clay to make bricks, the simplicity of construction is very quickly replaced by small mini-games that facilitate the production of objects and require concentration, skill and knowledge to perfect. For example, an early mini-game involves the production of charcoal. Charcoal is made in ovens in which the player must continuously regulate the temperature, the oxygen levels and the amount of water on the fire. Failure to do this results in the entire batch of wood used in production being wasted. More complex skills require even more balancing; glassmaking involves a similar process where the regulation of materials, pressure and temperature is needed: the glass will shatter if not kept at the proper heat. Production of wines needs complex cross-breeding of grapes and the long-term monitoring of barrels for factors, such as acidity, sugar level and strength. The concentration required to facilitate this process is intended to be a reflection of its difficulty in real life and the complexity of equipment required to make artefacts in the game. For example, this complexity means that each member of the community must by necessity specialize to produce things such as paints, gearboxes, food and mining equipment. This was witnessed by the author who lived near one of Egypt's few vintners for several months, as well as establishing connections with a miner, a fence who would sell goods for others as well as sourcing difficult-to-find objects and a couple who rented gearboxes for use in mining operations. The best hookah blower in the game however, lived at the opposite end of the map, and because he was only able to play infrequently, his glass bowls were considered of exceptional worth.

The superficial learning objectives of *A Tale in the Desert* are very visible to the players – in fact the game could almost be described as educational rather than historical in nature. Players need to know a great deal about construction, physics and natural sciences – over 240 different herbs require nine different types of harvesting techniques. Most of this knowledge can be acquired within the game – it is unnecessary to know much about 'real' glassblowing techniques, although this does help the player break less in its manufacture. Stealth Learning can be said to be taking place through this knowledge construction – for example, players often share information about how to make the objects in the game through an extensive wiki, by word of mouth and by doing research into the background behind each task. Often, they have also learned that knowing the coordinates on which to make a specific type of brightly coloured tiles in a kiln is a commodity that should not be shared and information frequently comes at a price within the game. Learning here is market knowledge of commodities.

A Tale in the Desert is intended to be a mature, world-building MMORPG in which players must learn together in order to succeed. It is possible to fail a Telling (the first and third Tellings were in fact lost by the players). However, from the first Telling, Andrew Tepper the game's designer, frequently introduces elements which are aimed to make players reconsider their relationships with other players and to learn among them. The elements are not necessarily benign in nature, instead they aim to challenge players socially and sometimes ethically.

A Tale in the Desert has a nominal backstory – it is set in an Elseworld based around Ancient Egypt. The ongoing narrative from the first three Tellings concerns Pharaoh (an avatar, controlled by Tepper) and his negotiations with the Stranger, who occasionally requests help from the players or sets them additional trials. In the fourth Telling, Pharaoh was reported dead, and the storyline revolves more around the doings of his two sons, the fun-loving but ultimately aimless Sami, and the driven but socially devious Wahim. Interventions from afar still come in the nefarious guise of Greeks bearing gifts – in this case the nefarious Nicomedes. However, these characters have little to do with the daily running of the game – instead they tended to be the instigators of role-playing events, or used to rationalize developments in the game, such as the introduction of new technology or Tests. Law keeping is left in the hands of the players. Moderators (or Demi-Pharaohs) are voted in by the players and allowed certain privileges, most notably the ability to totally ban up to seven other players, whereupon all their assets are lost and that player cannot return to the game in that form again. Players are allowed to introduce laws into the game which change the content. These laws are checked by Tepper for suitability (usually to see if they can be coded effectively) but are then voted on by the players. They often consist of visual changes, for example, a law to enable buildings to contain windows, or 'fixes' to bugged or overlooked content within the world, but can also be social in nature. For example, they may suggest that the contents of all mines become open access after a certain period or that a user may only take a certain percentage of goods from one of their resources at a time. Laws that demand people to act in a certain way are strongly challenged and debated, and can lead to considerable social strife within the game. Without the typical MMORPG outlet of violence, regular communal activity or rapid activity, different factions can form seething enmities for each other.

Andrew Tepper is unrepentant about this. His secondary objective, he claims, is to actively promote the social disharmony that can thrive from introducing such challenges:

> The intent was never to make a purely co-operative game . . . We give game projects that people have to co-operate in, and then we give them reasons why they would want to act selfishly. The tension between those two, knowing that you

have to co-operate to get certain things done, but also knowing that co-operating isn't the personal best route to do things, it creates an interesting decision. (Tepper in Gillen, 2007)

Arguably, then, the stealth content in *A Tale in the Desert* is not the high degree of technical awareness that players require, nor the background they might research about Ancient Egypt, it is their development over social obstacles placed in the game by its designer. Some players are very aware of this – they regard themselves as part of the social experimentation within the game and actively engage with it. They are not always as aware of this as they might like however; the Lung Spore Plague of 2007, which was transmitted by proximity and thus drove avatars away from each other, causing players to leave the game in droves rather than work together for a cure. A cure simply seemed to them too long in coming and too difficult to achieve. Players did not recognize that they were being asked to cooperate in new ways, as well as having to work together to solve a quest. Players simply saw the plague as a frustrating and ultimately disharmonious introduction to the already difficult gameplay. In the third Telling of *A Tale in the Desert*, it was also apparent that factions existing from earlier iterations of the game, or who had started playing when the Telling began, held a great deal of control within the game through prior assets based on previous knowledge, cooperation between each other which did not benefit from including lower-level players and the like. Since they already possessed all the equipment that they needed or did not require basic commodities that lower-level players could collect in gigantic amounts, barter was extremely top heavy. Some players tried to form collectives. Players can join as many guilds as they want in order to create communal areas stocked with equipment and supplies for new players. Arguably, this promotes social disharmony as players can end up with multiple, conflicting commitments. However, once these players moved away from the collective, they found themselves isolated and lacking in sufficient mid-level resources to continue. The natural social order that had formed had learned that new players were a cost rather than an asset.

Overall, the Stealth Learning in *A Tale in the Desert* has various effects. Players are aware of it to an extent. Since the player group in *A Tale in the Desert* is a mature one, players take pride in the difficulty of the game, and anticipate the problems it presents them with, even if they are not always able to cope with them fully. As Tepper outlines, 'what they latched onto at first was building. It's something everyone was familiar with, and we have hundreds of things to build and craft. Players learned to do this very quickly, and enjoyed it. At first it seemed the game was just about building'. However 'teaching people to get [. . .] into the social side of the game was a little harder than I expected,' (Tepper in Gillen, 2007). Tepper's use of 'learned' and 'teaching' is perhaps accidental. His insertion of social content into an already complex world is not.

Interlude: The thinking community of MMORPGs

Before we consider our second case study, it might be useful to comment on the process of socialization in MMORPGs. This is not simply a matter of players interacting in order to direct ludic play onwards and upwards. Players engage in many social activities, often precluding their own desire to succeed. MMORPGs are specifically built for players to spend long periods of time within them, and by their very nature, facilitate a huge need for human contact. This is also the first point at which learning ideals are put directly into play by the players, and arguably it is the immense capacity of MMORPGs to transmit knowledge through socialization processes which is their greatest strength.

Players are usually made to choose their skills, most MMORPGs force players to diversify in one particular class, such as mage, fighter, healer, as well as picking a number of secondary skills to complement these abilities, such as Farming, Alchemy, Engineering, Runecrafting. It is unusual that players have totally free agency in these choices although there are exceptions, *A Tale in the Desert* is one, although that initially had deliberate gender differences. The strongest healer, for instance, cannot possibly also be the most powerful warlock and crafting skills are often limited to a certain number per player. Players must usually also choose a class, a race and various other attributes when they create a character, giving them various individual skills. Within these classes there is also considerable specialization, for example, a priest might choose to be particularly good at banishing undead, but this might render them very poor at healing people. This means that players become highly specialized in different vocational and class-related skills and it also deliberately creates a reliance on other players, for example, three warriors cannot enter a dungeon without someone to heal them.

MMORPGs have social activity encoded into their ludic objectives for two reasons. In order to proceed through the harder stages of the game, players must band together to achieve collective tasks, usually by visiting dungeons, destroying the monsters inside and distributing the equipment that the creatures drop as a prize for doing so. This form of shared activity means that players must join together in order to succeed, and often form groups (usually called guilds or clans) in order to more easily collect people together when they are needed. Second, the amount of time needed to level a character and then provide them with all the things they need to sustain equipment and perform at optimum levels means that there are considerable periods where a player is either carrying out a repetitive activity. For example, picking herbs, or performing a task done before, such as repeatedly visiting one dungeon to acquire a certain piece of clothing, which will upgrade the avatar's perform-ance overall. This activity is commonly known as 'grinding'. During grinding, social activity, such as chatting to guild members, sustains the player through a period that can be boring and repetitive, despite their knowledge of the gain it will entail.

Players in a MMORPG usually drift into groups where 'no one knows eve-rything, everyone knows something [and] all knowledge resides in humanity' (Jenkins, 2006, 27). Since the skills, abilities and knowledge of each character, as well as the player's progression through the game, are different, players use what Pierre Levy calls 'thinking communities' in order to function:

> The knowledge of a thinking community is no longer a shared knowledge for it is now impossible for a single human being, or even a group of people, to master all knowledge, all skills. It is fundamentally collective knowledge, impossible to gather together into a single creature. (Levy, cited in Jenkins, 2006, 28)

Thus, what players cannot know or perform on their own, they may now be able to do collectively. Conversely, the things that are known to all become aspects needed to sustain the existence of the community, to fulfill goals and to prevent social disharmony. The most important central aspect is that shared information, assets and actions succeed where individualism cannot. This nat-urally brings people into social contact with each other.

Case study 2: Users are receptive to learning: *World of Warcraft*

Last night was a solid, successful and productive Karazhan raid and it showed I think that the ideologies and outlooks of both guilds are close enough to work without either side making too many allowances! ☺ Last night Teamspeak was fairly FC centric ☺ and this meant we got to use our strategies and methods a fair bit, as well as be fairly sarcastic and jovial, keeping the whole thing fun and light-hearted. Epix alone do not fun make! (Final Chapter Forums, 2008).

A Tale in the Desert has a small, primarily mature user group and so it might be argued that Andrew Tepper's 'social experiment' is simply an oddity in the world of MMORPGs. In many ways it is, the game is deliberately difficult to play and fraught with unexpected challenges that arise from peculiar positions created by Tepper. However, the attitude of the players is not unique. Aware of the complexities within the game, players embrace this as 'part of the social experiment' (Kovia, 2007), as well as regarding it as an enjoyable process that they must learn to overcome. Play, to players, means all sorts of agendas, from ludic to *paidea* to manipulative to simple discovery. This attitude among players is not uncommon.

The inherent trial-and-error nature of online gaming means that players of online MMORPGs recognize the need to learn and adapt within game contexts. They are also aware that this learning must come as a thinking community with all players reliant upon the diversity of each other's skills to provide the solution to a collective whole. When MMORPGs are released, the content is unmapped, often literally, as players roam across large-scale continents 'unlocking' content as they explore. Solutions to puzzles, locations of people and strategies for overcoming areas or monsters must be discovered by the player. MMORPGs are so large that not only are there thousands of individual things that need to be uncovered, but gameplay is broad enough that the player has some agency both in what they choose to do, and how they choose to go about it (Murray, 1998; Parsler, 2007). Players consider discovery as a naturalized part of their gaming experience. Often they express this as a need to 'learn' the game content.

World of Warcraft (*WoW*) is the most infamous of the MMORPGs. With 11.5 million active accounts in 2008 (Blizzard, 2008), it is also the largest, holding 62 per cent of the market share in online games (2008). *World of Warcraft* successfully combines elements of previous games, most notably *Everquest*, its predecessors, *Diablo, Starcraft* and the early *Warcraft* games to make a world that is rich in narrative and in gameplay, with complex economic systems and highly structured tiers of play. However, it is upon the attention to social grouping that has arguably led to its success and to its retention of players.

In *A Tale in the Desert,* the active user-base tops out at 1,750–2,500, about a month after a Telling begins, and then tends to stabilize at around 1,100 subscribers (Tepper, 2010). As Richard Bartle argues, 'community ties rank among the most powerful reasons for players to stay with a virtual world' (2004, 220), and it is perhaps an indication of the schisms that *A Tale in the Desert* deliberately sets out to provoke that account for its relatively small user-base.

By contrast, *World of Warcraft* is comparatively easy to pick up and play as a solo player and even at very high levels in the game the individual is kept busy. Indeed, the game provides literally hundreds of things for players to do, thereby ensuring that there is never a final point to the game. Large expansions and 'patches' containing new features and additional content are released on a regular basis, replacing the player's aims with ones yet higher and more exciting. However, the game also relies on a great deal of social activity. Players must form groups, or 'raids' in order to enter dungeons and get the best equipment together with dungeons previously requiring over forty people to complete. More recently, this has been reduced in size to twenty-five, when it was realized that these sizes were not, in fact, particularly self-sustaining.

Raiding and grouping is all about cooperation and learning, often requiring players to act collectively in highly complex ways. Wowwiki describes a section of the tactics required to kill the boss 'Lady Vashj'. This quote, as with the previous one from the guild Final Chapter (FC), also demonstrates the high level of technical jargon that has mainly evolved from a need to be concise and brief in situations where rapid instructions need to be given. Thus terms like 'DoTs' for 'damage over time spells', catch-all terms like 'ranged', 'kited' or 'tanks' which describe actions, groups of players or types of behaviour, or abbreviations such as 'At 70%' ('at the point where the monster has 70% of its health bar remaining') are all interspersed with the description of technique in order to give a precise, rapid explanation of what is required for players

At 70% [Lady Vashj] runs to the middle of her platform and surrounds herself in a shield making her invulnerable. To take down the shield the 4 Shield Generators around her must be deactivated, by using a Tainted Core (from the Tainted Elementals) on each. During the entire phase, four different types of adds spawn, each of which need to be dealt with:

1. Coilfang Elites are tanked and killed by the tanks and melee damage dealers
2. Coilfang Striders are kited and killed by DoTs. Every class able to cast a DoT should help on this (even healers)
3. Killing Enchanted Elementals is the main business of all ranged damage dealers
4. Tainted Elementals must be killed, their Tainted Cores looted and used to switch off the shield generators. This task requires teamwork, each raid has to work out what's best.

At the start of phase 2, there's a brief lull for about 40 seconds, during which time everybody can make sure they're at the right position. There are 12 stairs, many raids divide them into four sections of 3 stairs (N, W, S and E), and assign a team of two ranged damage dealers and one healer to each section. (Wowwiki, 2008)

This description is complex and requires a group to act in unison, while at the same time trusting everyone to perform different tasks, also acknowledging that experimentation and group work is key to success. Since high-level content, specifically the equipment that these bosses drop and the kudos that accompanies 'downing' or killing one, is desired by players, and guilds, and raiding teams often form as a result of this need. Players practise together, organize specific times to raid and help each other maximize their chances of succeeding by 'farming' or 'grinding' food, potions and other resources that they may need. In forming guilds, players are more easily able to assemble groups, and the regular social contact this entails means they are also more likely to know each other's strengths and weaknesses within the framework of the team. Groups within MMORPGs are not restricted to these ludic aims, however, it is common for groups to form with other intentions in mind, for example, player versus player enthusiasts, solo players, role players who want to enact their characters' personas with others, and smaller groups who will never reach the high-end content but are happy to remain together as social groups. Since a great deal of grind is required for all of these tasks, all guilds use shared chat channels to pass the time when they are not actively playing together but are instead carrying out individual tasks or quests in the world.

World of Warcraft's social structuring arises from a commercial desire to retain players. At the same time the bonds formed and the ways in which players learn how to learn as a co-operative group together shows how receptive they are to absorbing new information. Considerable research outside the game is required or produced as a result – players look up and write how-to guides, but they also research oddities, for example finding out if the Wolpertinger pet given as a prize during the annual Brewfest event is mythical or simply an invention of Blizzard. Players also record tactics on forums or as machinima, programme add-ons that allow the cool-down times of spells to be visualized more effectively or which display the relative threat of one player against another. In addition, planning and meeting people in real life, negotiating and delegating between antagonistic or disruptive players, all of these aspects result from socialization originating within *World of Warcraft*. Players form intense social links which extend outwards across racial and social barriers, it is common, for example, for players to ask the meaning of words or to ask each other for help understanding each other. This sort of behaviour arises from an atmosphere in which each individual takes learning for granted and then begins to extend it outwards as they gain trust of their peers.

Players freely learn *around* the game as well as recognizing their status as a thinking community where knowledge needs to be portioned out. They regard this, as the quote from Final Chapter demonstrates, as a rewarding part of the game. The social organizations that they form work together very much like one in the employment field. Beck and Wade (2006) have suggested that this type of learning produces more effective, experimental workers, supporting the idea that the diffracted methods of learning within MMORPGs are not simply limited to the game. Crucially, *World of Warcraft*, probably the least ostensibly educative MMORPG currently running, contains significant subtexts, not least through its generation of social activity, which encourages a learning agenda.

Case study 3: educative agendas within existing frameworks: *Runescape*

Runescape (Jagex, 2001–present) is a simpler MMORPG than the two previously described, but it is also the second most popular MMORPG currently in existence with numbers to rival that of *World of Warcraft*. In 2008 its users were regularly three times more than that of *Second Life*. On 12 March, 2008, *Runescape* players averaged between 44,805 players and 123,250 players online concurrently (*Runescape*, 2008a), *Second Life* between 59,740 and 29,437 (Massively: 2008a). By 2010, these figures were still consistently higher – *Runescape* had 113,351–72,215 players (*Runescape*, 2010) whereas *Second Life* had 50,561–29,002 (*Second Life*, 2010).

Runescape runs entirely from a web browser and has been variously praised for its simplicity or derided for its relatively low-fidelity graphical representation. Either way, *Runescape* is cheap (or free) to play and popular with younger players. Because of this, the game has a preoccupation with security and the safety of its users.

> Here at Jagex, we understand the importance of learning, education and experience. In our Keeping Healthy and Responsible Gaming Policy sections, we emphasize the importance of maintaining a balanced life, helping our players realize that work and study are hugely important, as is getting regular exercise, taking regular breaks from your computer and socializing away from an online environment.

> This stance on responsible gaming is as true of our game as it is of our policies.
> We try to help bridge the gap between education and entertainment by present-
> ing players with thought-provoking challenges that make for a fun and stimulat-
> ing experience.

From reading the socially conscious webpages of *Runescape*, this 'stance on responsible gaming' seems to be a rather platitudinous utterance designed to subdue worried parents. However, *Runescape* takes its policies far more seriously than this, embedding safety, as well as educational content, within the actual framework of the game. Crucially, this hinges on how players gain 'experience points' in the game, the statistics needed to make them stronger, better players.

At the beginning of the game, players are led through a tutorial area. After being told how to move by clicking the mouse and how to build fires, they are then told not to give their password to anyone. Jagex representatives will never contact them except through the in-game mail, they are informed, before being shown how to cast magic bolts and then instructed on good practice in setting recovery questions and a pin number for their *Runescape* bank box. This interchangeability is typical of the whole game, where net safety and learning objectives are a marked element of daily life within the world simply because so many Non-Player Characters (NPCs) within the world keep reminding players of these aspects.

The ways that experience points are gained within *Runescape* are also atypical. Players gain points in a variety of different skills that level up independently of each other, rather than adding to a cumulative whole. The majority of these twenty-six skills are related to crafting or physical activity rather than offensive capabilities. Thus players receive points in specific categories for related skills rather than having a generic experience pool whereby any activity feeds into the characters' level. This allows *Runescape* to structure its experience point system in different ways. There is often a learning agenda where a player gets more points for a learning activity rather than a 'doing' activity can be easily inserted into the gameplay. In the main city of Varrock is a museum, where the player can view exhibits of archaeological finds, mythical and real animals and a history of Gielinor (the *Runescape* world). The museum is dryly witty, players can press buttons on the animal exhibits which cause them to move. The dragon flaps its wings and the mole pops out of its burrows. But the mole is lifted up by a pole and the giant leeches run round their exhibit on a track, all of them are clearly inanimate objects. The museum animals combine real with fictional, in a recursive joke. Even though some of the information is genuinely informative and animals such as the terrorbird and wyvern still obey the laws of nature. Players can additionally donate quest items to the museum's historical archive when they have finished with them, they can clean archaeological finds, only after giving the beleaguered workers at the dig site cups of tea and they can embark on a mini-quest to correct the labels on the animal exhibits. All of these activities earn the player 'kudos' points at the museum which, when they speak to the head-curator, are translated into experience points for the 'slayer' skill. Knowing about the animals helps the player a great deal more than simply going out and repeatedly killing rabbits for experience in the same category. The message here is obvious to an older player, but perhaps less so to the target demographic. Learning is not only good, it is rewarded by a significantly large amount of points.

This type of content, where learning directly intersects with gameplay, can be seen throughout *Runescape*'s world. The Stronghold of Security is a dungeon in which the doors will only open if the player can answer questions about online safety. The game times out and player are disconnected after two minutes, preventing long periods of stasis but also keeping their accounts safe. Using one's wits and following the often complex quest lines provide a great deal more points in various skills than simply walking outside and hitting things. Overall, although quests may be silly or fantastic in nature, they are based on logic and the sensible application of skills. Not only is it possible to attain high levels in the game with relatively little combat, but the knowledge required to do so is complex, thoughtful and cleverly intersected into the main body of the narrative.

Runescape is a strong example of how games can include Stealth Learning as an embedded topic and still be successful. Conversations with non-player characters (NPCs) are witnessed by the player, who sees their own avatar speaking in the manner of a point-and-click adventure, where the player is given options to ask the NPC questions from which a set piece of dialogue will ensue. This means that players witness their online 'selves' at a remove from which instructions, information and ideas can in some ways be directed by the Games' scriptwriters. Usually, this dialogue is dry or comic, but it also allows the player to look objectively at their 'self' within the game, carefully navigating the divide between the fourth wall, in this case the remove between player and player avatar, rather than player and screen (Conway, 2010). To an older player, the learning content might seem obvious yet it is still not crude, all of it seems to fit well within the world sphere, and there is a secure narrative, which includes the distancing effect of player/avatar, to reinforce the viability of this within the gameworld. *Runescape* teaches partly through a consciousness of its players, but also, partly with the intent of showing its players that learning has a greater gain than monster mashing.

Conclusion

MMORPGs provide new ways of learning, ways that have not been investigated in any depth but are already implicit in existing gameplay. The communities that have developed within these worlds have a proactive attitude towards learning if it is of benefit to gameplay, this includes teaching appropriate social behaviours, learning to work in large groups and sharing the required tasks between many, as well as achieving ludic agendas configured within the game.

Learning of this nature is intrinsic to the style of MMORPG design, where initially there appears to be no educational content. These worlds are so multifaceted that learning simply how to navigate them teaches skills. These can include very intricate or in-depth understandings and knowledge as widely diverse as how to tailor the most aesthetically pleasing robes to convoluted statistical awareness and analysis of a character's relative power in the world. Simple learning objectives are as basic as reading and comprehending the instructions given in a small quest narrative, but they are a part of a player's daily life within each world, something which they both accept and celebrate.

As players become older, the desire for more complex, mature texts has led to a groundswell of MMORPGs, such as *Roma Victor* or *A Tale in the Desert*. Both games are specifically targeted at more thoughtful players and engage both historical and scientific principles as a central tenet of daily gameplay. These games are particularly interesting as they eliminate combat from gameplay and require their players to consider ethical and moral aspects of the world they inhabit. At the same time, the challenges of each game often results from the fact that the complex social structures, narratives and codes of behaviour placed in the more mainstream MMORPGs are absent.

Embedded content is something that has not been addressed in detail within the context of MMORPGs and educative frameworks. Nevertheless, it is not only present, but players actively engage with it. Players equate their experiences with 'learning' even if they do not regard this learning as 'educational'. This does not have to be an issue however, as players are happy to absorb good content in great detail, and will often overlook elements like implementation of net safety agendas into games like *Runescape*, if they still feel that their ludic and social play is deep enough. When educative aims eclipse the agency of the ludic and the social, however, players are less likely to engage in content and more likely to regard it with suspicion or simple lack of interest. Aspects of learning that get in the way of fulfilling play are not appreciated, whereas integrated elements, such as the Museum in Varrock, prove more successful.

Stealth Learning is a way of viewing these constructions, and in some ways it also helps to refute the lack of evidence about learning in games. This is because it acknowledges that secondary outcomes can often be more valuable as learning outcomes than the stated aims of the game. Players in the Stronghold of Security would tell you that they were trying to get to the deepest chamber and that they already 'knew' the answers about net safety, in fact they have learned or remembered these answers while trying to achieve this goal. The learning content is still present, but the players do not see it as the root of the game. Similarly, an obvious game agenda can be supplanted by the means to get there, by the diffracted patterns of learning that have allowed players to reach that point in the game. Often, these cannot be quantified, for every player's MMORPG journey varies, but they can be explained or even anticipated.

References

Bartle, R. (2004). *Designing Virtual Worlds*. New York: Pearson Educational.

Beck, J. and Wade, M. (2006). *The Kids are Alright; How the Gamer Generation is Changing the Workplace*. Massachusetts: Harvard Business School Press.

Booth, M. (2007). Code Monkey, at http://www.youtube.com/watch?v=v4Wy7gRGgeA&feature=related

Conway, S. (2010). 'A Circular Wall? Rethinking the Fourth Wall for Videogames'. *Journal for Computer Games and Virtual Worlds*. Vol. 2, No. 3, page reference

Dybwad, B. (2008). SXSW08: How gamers are adopting the wiki way. Available at http://www.massively.com/2008/03/08/sxsw08-how-gamers-are-adopting-the-wiki-way/. Last accessed 25.4.10.

Egenfeldt-Nielsen, S. (2005). Beyond Edutainment: Exploring the Educational Potential of Computer Games. PhD Thesis. IT University. Copenhagen. 27 May 2005.

Final Chapter Forums (2008). Last night in Karazhan at http://www.finalchapterguild.com/viewtopic.php?t=851. Last accessed 25.4.10.

Gee, J. P. (2003). *What Video Games have to Teach Us about Learning and Literacy*. New York: Palgrave.

Gillen, K. (2007). The making of: *A Tale in the Desert* (interview with Andrew Tepper) at Rock Paper Shotgun. 14 September 2007. Available at http://www.rockpapershotgun.com/?p=261 Last accessed 25.4.10.

Jenkins, H. (2006). *Convergence Culture: Where Old and New Media Collide.* New York: New York University Press.

Klastrup, L. and Tosca, S. (2010). When Fans become Players: *LOTRO* in a transmedial world perspective. In *Ringbearers, Lord of the Rings: Online as Intertextual Narrative.* Manchester: Manchester University Press.

Kovia (2007). Conversation in *A Tale in the Desert* with player 'Kovia'.

Massively (2008a). 'Yesterday in *Second Life*, March 13 2008'. http://www.massively.com/2008/03/13/yesterday-in-second-life-second-life-daily-news/.

Mortensen, T. (2007). Me, the other. In P. Harrigan, and N. Wardrip-Fruin, eds. *Second Person, Roleplaying and Story in Games and Playable Media.* Massachusetts: The MIT Press.

Murray, J. (1998). *Hamlet on the Holodeck.* Massachusetts: MIT Press.

Parsler, J. (2007). A Taxonomy of Agency. Unpublished thesis paper, University of Brunel.

Prensky, M. (2001). *Digital Game-Based Learning.* New York: McGraw-Hill.

Prensky, M. (2006). *Don't Bother Me Mom, I'm Learning!* Minnesota: Paragon House.

Runescape main page (and loading screen for the game) (2008) at http://www.runescape.com.

Squire, K. (2002). Rethinking the role of games in education. *Game Studies, Vol. 2, No. 1.*http://gamestudies.org/0201/Squire/. Last accessed 25.4.10.

Taylor, T. L. (2006). *Play Between Worlds.* Massachusetts: MIT Press.

Tepper, A. (2010). 'T4 NewsLetter Issue 4, 02/12/2010' at http://www.atitd.com/news/t4_newsletter_4.html Last accessed 25.4.10.

Murder on Grimm Isle: The Design of a Game-based Learning Environment

6

Michele D. Dickey

Introduction

For the past two decades, the design of digital games has been a source of study for educational researchers and instructional designers investigating how various aspects of game design might be appropriated, borrowed and repurposed for the design of educational materials (Bowman, 1982; Dickey, 2005a, 2006a, 2007a; Malone, 1981; Prensky, 2001; Provenzo, 1991; Rieber, 1991; Squire, 2003). While much scholarship has been invested in the benefit of using games and game-based elements for learning, educators and designers are now addressing how to design game-based learning environments. A variety of noteworthy scholars and designers have contributed to the discussion (Amory, 2001; Amory and Seagram, 2003; Barab et al., 2005; Barab et al., 2005; Barab et al., 2004; Nelson et al., 2007; Rieber and Matzko, 2001; Rieber, 1996). However, much of the research has focused primarily on the learning design.

While certainly learning design is the most important aspect of designing a game-based learning environment, there are other areas of design significant in the process which also impact cognition and learner perception.

The purpose of this chapter is to present a case study of the design of the game-based learning environment, *Murder on Grimm Isle*, and to highlight how research from such diverse sources as literature, behavioural psychology, architecture, animation studies and the emerging field of game design informed the design. Specifically, this chapter addresses (a) narrative design, (b) character development, (c) environmental design and (d) interactive design. The goal of this chapter is to illustrate how research from various fields of the Arts and Sciences can inform the design of interactive and game-based learning environments.

One of the current movements within the field of instructional design is towards the cultivation and development of interactive learning environments (Winn, 2002). This development towards learning environments has been in part fuelled by the epistemological shift towards constructivism and in part fuelled by the impact and integration of technology and learning. The focus of learning environments is on meaningful, active learning in complex, multimodal environments (Hannafin et al., 1994; Hannafin and Land, 1997; Hannafin et al., 1999; Jonassen, 1999; Land and Hannafin, 1996; Land and Hannafin, 1997). The theoretical assumption is that learners construct understanding by interacting with information, tools and materials, as well as by collaborating with other learners. Because of the interplay between all of these dynamics, digital games are becoming a popular source of inspiration for models, strategies and techniques for designing interactive and by extension, game-based learning environments. However, while the field of game design provides a natural point of departure, the field of game design has a history of borrowing and appropriating research, methods and techniques from various disciplines within the arts and sciences. There is much to be gleaned from various disciplines in the Arts and Sciences, which may help inform the design of engaging and accessible interactive and game-based learning environments.

The focus of this chapter is to present a case study of the design of a game-based learning environment and to highlight how research from such diverse sources as literature, behavioural psychology, architecture, animation studies and the emerging field of game design informed the design of a game-based learning environment. The following presents first an overview of *Murder on Grimm Isle*, followed by four sections discussing the narrative, character, environment and interactive design. Each section also includes an overview of the academic foundations of each of these elements, along with the value of these elements for learning. Also included is a discussion of how each of these elements informed the design of *Murder on Grimm Isle*.

Overview: *Murder on Grimm Isle*

Murder on Grimm Isle (Dickey, 2006b, 2007b, 2008) is a 3D adventure-style game-based learning environment designed to foster argumentation writing skills for grades 9–14 language arts. The premise begins with a back-story involving the murder of a prominent citizen of the fictional Grimm Isle. Learners are cast in the role of an investigator probing the crime scene along with other locales on Grimm Isle to determine the culprit. As learners move throughout the environment, they encounter and collect evidence to help them determine motivation and construct arguments about their beliefs of the crime and the culprit. Part of the underlying instructional design relies upon Toulmin's model for argumentation (Toulmin et al., 1979). The evidence that learners encounter provides support for their arguments. The following is a discussion of how various fields such as literature, behavioural psychology, architecture, animation studies and game design served to inform and guide the narrative, character, environmental and interactive design of *Murder on Grimm Isle* (MOGI).

Narrative and game design

The use of narrative is important in learning environments because narrative is ubiquitous in human reasoning and allows humans to assign meaning to their experiences (Bruner, 1990; Scholes and Kellogg, 1969). Humans use narrative to not only frame thought, but to guide actions (Polkinghorne, 1988). According to Robinson and Hawpe (1986), narrative is a type of causal thinking in which the narrative (cognitive) schema identifies categories, for example protagonist, situation, conflict, outcome and relevant types of relationships, for example temporal, motivational and procedural. The importance of narrative in game-based learning is that it provides a cognitive framework for problem-solving. According to Rieber (1996), when learners (players) are presented with a problem, a learner (player) 'will seek resolution if a solution seems possible and within reach' (p. 49).

Two common narrative devices used in digital games are the quest and plot hooks. Both are borrowed from literature yet provide key structure for games.

While the quest provides structure for the entire duration of a game, plot hooks are devices that are used to both frame and draw players into the storyline of a game and are used in key junctures within a game.

The most common narrative structure found in digital games is the quest. The quest is a familiar structure that occurs throughout Western literature ranging from works by Homer, Chaucer, Cervantes and Joyce, to more recent popular films such as *Star Wars*, *Sleepless in Seattle* and *Finding Nemo*. The classic structure of the quest typically involves a hero/heroine who for various reasons must embark on some type of journey. During this journey, the heroine or hero has to overcome various conflicts encountered along the way, typically culminating in a large struggle or conflict before returning to everyday life. This is a popular narrative structure used for games because it affords many opportunities for exploration and conflict.

In the literature of game design, one of the more frequently cited sources of guidance for narrative design is Vogler's (1998) work on mythic structures and writing (Crawford, 2003; Dunniway, 2000; Rollings and Adams, 2003). Vogler (1998) draws heavily upon the work of a foremost scholar of mythology, Joseph Campbell. In *The Hero with a Thousand Faces* (1973), Campbell outlines the reoccurring myths or mono-myths that transcend both time and culture. Vogler (1998) identifies and outlines these in the following twelve stages of the hero's journey as it relates to contemporary storytelling.

1. Ordinary World
2. Call to Adventure
3. Refusal of the Call
4. Meeting with the Mentor
5. Crossing the First Threshold
6. Tests, Allies, Enemies
7. Approach to the Inmost Cave
8. Ordeal
9. Reward (Seizing the Sword)
10. The Road Back
11. Resurrection
12. Return with the Elixir

An example of the use of the quest in a game is the popular adventure game, *Syberia*. In *Syberia*, a New York-based lawyer, Kate Walker, is sent to the remote alpine village of Valadilene to conclude the acquisition of a famous mechanical toy factory. However, upon arriving in Valadilene, she discovers the owner of the factory has recently died. Though her inclination is to return to New York, during her initial interactions in Valadilene, she finds, that the owner may have a brother who in turn would inherit the factory. Kate reluctantly undertakes a journey to find the missing brother. Throughout her journey, she encounters a variety of challenges, both personal and physical, in order to reach her goal. For the design of game-based learning environments, the quest is a useful structure because it provides a natural design heuristic for how to frame narratives in game-based learning environment (Dickey, 2006).

Another common way to frame a narrative and to entice an audience is the use of plot hooks. Plot hooks are a strategy common to many types of literary genres, such as soap operas, romance and other serial fiction. Plot hooks are also commonly used for table-top role-playing games (Dansky and Kane, 2006). Plot hooks frame a storyline by presenting unanswered questions and uncertainties that focus attention of readers, viewers, and in the case of games, players, by planting questions that one feels compelled to answer. The purpose of plot hooks are to arouse curiosity, create intrigue and frame puzzles which all lead to the question, 'what is going to happen next?' In games, good plot hooks put players in the middle of an action without providing much exposition. Plot hooks can play a key role in structuring narrative for games because they allow for player choice.

An example of how a plot hook can draw players into a game is once again the example of the adventure game *Syberia*. The initial plot hook is presented at the beginning of the game in a short animation cut scene. The scene begins on a grey rainy day. Kate Walker, with suitcase in hand, has just arrived in the remote alpine village of Valadilene to meet with Anna Voralberg to conclude the purchase of Anna's factory. However, the game opens with Kate encountering a funeral procession by a mechanical human drummer. A wagon, bearing a casket and a wreath with the name 'Anna' on it passes by Kate, followed by an array of mechanical human mourners. As Kate walks towards the hotel, she is greeted once again by a mechanical human. In the case of *Syberia*, the player is placed in the centre of the action without much exposition but with the choice of playing the game in order to answer the question, 'what happens next?'

Narrative design: *Murder on Grimm Isle*

The narrative of *Murder on Grimm Isle* employs both a loose quest and plot hooks. The entire adventure is loosely framed as a journey with learners beginning in everyday life. The beginning of *Murder on Grimm Isle* begins with an animation cut scene. The scene begins with a fade-in shot of a dark and foreboding mansion framed against a stormy night sky (see Figure 6.1). As the camera slowly pans up, there is the sound of a man crying out in anguish followed by a thud and the sound of a glass hitting the floor. Next, the camera moves into the house to reveal a close-up of a hand and a wine glass both lying still (see Figure 6.2). As the animation progresses, a scenario is revealed in which learners find out they are criminal investigators being sent to Grimm Isle to investigate the murder of the wealthy attorney and environmentalist, Robson Wolfe. They also learn of the long-standing feud between two powerful families on Grimm Isle: the Wolfes and the Ryding-Hoods. Learners are granted a search warrant to search the homes of three main suspects: Scarlett Ryding-Hood (young fashionista), Mimi Ryding-Hood (Scarlett's step-grandmother) and Mark Woodsman (handy man on the Ryding-Hood estate). They are provided with some additional back-story about some of the complex interplay of dynamics between all four characters. Additionally, they are informed that a hurricane is headed towards Grimm Isle, hence the need to remain on task. They are also provided with some initial instructions about how to 'travel' within Grimm Isle and how to identify and 'bag' evidence.

Figure 6.1 Beginning of animated cut scene in *Murder on Grimm Isle*

Figure 6.2 End of opening animated cut scene of *Murder on Grimm Isle*

At the end of the animated back-story, learners are transported to the 3D environment of Grimm Isle. Learners initially 'land' outside of the Wolfe mansion (in the 3D environment – see Figure 6.4). Learners are free to begin collecting evidence. They may choose to begin at the Wolfe mansion or because *Murder on Grimm Isle* is a 3D environment, they are free to travel to any other location on the isle. As learners encounter objects which are evidence, they are able to click on the evidence to reveal more information about the evidence. Learners are able to 'bag' the evidence to study at a later time. Evidence objects include such items as book covers, a forensic report, a last will and testament, a valentine and audio voice mail.

The narrative design of *Murder on Grimm Isle* is loosely based on the adventure game genre, for example *Myst, Syberia, the Nancy Drew Series, Broken Sword*. Typically most adventure games begin with an intriguing, yet somewhat vague back-story that usually presents some type of mystery or conflict. Players are then able to move throughout parts of the environment and encounter various obstacles in forms of puzzles to solve. The correct solution to the puzzle often activates another cut scene to reveal the next part of the story. Players move through the game solving puzzles to uncover the linear narrative. Usually the gameplay puzzles are related to the blossoming narrative storyline. Although the design of *Murder on Grimm Isle* is based on some of the conventions of an adventure game, it is not an adventure game. Within *Murder on Grimm Isle*, there is no one central narrative to uncover. Instead, learners uncover lines of evidence that suggest possible scenarios.

The narrative design of *Murder on Grimm Isle* draws upon the narrative conventions of both literature and by extension, games. The initial plot hook is a 'whodunit'. Learners embark upon a quest of sorts as they travel through the environment in pursuit of their goal. Depending upon the evidence learners' encounter, they may construct very different storylines. Much of the narrative relies on common mystery conventions that help suggest motives for each of the characters. For example, a boot print found at the crime scene may match the boots found in another character's home. Learner interpretations, and subsequent arguments of motive and guilt, vary depending upon the homes visited and the evidence collected. While this design draws upon adventure style-games, it is important to note that *Murder on Grimm Isle* is not a game *per se*, but rather a game-based learning environment. The lack of one single narrative storyline is purposeful. It is designed to keep learners focused on the goal of developing their arguments rather than focused on merely revealing a storyline to win a game.

Character design

Although much of the educational focus of character design has been situated in the realm of pedagogical agents, the potential impact and importance of character design for game-based learning environments should not be understated. Great characters in games, movies and literature can motivate, inspire, teach and provide insight and opportunities for reflection. A great character in a game can serve a variety of functions and reinforce a sense of immersion in the environment as well as providing guidance and information.

Character design within games consists of both the role and function of the character as well as the visual manifestation of the character. While fields, such as literature and even behavioural psychology, can help inform about aspects of role and function, visual fields, such as comics and animation provide guidance in how characters convey those aspects.

Vogler's (1998) analysis of the quest also offers insight into character design. Within the scope of the quest, Vogler identifies the seven character archetypes: Hero, Mentor, Threshold Guardian, Herald, Shapeshifter, Shadow and Trickster based upon Jung's (1953) archetypal patterns of the collective unconscious.

Vogler (1998) stresses that archetypes should not be considered as fixed roles, but rather as functions within a storyline. The hero's role functions as the main agent of action who undertakes the journey from a first-person perspective. The mentor functions to provide guidance. The threshold guardian functions as a character or even a situation which in some way tests the hero with some obstacle. The herald functions to signal change and new information. The shapeshifter functions as a character or situation in which doubt must be overcome. The trickster functions as another type of obstacle in the form of a character who causes problems or provides obstacles either by design or by accident. Finally, the shadow functions as the main antagonist in the form of a character or as a situation.

The function of a character is a key aspect for character design because it serves to define the role; however, the appearance, movement and dialogue of a character also are important for conveying these roles. There is a significant body of research from various fields of psychology which help to inform the design of pedagogical characters based on public perceptions of attractiveness, agreeableness and dominance. Much of this work has been leveraged in the design of pedagogical agents and characters (Bates, 1994; Isbister, 2006; Isbister and Nass, 2000; Nass et al., 2000; Johnson et al., 2000). According to Isbister (2006) both agreeableness and dominance of a character can provide more depth in character development. Based on research about perceptions of personality, Isbister argues that agreeableness impacts how game players perceive their relationship to a character. People tend to have a positive association with characters deemed attractive (Zebrowitz, 1997).

Both comic artists (McCloud, 1994) and animators (Thomas and Johnston, 1981) have a long history of intuitively using this type of knowledge. Characters designed and portrayed by animation pioneers, such as Tex Avery and Chuck Jones, provide studies in how design, motion and action convey and reinforce character design. Thomas and Johnston (1981) of Disney's infamous 'nine old men' outlined the following eleven principles of animation which are foundational for giving characters personality and the illusion of life.

1. Squash and stretch
2. Timing and motion
3. Anticipation
4. Staging
5. Follow through and overlapping action
6. Straight ahead action and pose-to-pose action
7. Arcs

8. Slow in and out
9. Exaggeration
10. Secondary action
11. Appeal.

In turn, Lasseter (1987) integrated these elements in foundational work with Pixar in creating 3D computer-based characters.

Character design: *Murder on Grimm Isle*

Within the storyline of *Murder on Grimm Isle*, there are four main characters: Robson Wolfe (deceased), Scarlett Ryding-Hood, Scarlett's step-grandmother, the young Mimi Ryding-Hood and Mark Woodsman. However, these characters do not appear in the environment nor do any images of them appear beyond the inanimate hand of Robson Wolfe in the opening animated cut scene sequence. This design is purposeful for several reasons. First, full character rigging and animation of human characters is difficult and time consuming. Second, and more importantly, the focus of *Murder on Grimm Isle* is for learners to construct an argument based on found evidence. Animated characters could have potentially swayed learner opinions based on their perceptions of the appearance and animation of a character, rather than their collection of evidence. Finally, in an attempt to foster inclusive design, *Murder on Grimm Isle* is intended to allow learners to create their own images and sense of the characters without imposing aspects of race and ethnicity. The lack of characters is explained by the impending hurricane, which in turn also provides a narrative explanation for time limits imposed on learners.

In the initial version of *Murder on Grimm Isle*, the characters appeared, so much of the visual design and animation draw upon the works of Bates (1994), Isbister (2006) and Thomas and Johnston (1981). However, in the final version, the characters do not appear, instead their presence is constructed through their homes, home furnishings and voice mail messages. In order to fully express these characters, they were designed to play upon common stereotypes and common literary conventions. For example, Mimi Ryding-Hood might be easily characterized as a young 'gold digger' who upon the death of her elderly husband inherited the entire Ryding-Hood estate. Scarlett could be characterized as a disinherited heiress and former fashionista. Mark Woodman might be characterized as a 'player'. While there are no explicit elements in the game-based learning environment describing any of the characters this way, both their homes and artefacts found within each character's home and the homes of other characters are meant to evoke these stereotypes. The character design is purposeful. Each character is designed to evoke a motivation for potentially harming Robson Wolfe, such as love, greed, jealousy and/or revenge. Additionally, the evidence, though consistent for each character, was also designed to cross-link characters and provide additional insight into motivation.

Environmental design

Like character design, environmental design begins with abstract elements and moves into the pragmatic realm of visual expression. While the field of game design is a good point of departure for the design of abstract elements, such as temporal, emotional and even ethical dimensions, the field of architecture provides grounding in how the environmental design can be conveyed in an accessible way that fosters way-finding and navigation.

Within different game genres, the setting plays a variable role in the design by supporting the narrative, providing a sense of immersion and by defining the 'gamespace' (Laramée, 2002; Rollings and Adams, 2003). According to game designers, Rollings and Adams, a game setting can be defined by physical, temporal, environmental, emotional and ethical dimensions (2003). The physical dimension defines the physical space in which the player's character/avatar or game pieces move around (Adams, 2003; Rollings and Adams, 2003). This dimension is comprised of scale and boundaries which define the size and edges of the playing environment. The temporal dimension defines the role of time in the game (Rollings and Adams, 2003). It describes not only temporal aspects, such as how much time a player has to complete an action, but also defines whether the game will include nightfall, seasons, time passage, as well as delineating the impact that time passage will have on gameplay. The environmental dimension (Rollings and Adams, 2003) defines both the game setting appearance and atmosphere. It characterizes the game setting as fantasy or realism, the historical context and the geographical location, and the overall mood and tone. The environmental dimension is manifested in the use of colour and lighting, the shape, size and placement of objects within the environment and the supporting materials, such as menus and documentation. The emotional dimension describes the emotions of both the characters in the game and the types of emotions that the design hopes to invoke within the game. The ethical dimension defines the moral aspects of the game (Rollings and Adams, 2003). It is by defining this aspect that character and roles logically follow rules that govern conventions within the context of the game.

Outlining the various dimensions of a game-based learning environment can help designers and educators create environments that are both plausible and support the learning task. Research into narrative notes the importance of plausibility in storyline. A story does not have to be realistic, but it must be plausible. Outlining the various dimensions can help identify weaknesses in plausibility and reinforce the narrative storyline for a game-based learning environment.

As game-based learning environments become more complex, coupled with the greater accessibility of 3D authoring environments, such as *Active Worlds* and *Second Life*, it is important to look at methods for designing environments that not only support the physical, temporal, environmental, emotional and ethical dimensions, but also as importantly, methods for designing accessible navigation within an environment. Charitos' (1997) research into the design of virtual environments to support way-finding and narrative holds much relevance for the design of game-based learning environments. The inclusion and placement of objects, such as landmarks, signs, boundaries and thresholds, which serve as way-finding guides in real-world environments are also the types of objects requisite for creating accessible virtual learning environments (Dickey, 2004).

Within real-world environments, a landmark is a prominent object in the environment that has physical characteristics that distinguish it from the surrounding environment (Lynch, 1960; Passini, 1984). The prominence and distinguishing characteristics of a landmark serve as a type of navigational guide by marking fixed points in space (Passini, 1984). Landmarks can help orient learners in a virtual environment. Signs, for example directional, identification and reassurance, also play a primary role in aiding in way-finding in an environment by providing key information necessary for decision-making. Directional signs specify the direction of a location, object or event, while identification signs identify a place, object or even a person. Reassurance signs function as checkpoints during the way-finding process. They provide reassurance to users that the chosen path will lead to the desired destination.

In addition to landmarks and signs, in a real-world setting, boundaries construct and define a space. Boundaries may take the form of something solid, such as a wall that defines a room or a building, hedges, curbs and partitions or they may be constructed of something formless, such as light or regions of contrast (Lynch, 1960). Thresholds are a type of object or opening that 'signifies the transition between spaces' (Charitos, 1997). Thresholds might include openings, for example doors and windows, or in the case of a virtual environment, even a device that sends a user into another setting or location within a setting (teleport).

Another element of way-finding is a path. We encounter paths of many kinds as we navigate through environments in our daily lives and in game-based learning environments, paths in the form of sidewalks, streets, roads and even worn areas on the landscape serve to foster learner movement from one locale to another. Along with paths are intersections. Intersections are points along paths where decisions must be made. For example, a crossroads in which two roads intersect forces the user to make a navigational choice. Charitos (1997) argues that because interactions are decision points, it is imperative that they be considered a discrete spatial element. In game-based learning environments, both the use of architectural elements can help aid learners in way-finding and navigating virtual environments (Dickey, 2004).

Environmental design: *Murder on Grimm Isle*

Within *Murder on Grimm Isle*, the physical, temporal, environmental, emotional and ethical dimensions helped shape not only the visual environment, but also helped guide and inform aspects of the cognitive design. *Murder on Grimm Isle* was initially authored as a 2D environment with images; however, learner feedback and more accessible means of authoring in 3D platforms prompted the move to a 3D environment using the *Active Worlds Educational Universe* (AWEDU) as the authoring platform. The affordances (Gibson, 1977) of *Active Worlds Educational Universe* allowed for easy construction of an island to support the physical dimensions. The intent of the temporal dimensions is to keep the environment as present, but somewhat timeless. Part of the narrative storyline includes an impending hurricane headed towards the island that in turn helps keep learners on task by limiting the time they have to gather evidence. The narrative also supports the lack of characters present on the island, everyone has been evacuated. The environmental dimension is illustrated in both the colour palette for the island, for example dark and foreboding, but is also illustrated in the individual homes of the characters. The selection colour, scale and texture are designed to be somewhat realistic, but with a playful sense of kitschy drama. This in turn is reinforced in the opening cut scene and in the evidence. The emotional dimensions are first established in the opening cut scene. Because none of the characters appear, the emotional dimensions are also conveyed through the homes of each character, both in the home furnishings and through the evidence. For example, the interior of

Robson Wolfe's home is enclosed in dark wood-panelled walls lined with bookshelves to convey both a sense of the character's tie to nature, as well as being well-educated, whereas Mark Woodman's squalid little room is dominated by a television, stereo and hunting and trapping gear. Emotional dimensions are also reinforced in the voicemail messages of each character.

Architectural elements helped inform the design of the physical environment. The game-based environment for *Murder on Grimm Isle* resembles a tree-covered island, surrounded by water. The island includes two large houses: the Wolfe mansion and the Ryding-Hood estate. Along with the house on the Ryding-Hood estate are both the servant's quarters which house one character and a cottage that houses another. The homes define the characters and define the space used to represent the characters. In addition to the characters' homes, there is a small village to help reinforce the notion of a larger community.

Gates and fences are used to reinforce the scale and boundaries of the two main estates. There are stone and brick paths which lead from each home to one of the two main roads. They also aid in way-finding because these paths are specifically designed to lead learners from one locale to another and to visually provide clues and remind learners of the connections between characters. Because of the visual reinforcement with colour of the paths, few signs are used and those that are present serve primarily for identification. However, because of the placement of intersections, a few of the identification signs also serve as directional signs as well.

Interactive design

Typically, most gameplay is goal-oriented. The focus of the setting, story and character is on the player/character achieving a particular goal. Interaction within the gameplay is also usually rule-bound. Rules define what the player/character can and cannot do and they define victory and loss conditions. Various game mechanics provide the types of interaction. As there are many different genres and combinations of genres in games, so are there varying types of game mechanics. Because games often blur and blend genres, it is difficult to concretely align game mechanics with various genres, however, at the risk of over-generalizing, some common game mechanics manifested that can be found in action, simulations, role playing, strategy, arcade-style and sports games include the following:

1. Collection
2. Elimination
3. Avoidance
4. Resource management
5. Races
6. Construction

Collection mechanics include gathering/collecting a specified amount of objects such as points, bounty and territory. Elimination mechanics often require players to defeat a specified enemy(s) or objects. Avoidance mechanics require players to avoid losing objects or territories. Resource management mechanics require players to balance and negotiate resources, such as tokens, money, health, character attributes and traits, to achieve a goal. Races mechanics require players to beat an opponent(s) in some type of race negotiating space, time or both. Construction mechanics require players to build, construct and/or alter an environment. It is important to note that several of these mechanics may be manifested in various ways in different genres.

Often adventure games may include several common game mechanics, most notably collection and resource management, yet also typically include an assortment of puzzles. There is a wide variety of types of puzzles, but the most common include the following:

1. Inventory manipulation
2. Dialogue-based puzzles
3. Mazes
4. Environment puzzles
5. Jigsaw puzzles
6. Slider puzzles
7. Audio puzzles
8. Combination puzzles

While game mechanics specify types of interaction, the player must perform in order to interact with the game and to achieve goals, there are other elements of game design that also impact interactions, such as turn-taking, exploration, trading and customization.

Ultimately, the design of a great game is a unique combination of game mechanics and interaction along with narrative, character design and the interests of the player. Additionally, an understanding of game mechanics and interactive elements can inform designers and educators about the array of interactive mechanics. One of the concerns about using educational games and game-based learning environments is that in order for game-based learning environments to be most effective, the mechanics must be contextually intertwined with the learning goal or there is the risk that learner will be able to focus on winning the game or more precisely, beating an algorithm rather than engaging with the learning task and content (Scoresby and Shelton, 2007; Streibel, 1986; Turkle, 1997).

Interactive design: *Murder on Grimm Isle*

As previously stated, *Murder on Grimm Isle* is loosely based on the adventure game genre. Two key aspects of the adventure game genre include a strong storyline coupled with exploration. Typical game mechanics in adventure games include collection tasks and puzzles. Although *Murder on Grimm Isle* is based on adventure games, there are no puzzles. There is, however, heavy reliance on collection mechanics. Because the goal of *Murder on Grimm Isle* was to match game mechanics with the learning task, collection mechanics are a natural fit within the learning task. Learners collect evidence which is the data used to construct their arguments. However, in adventure games, puzzles are typically used to unlock part of the narrative and within *Murder on Grimm Isle*, there is no one single narrative storyline, but instead, the narrative is learner co-constructed.

The environment for *Murder on Grimm Isle* both supports and limits exploration. Learners may travel to any of the homes in any order and are free to roam around the outside of each home, yet road blocks, trees, fences and cliffs prevent learners from roaming too far from where evidence is located. Because the goal is to discover evidence, the environmental and story-driven barriers within the environment help keep learners on task.

Murder on Grimm Isle was authored using the *Active Worlds Educational Universe* (AWEDU) which affords a degree of interactivity in both the 3D environment and through the availability of the integrated web-browser. Learners are represented in the 3D environment in the form of an avatar. Within *Active Worlds Educational Universe*, world owners have the option of choosing a selection of avatars from a library provided by *Active Worlds Educational Universe* or creating unique avatars. Learners can move their avatars throughout the environment. Additionally, learners have the choice of toggling between points-of-view of first-person (through the eyes of their avatar) and from third-person (orthographic). When an avatar encounters a solid object, for example a wall of a building, the avatar will register a slight impact and be prevented from moving through the wall. Because *Active Worlds Educational Universe* is a networked environment, not only can users see one another in the environment, but they can also communicate through the use of a chat tool.

Within *Active Worlds Educational Universe*, world owners and builders can enhance their 3D worlds, by placing sensors and triggers within the environment. As one learner's avatar encounters a sensor or trigger, a variety of pre-specified actions may occur, such as activating a sound file and animation or even activating a webpage to load in the integrated web-browser.

There are many opportunities for learner exploration within the *Active Worlds Educational Universe* environment. Learners may move through the environment encountering other learners and objects. However, opportunities for manipulation are still fairly limited. Other than navigation, learners have little control over their avatar's body. For example, it is not possible for avatars to simulate picking up an object, however, for collection activities there are ways to work around this limitation.

Within *Murder on Grimm Isle* each piece of evidence was scripted with a sensor that activated a webpage to load in the integrated web-browser providing information about the evidence. When a learner encounters evidence, then their cursor will change to a hand, which signals to the learner that they can click on that object to learn more about it. Upon clicking on the object, a corresponding webpage is activated in the integrated web-browser (see Figure 6.3). Within this webpage, learners are able to type notes about the location of the evidence and 'bag' the evidence to be studied at a later time. Although the interface for the evidence is actually a website with a database, *Active Worlds Educational Universe* offers many easily accessible interactive options for non-programmers, such as triggers and sensors and the use of an integrated web-browser.

In addition to the use of triggers and sensors in the 3D environment, the *Active Worlds Educational Universe* browser also offers a degree of customization through the use of bots and other customizable features. While this does require some programming knowledge, there is supporting documentation. In *Murder on Grimm Isle*, a bot was scripted to allow learners the option of turning on a head-up display (HUD) map of the island and key locations. This map also provides updated information as to their present location. This was developed through the use of a bot to track individual learner locations within the

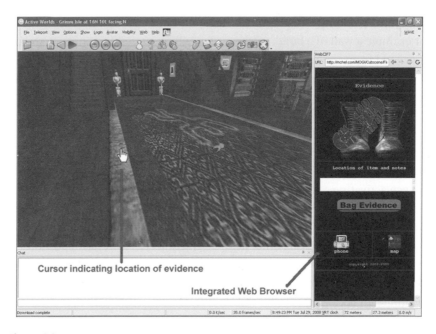

Figure 6.3 Discovering and 'bagging' evidence

Figure 6.4 The Wolfe mansion, with HUD map of Grimm Isle (top left)

3D environment and by sending that information to a semi-transparent map of the island which is overlaid in the upper-right corner of the 3D window. This map option is provided to help orient learners and inform them about other locations on the island (see Figure 6.4).

Conclusion

The design of *Murder on Grimm Isle* was informed by a range of disciplines from such seemingly incongruent fields as literature, psychology and architecture yet each foundation provided assistance on how to best construct an environment to engage students in learning. Within the field literature, conventions such as plot hooks and the quest structure provided insight into how to create a narrative structure that is (hopefully) engaging, while at the same time allowing learners to rely upon narrative conventions to accomplish their learning goals. Research from diverse sources, such as psychology, animation and literature provided insight into how to construct characters that could be easily understood but with enough complexity to support the overarching learning goal. Both the fields of game design and architecture provided structures for the design, in terms of defining the place, space and movement of learners through the environment. Finally, the fields of interactive design helped inform the mechanics of the game-based learning environment.

The purpose of the chapter is not to advance a model or system for designing game-based learning environments nor is the intent to assert that *Murder on Grimm Isle* is a model for design. Rather the purpose is to address the complex nature of designing a game-based learning environment and to illustrate how various fields served to inform the design of one game-based learning environment. It should be noted that this overview is by no means comprehensive in nature but rather focuses on key aspects of design that helped shaped the design of *Murder on Grimm Isle*.

The theoretical assumption essential to game-based learning environments is that learners construct understandings by interacting with information, tools and materials as well as by collaborating with other learners. However, game-based learning environments must also help scaffold the learning process. Game designers are well versed in devices and techniques for constructing compelling and engaging environments, which allow for immersion and agency, demand the participation of users and yet also provide scaffolding for problem-solving. Looking at the types of structures and the underlying research which supports various elements found in game design and how these elements support problem-solving environments will help inform designers and educators of how to meaningfully integrate these elements into the design of game-based learning environments. In addition to game design, disciplines within the arts and sciences such as literature, behavioural psychology, architecture and animation studies, provide resources, inspiration and research that may aid designers and educators in the design of rich and engaging game-based learning environments.

References

Adams, E. (2003). Defining the physical dimension of a game setting. *Gamasutra*, 04.30.03. Available: http://www.gamasutra.com/features/20030430/adams_01.shtml. Last accessed 9.4.10.

Amory, A. (2001). Building an educational adventure game: theory, design and lessons. *Journal of Interactive Learning Research*, Vol. 12, pp. 249–64.

Amory, A. and Seagram, R. (2003). Educational game models: conceptualization and evaluation. *South African Journal of Higher Education*, Vol. 17, No. 2, pp. 206–17.

Barab, S. A., Arici, A. and Jackson, C. (2005). Eat your vegetables and do your homework: a design-based investigation of enjoyment and meaning in learning. *Educational Technology*, Vol. 65, No. 1, pp. 15–21.

Barab, S., A., Thomas, M., Dodge, Squire, K. and Newell, M. (2004). Critical design ethnography: designing for change. *Anthropology & Education Quarterly*, Vol. 35, No. 2, pp. 254–68.

Barab, S. A., Thomas, M., Dodge, Carteaux, R. and Tuzun, H. (2005). Making learning fun: Quest Atlantis, a game without guns. *Educational Technology Research and Development*, Vol. 53, No. 1, pp. 86–108.

Bates, J. (1994). The role of emotion in believable agents. Communications of the ACM, Vol. 37, No. 7, pp. 122–25.

Bowman, R. F. (1982). A 'Pac-Man' theory of motivation: tactile implications for classroom instruction. *Educational Technology*, Vol. 22, No. 9, pp.14–17.

Bruner, J. (1990). *Acts of Meaning*. Cambridge, MA: Harvard University Press.

Campbell, J. (1973). *The Hero with a Thousand Faces*. Princeton, NJ: Princeton University Press.

Charitos, D. (1997). Designing space in virtual environments for aiding way-finding behavior. The fourth UK VR-SIG Conference, Brunel University, 1 November 1997.

Crawford, C. (2003). *Chris Crawford on Game Design*. Indianapolis, IN: New Riders Publishing.

Dansky, R. and Kane, B. (2006). Book Excerpt and Review – Game Writing: Narrative Skills for Videogames. http://www.gamasutra.com/view/feature/1838/book_excerpt_and_review__game_.php?page=1.Last accessed 10.9.07.

Dickey, M. D. (2004). An architectural perspective for the design of educational virtual environments. *Journal of Visual Literacy*, Vol. 24, No. 1, pp. 49–66.

Dickey, M. D. (2005). Engaging by design: how engagement strategies in popular computer and video games can inform instructional design. *Educational Technology Research and Development*. Vol. 53, No. 2, pp. 67–83.

Dickey, M. D. (2006a). Game design narrative for learning: appropriating adventure game design narrative devices and techniques for the design of interactive learning environments. *Educational Technology Research and Development.* Vol. 54, No. 3, pp. 245–63.

Dickey, M. D. (2006b). 'Ninja Looting' for Instructional Design: The Design Challenges of Creating a Game-based Learning Environment. Paper presented at the annual meeting of SIGGRAPH. Boston, MA.

Dickey, M. D. (2007a). Game Design and learning: a conjectural analysis of how Massively Multiple Online Role-Playing Games (MMORPGs) Foster Intrinsic Motivation. *Educational Technology Research and Development,* Vol. 55, No. 3, pp. 253–73.

Dickey, M. D. (2007b). The Design of a Game-based Learning Environment: Murder on Grimm Isle. Paper presented at the annual meeting of the annual meeting of the American Educational Research Association. Chicago, IL.

Dickey, M. D. (2008). Murder on Grimm Isle: The Impact of Game Narrative for Fostering Argumentation Writing. Paper presented at the annual meeting of the annual meeting of the American Educational Research Association. New York, NY.

Dunniway, T. (2000). Using the hero's journey in games. *Gamasutra* 27.11.00 http://www.gamasutra.com/view/feature/3118/using_the_heros_journey_in_games.php. Last accessed 28.4.10.

Gee, J. P. (2003). *What Video Games Have to Teach Us About Learning and Literacy.* New York: Palgrave.

Gibson, J. J. (1977). The theory of affordances. In R. Shaw and J. Bransford, eds. *Perceiving, Acting, and Knowing: Toward an Ecological Psychology,* pp. 67–82. Hillsdale, NJ: Erlbaum Associates.

Hannafin, M. J. and Land, S. (1997). The foundations and assumptions of technology-enhanced, student-centered learning environments. *Instructional Science,* Vol. 25, pp. 167–202.

Hannafin, M. J., Hall, C. Land, S. and Hill, J. (1994). Learning in open environments: assumptions, methods, and implications. *Educational Technology,* Vol. 34, No. 8, pp. 48–55.

Hannafin, M. J., Land, S. and Oliver, K. (1999). Open learning environments: foundations, methods, and models. In C. M. Reigeluth, ed. *Instructional-Design Theories and Models: A New Paradigm of Instructional Theory.* Vol. II. pp. 115–40. Hillsdale, NJ: Lawrence Erlbaum Associates.

Isbister, K. (2006). *Better Game Characters by Design: A Psychological Approach.* NY: Morgan Kaufmann.

Isbister, K. and Nass, C. (2000). Consistency of personality in interactive characters: verbal cues, non-verbal cues, and user characteristics. *International Journal of Human-Computer Studies,* Vol. 53, No. 2, pp. 251–67.

Johnson, W. L., Rickel, J.W. and Lester, J. C. (2000). Animated pedagogical agents: face-to-face interaction in interactive learning environments. *International Journal of Artificial Intelligence in Education,* Vol. 11, pp. 47–78.

Jonassen, D. (1999). Designing constructivist learning environments. In C. M. Reigeluth, ed. *Instructional-Design Theories and Models: A New Paradigm of Instructional Theory.* Vol. II, pp. 215–40. Hillsdale, NJ: Lawrence Erlbaum Associates.

Land, S. M. and Hannafin, M. J. (1997). Patterns of understanding with open-ended learning environments: a qualitative study. *Educational Technology Research & Development,* Vol. 45, No. 2, pp. 47–73.

Laramée, F. D. (2002). *Game Design Perspectives.* Hingham, MA: Charles River Media.

Lasseter, J. (1987). Principles of traditional animation applied to 3D computer animation. *ACM Computer Graphics,* Vol. 21, No. 4, pp. 35–44.

Lynch, K. (1960). *The Image of the City.* Cambridge, MA: MIT Press.

Malone, T. W. (1981). Toward a theory of intrinsically motivating instruction. *Cognitive Science,* Vol. 4, pp. 333–69.

McCloud, S. (1994). *Understanding Comics: The Invisible Art.* New York: Harper Perennial.

Nass, C., Isbister, K. and Lee, E. J. (2000). Truth is beauty: researching embodied conversational agents. In J. Cassell, S. Prevost, J. Sullivan and E. Churchill, eds. *Embodied Conversational Agents.* Boston, MA: MIT Press.

Nelson, B., Ketelhut, D. J., Clarke, J., Dieterle, E., Dede, C. and Erlandson, B. (2007). Robust design strategies for scaling educational innovations: The River City MUVE case study. In B. E. Shelton and D. A. Wiley, eds. *The Educational Design and Use of Computer Simulation Games.* Rotterdam, Netherlands: Sense Press.

Passini, R. (1984). *Wayfinding in Architecture.* New York: Van Nostrand Reinfold.

Polkinghorne, D. E. (1988). *Narrative Knowing and the Human Sciences.* Albany: State University of New York Press.

Prensky, M. (2001). *Digital Game-Based Learning.* New York: McGraw-Hill.

Provenzo, E. F. (1991). *Video Kids: Making Sense of Nintendo.* Cambridge, MA: Harvard University Press.

Rieber, L. P. (1996). Seriously considering play: designing interactive learning environments based on the blending of microworlds, simulations, and games. *Educational Technology Research and Development,* Vol. 44, No. 2, pp. 43–58.

Rieber, L. P. and Matzko, M. J. (2001). *Serious Design of Serious Play in Physics. Educational Technology,* Vol. 41, No. 1, pp. 14–24.

Robinson, J. A. and Hawpe, L. (1986). Narrative thinking as a heuristic process. In T. R. Sarbin, ed. *Narrative Psychology: The Storied Nature of Human Conduct,* pp. 3–21. New York: Praeger.

Rollings, A. and Adams, E. (2003). Game Design. (Pre-Publication Galley Proof). Indianapolis, IN: New Riders.

Scholes, R. and Kellogg, R. (1969). The nature of narrative. *Comparative Literature,* Vol. 21, No. 2, pp. 177–79.

Scoresby, J. and Shelton, B. E. (2007). Linking gameplay activity and learning objectives through a videogame motivational model. Paper presented at the annual meeting of the American Educational Research Association, Chicago, IL.

Squire, K. (2003). Video games in education. *International Journal of Intelligent Simulations and Gaming,* Vol. 2, No. 1, pp. 49–62.

Streibel, M. J. (1986). A critical analysis of the use of computers in education. *Educational Communications and Technology – A Journal of Theory, Research and Development,* Vol. 34, No. 3, pp. 137–61.

Thomas, F. and Johnston, O. (1981, reprint 1997). *The Illusion of Life: Disney Animation.* NY: Hyperion.

Toulmin, S., Rieke, R. and Janik, A. (1979). *An Introduction to Reasoning.* London: Collier Macmillan.

Turkle, S. (1997). Seeing through computers: education in a culture of simulation. *The American Prospect,* No. 31, March–April 1997.

Vogler, C. (1998). *The Writer's Journey: Mythic Structures for Writers.* Studio City, CA: Michael Wiese Productions.

Winn, W. (2002). Current trends in educational technology research: the study of learning environments. *Educational Psychology Review,* Vol. 14, No. 3, pp. 331–51.

Zebrowitz, L. A. (1997). *Reading Faces: Window to the Soul?* Boulder, CO: Westview Press.

7

Are Games All Child's Play?

Scot Osterweil and Eric Klopfer

Chapter Outline

Two views of learning games

Those who believe in using games in education usually start from a common set of assumptions. They observe that game players regularly exhibit persistence, risk-taking, attention to detail and problem-solving skills, all behaviours that ideally would be regularly demonstrated in school (Jenkins et al., 2006). They also agree that game environments enable players to construct understanding actively, and at individual paces, and that well-designed games enable players to advance on different paths at different rates in response to their interests and abilities, while also fostering collaboration and just-in-time learning. Much has been written on this subject, but nowhere so comprehensively as in James Paul Gee's *What Video Games Can Teach Us About Literacy and Learning.*

Even starting with these shared notions, advocates for game-based learning tend to adopt one of two very different approaches to the question of games in formal education. One group sees the skills students develop playing games as essential to a twenty-first-century education, and conversely despair of anything meaningful happening in schools still shackled to a nineteenth-century factory model. They focus on the habits of mind and dispositions needed to collaborate, innovate, problem solve and communicate effectively in a knowledge-based economy. They observe with some accuracy that these skills can all be gained from engagement with commercial off-the-shelf (COTS) games, or through social networking, blogging and other forms of user-generated content that fall under the larger banner of participatory culture. They focus on these skills largely to the exclusion of traditional academic subject matter, and at least insofar as game-based learning is concerned, they assume the institution of school is highly resistant to reform and find alternate venues and opportunities to foster learning. They imagine the important learning will take place outside of school, questioning what value school adds to the process. This group has demonstrated through its research that young people can and do use COTS games in many interesting ways and have shown that players can learn exciting and powerful new ideas, relevant to surviving and thriving the twenty-first century, through this play. They have done this primarily in the context of self-organized and self-motivated play or through informal extracurricular organizations.

In contrast, the second group tends to concentrate only on applying games in school settings. They may pay lip service to twenty-first-century skills, but they look at the learning that occurs in COTS games and ask, 'why can't we have games that foster the same learning in more traditional academic areas?' In order to integrate games into the existing school environment, they must address several common concerns of the educational community, particularly teachers:

- The need to cover mandated content areas;
- Healthy scepticism of new technologies;
- Unfamiliarity with games and no easy route to game competence.

In addition, proponents of games in school also have to overcome the objections of those parents, teachers and administrators who see games as insufficiently serious. The current solution to all these difficulties tends to be games that can be played in very short bursts of class time, games whose simplicity make them easy to grasp immediately and games that are packed with what can be recognized as factual content. These games are often curricular, attempting to teach subject matter that is otherwise advanced through textbooks, lectures or problem sets. Sadly, they usually end up being nothing more than interactive quizzes. The surface resemblance to a game means little when the activity involves answering multiple-choice questions and when success (or score) is measured solely as the percentage of correct answers given. If the first group embraces games and ignores school, this second group often embraces school to the detriment of anything that looks like real gaming.

In spite of their striking differences, we have pointedly avoided suggesting that these impulses, to promote new modes of learning on the one hand, and to adapt to the classroom on the other, are mutually exclusive. One might advocate that games can both build twenty-first-century skills and channel those skills in traditional academic fields. One could also argue that just because such games might be in the service of school, they do not necessarily have to be designed to blend into outmoded forms of schooling. Schools also have an opportunity to provide a needed service of reaching all students and doing so in a way that may be facilitated by professionals trained in fostering learning. We should avoid these polarized viewpoints in order to both learn from and advance the cause of learning games.

We start with some sympathy for those who favour unrestrained gaming over schooling. We see enormous creativity in gamers. Mastering a game involves entering into often chaotic environments, learning through trial and error, observation, analysis and systematic testing (Jenkins et al., 2009). When challenged, persistent players often engage in outside research, going to game FAQS and other websites to seek solutions to vexing problems. And gameplay is often collaborative, as players share knowledge with fellow gamers both in person and online (Gee, 2003). Indeed, the culture of problem-solving that surrounds gaming reveals the very dispositions desired in the twenty-first-century workforce.

On the other hand, while many young people learn extraordinary things from games, we believe that the children who make the most of these technologies tend to do so in the context of families or mentors, and sometimes schools, that support their efforts, or at the very least have modelled some of these same dispositions. For example, a study from the University of Michigan of children using computers in public libraries suggested that disadvantaged children were far less likely to spend time with single applications or sites, and tended to skim surfaces rather than dive deeply (Neuman and Celano, 2006). Structure and support from outside influences such as after-school programmes, parents or a teacher in the classroom are needed for most kids to excel with these technologies. As such, we are not ready to concede there is no role for school in helping them make the most of these experiences. Quite the opposite in fact, we believe schools can and should play a critical role in fostering learning in association with gameplay. While schools have much room for improvement, many of the existing assets of school can contribute positively.

Whatever the failings of school, the academic disciplines of Maths and Science, History, Literature and Language study remain vitally important, as do the abilities to read critically and communicate persuasively both in and out of school. In all of these fields, talented teachers and researchers have identified pedagogical approaches that are forward-looking and well-adapted to the changing environment of the internet age, approaches that rely on the same thinking skills that games exercise. There is no reason to believe that the kind of creative energy exhibited in games would not apply to these disciplines. Talented teachers have long known that non-academic texts from novels to theatre to film all have a role in sparking interest and curiosity in students, as have informal experiences, such as museum visits and competitive challenges such as science fairs.

Therefore, we are prepared to argue that:

1. games can engage players in learning that is specifically applicable to 'schooling'; and
2. teachers can leverage the learning in such games without disrupting the worlds of either play or school.

To succeed, we must look at where the strengths and challenges of both classrooms and games lie and situate learning games at the most productive intersection of these separate environments. We will examine these issues through concrete examples of existing best practices, and speculative designs currently under development at MIT's *Education Arcade*, and elsewhere (Jenkins et al., 2009).

The role of play

The starkly obvious difference between games and traditional schooling is that good games always involve play and schooling rarely does. Before we discuss what constitutes play in games, it is worth stepping back to look at play in the broader sense.

Think for a moment about a child at play with dolls or action figures or Lego blocks. To the outsider, the play is likely to look somewhat scattered: the child will be working fiercely one moment constructing a building or acting out a story, and then just as abruptly the child will shift gears, knocking down what they have built, or hurling dolls across the room in gleeful enactment of imagined disasters. Whether the child has been exploring the physical nature of things, their nascent understanding of familial and social roles, or obliterating everything they have just accomplished, the child at play is exercising freedom along four distinct axes:

1. freedom to fail;
2. freedom to experiment;
3. freedom to fashion identities; and
4. freedom of effort.

Freedom to Fail: One does not actually fail at play *per se*, but one is free to do things at play that would look like failure in other contexts. Think of the block tower that inevitably collapses or the sand castle fated to disappear with the tide. At play the child has unlimited freedom to undertake such doomed enterprises and learns as much about the nature of things from failure as from success. Every fall off a bicycle, every crumpled up drawing, every lost game of *Candyland* is a small failure. Fortunately, children at play do not have adults looming over them, fretting about the cost of these failures, and so children are free to learn from failure and move ever closer to mastery of their world.

Freedom to Experiment: This correlates closely with the freedom to fail but suggests in addition that within the play space the player has some room to manoeuvre and invent new approaches to whatever task is at hand. It is not sufficient that the child can build towers with blocks, but in fact they can engage in a wide array of activities with those blocks, experimenting with uses *they* have invented. Experimentation would be meaningless without the ability to fail regularly and the freedom to fail would amount to little if players were constrained in where they could seek that failure.

Freedom to Fashion Identities: At play, the child is not simply examining the nature of the physical and social worlds but is also exploring the identity in those worlds. That identity is not a fixed thing, but rather something that is itself 'in play'. Using dolls, a child will try out the roles of both mischievous child and stern parent. In fairy tales, children imagine what it means to be a dragon, and what it means to slay one. The child is practising when to be aggressive, when cooperative, when assertive and when docile. Only by trying on these identities do children begin to define themselves.

Freedom of Effort: Watching children play tag, Peter and Iona Opie (1969) noticed that a child will run vigorously for 20 minutes to evade the tag and then abruptly stop in the middle of the school yard to receive the tag. They observed that children regularly exhibited this pattern of alternating between intense and relaxed play. It is easy to overlook this quality of play, but if we stop to imagine play in which a uniform effort is expected, we quickly sense the presence of a controlling adult.

Play and games

What we have largely described above is free play: the sort of play a child pursues entirely on their own terms. This play has no agenda and the child's goals are entirely intrinsic and personal. Games by contrast, tend to have defined goals. Most games have 'win' states, and even those that do not end in victory usually have clear ways of demarcating success through points or other quantifiable outcomes. In addition, games have rules that structure the play and that guarantee fairness by being applied transparently and equitably to all players.

At first blush, games, with their rules, constraints and externally defined goals seem to be at odds with the freedoms of play. But within the prescribed space of a game, players regularly exhibit all of the freedoms of unstructured play. Most players undertake games in the knowledge that failure is a possibility. They show a willingness to experiment in their gameplay and to try on different roles from leader to follower, novice to expert. Finally the freedom of effort described above remains present in any voluntary game.

By offering challenges that seem worth attempting, games actually focus and channel players' efforts, while still allowing them the freedom needed to manage their individual experience in ways that are self-directed and beneficial to their own development. In games, children submit to arbitrary rules and structures, but only if they can continue to be playful. The promise of games is that we can harness the spirit of play to enable players to build new cognitive structures and ideas of substance.

Play and adults

By providing the above examples, we have stuck with descriptions of young children at play, as it is in childhood, play that these features are most easily recognized. But the same freedoms are visible in the play of adults. Mastering golf would be impossible without the ability to fail often and quite spectacularly.

And no one would get good at Poker if they could not experiment or try on different identities. Anyone who regularly plays tennis knows that sometimes you come to play hard and sometimes you decide to relax and just volley. Without the four freedoms of play none of these activities would be worthy of the name leisure.

Games vs. school and the freedoms of play

One might argue that the same freedoms should be present in learning and indeed many good teachers make room for all these freedoms in their classrooms. But much of the structure of school militates against the exercise of those freedoms. The emphasis on grades and high stakes testing leave few opportunities for failure or varied effort. Experimentation does not even make it into the one place you would expect to find it, the traditional Science class, where labs are usually done according to rigid recipes with pre-ordained outcomes and the need for classroom order and regularity rule out the possibility of playing with one's own identity.

If the spirit of play sits uncomfortably in too many classrooms, the logistics of gameplay are even more problematic for schools. The mere process of implementing computer-based learning activities typically requires dealing with the 'computer room' in the school. The computer room has a multitude of associated difficulties. First it involves transporting a class full of students from one location to another, which takes time in an already crowded schedule. Second, that room is often crowded with computers and not particularly hospitable to activities that take place off the computer. Third, due to under-staffing, the computers in these rooms are simultaneously locked down to prevent unauthorized software from being installed (including games), and are notoriously unreliable. Finally, sustained activities are difficult to take on, due to over-scheduling of the existing resources. These challenges create an obstacle that few teachers feel prepared to tackle, even if they have the motivation to integrate games into their teaching.

Providing further obstacles is the need to march students through mandated curricula with little time for exploratory and creative activities. Nearly all classroom activities have to be justified through their relevance to the local standards, which are bogged down in the details of content and scarce on twenty-first-century skills, such as 'new media literacies' (Jenkins et al., 2006). Combining all of these factors with the very real concerns of teachers when confronted with new and unfamiliar technologies creates an environment in which games just are not likely to be adopted, or when they are, to be used in limited and unproductive ways.

If we have highlighted here the disparity between the worlds of games and schools, our purpose is not to offer discouragement, but rather to encourage a clear-eyed sense of the challenges in integrating the two. The design of good learning games can only emerge when the obstacles that stand in their way are fully accounted for. We believe that the answer lies both in the design of games meant to fortify academic learning and in new and creative ways of imagining the integration of those games into schooling.

Design principles for learning games

We argue there are a number of design principles that should be taken into account in the creation of learning games. These principles can be grouped under the broader categories of activity, structure and narrative. We will define these terms and consider each in turn. But first, as a basis for this discussion, we will describe *Lure of the Labyrinth*, a game designed by the *Education Arcade* and currently being developed in collaboration with Maryland Public Television, Fablevision, Johns Hopkins University and Macro International. It is funded by the US Department of Education as part of its Star Schools programme. We will start with a brief description of the game and one of the puzzle environments within it.

The story

Lure of the Labyrinth's target audience is middle-school students and its primary goal is the enhancement of pre-algebra mathematics learning with a secondary goal of improving literacy. It is a long-form puzzle adventure game played over many sessions, with a persistent narrative that evolves over time. In the story of the game, the player's avatar is a young person trying to recover a pet that has disappeared. Following clues, the player is led into a fantasy world, an underground factory complex populated by mythical monsters, who are kidnapping pets and using them for nefarious purposes. By the game's conclusion, players will have recovered their own pets, freed many others and halted the monsters' plans by destroying their factory. In order to accomplish this, players must explore the space, learn how to navigate it and collaborate with others to accumulate credits by solving puzzles. These credits will in turn be used to free pets and to thwart the monsters' plans.

Labyrinth's story is told in comic form. Comics enable us to deliver a significantly more involved story for our production budget than would traditional animation but our enthusiasm for the form is not primarily economic. Comics promote both verbal and visual literacy and they leave more room for players' imaginations, both in the ways they imagine the voices of the characters and sound effects, and in the ways they fill in the visual details between each comic frame. With comics, players remain in control of the element of time. Rather than absorb a story told to them at a fixed pace, they take it in at their own pace. They read rather than simply watch.

Delivery

Labyrinth is developed in Flash and available over the web. It can be played from within the browser of any reasonably current internet-enabled computer. The game's server keeps track of individual log-ins and tracks player progress, so once players have enrolled, they can rejoin their games from any connected computer. This form of delivery offers several powerful advantages:

- The game does not need to be installed on individual computers, something that is often a challenge in schools or libraries.
- Because the game server keeps track of each player's unique log-in, the game does not depend on players always using the same machine. This enables players to play from home as well as school, and it is particularly important for disadvantaged students who may only get to play in libraries or after-school settings.
- Saving player progress makes it possible to deliver a long-form game. *Labyrinth* might take as many as 15 hours to play. This enables a more involved narrative, which in turn promotes a greater degree of investment on the part of the player. It also makes it possible for the game to pose challenges of greater intellectual depth, as we can anticipate that players will have more time to reflect and solve each puzzle.
- Since the game keeps track of player's progress, teachers can use this data to better assess and supplement their students' achievements.

As we have suggested above, we designed *Labyrinth* to be played at home or in other informal settings as well as in school. This is a critical factor in our vision of the integration of the worlds of play and school and one which we will expand upon further in this chapter.

A typical puzzle

Typical of *Labyrinth's* puzzles is one involving a strange vending machine serving unappetizing snacks that only a monster could love. Upon entering the puzzle, players only know that they are supposed to get food from the machine. Lacking other instructions, they must figure out how the whole puzzle works. What the player sees is the machine, with a number of food items behind glass doors. Under each item is a different number. To the right of the machine are three piles of round discs, each pile a different colour.

Playful players, as most kids are, immediately begin clicking around the screen. They discover that clicking on items has no effect and eventually discover that the coloured disks can be picked up and moved around the screen. In time they also notice that the machine includes three slots into which these disks can fit. When the slots are all filled, the disks fall into the machine, sounding like coins and an item drops out. It is up to the player to interpret what has happened. Initially players usually try one coin of each colour, and their second try is frequently the same three colours, but placed in different slots. When players realize that simply placing the same coins in a different order always yields objects of the same numerical value, most conclude that the disks are coins of different denominations adding up to the value of whatever item the machine vends. At this point they begin trying to deduce the values of each coin by trying different combinations, and eventually they use this knowledge to retrieve certain items that they come to recognize as 'target' items. As you may have gathered, solving this puzzle requires algebraic thinking, as players must solve for the variables represented by the unmarked coins.

Players do not usually succeed on the first try. It may take a while to figure out the apparatus or to recognize that there are target items. In these early attempts, players run out of turns, the machine powers down and they must start again. But even as they are not fully succeeding, they are getting some items out of the machine and for their efforts they are earning points. In every *Labyrinth* puzzle, players earn some points for effort, or for partial successes, though never as many as when they completely solve the puzzle. As such, while failure has consequences, it is easy to pick oneself up and try the puzzle again.

While players are still trying to master a puzzle they are not confined to working solely on that particular puzzle. Players can quickly earn access to all the puzzles in the game. The game also involves a large virtual space that the players can wander through and explore. Through this exploration they will discover other items that must be collected to win the game. In other words, players enter into an environment in which a wide range of activities are always open to them, all in the service of achieving their game goals.

Players who do work on solving the puzzle learn that every time they play it, the values of the coins are different. They discover that their challenge is not in memorizing the value of the coins, but rather in developing foolproof strategies that will enable them to solve for any possible array of values, and often unbeknownst to them, tackling fundamental algebraic understanding in the process. Once they have mastered the puzzle, they are rewarded for their success, but also challenged to try solving more difficult versions of the same puzzle.

Finally, throughout the game, players are in communication with team-mates via an in-game message board. Players can seek or give advice about solving individual puzzles or about the overarching game goals. Since answers to puzzles are never the same twice, in order to help each other team-mates must write about what strategies they use for solving them. They must write about the underlying mechanisms of the puzzles, not just their solutions. This skill of describing the puzzle's structure and articulating a problem-solving strategy, makes them valuable team members, and also builds skills required on many standardized assessments.

Design principles: activity

A game's activity, what is often referred to as its 'mechanic', is that action the player performs in playing the game. The activities in individual *Labyrinth's* puzzles are different at their basic level, putting coins in slots in the example above, mixing quantities of liquids in another one, but at a larger level, all the *puzzles are about learning to act like a scientist, mathematician or engineer*. Players enter a chaotic environment in which nothing initially makes sense. Through probing, sometimes random, sometimes focused, players initiate actions and see results. Players must carefully observe the environment's response to the stimuli they introduce. They gradually form hypotheses about what processes are at work, and learn to test those hypotheses by altering single variables as they initiate new actions.

Playing the game is not about memorizing solutions, but about learning strategies, processes and habits of mind. As such, it aligns with the so-called twenty-first-century skills, but in reality it is mirroring the habits of mathematicians and scientists from the Enlightenment forward. While it is arguable that these kinds of process skills should have always been the goal of a good education, in the internet age, with mountains of data at almost everyone's fingertips, it is ever clearer that memorizing facts is no substitute for having solid strategies for manipulating abstractions, data and ideas. Although *Labyrinth* focuses on the process of mathematics, one can imagine that games would similarly model the behaviour of historians, policy-makers or designers.

Players intuitively understand that 'wrong' answers are part of getting the right answer. Because solving a puzzle involves probing and interpreting responses to successful *and* unsuccessful stimuli, the game models the notion that small failures often lie on the path to larger successes. While this may be self-evident about games, it is worth noting that many academic exercises and many 'educational' games do little more than tell a student that they are wrong without giving feedback that would make it possible to reason about what is correct.

Players engage with content in a context. The game looks for ways to make the abstractions of mathematics concrete. Although it does so in the mythical world of a fantasy game, the activities nevertheless have real-life parallels. Indeed, the game uses relatively little mathematical notation and where it can enables the players to reason about numbers as quantities, volumes or magnitudes, not just numerals on a screen.

Activities are tactile and offer sensory satisfaction. Although computers have limited inputs and outputs, clever use of animation and sound can make the activity pleasing, thereby fostering greater engagement and investment in activities. When items come out of the vending machine in *Labyrinth* with a satisfying 'ca-ching', the game is providing sensory reinforcement to the intrinsic pleasure of successful problem-solving. It is not sufficient for designers to create mechanisms that distinguish right from wrong answers and reward points accordingly. They must also create worlds where the intrinsic satisfaction of successful play is sufficient to overcome the frustration of initial failures. Indeed, in *Labyrinth* we strove to make the feedback for wrong answers as entertaining and amusing as for right answers. Far from feeling the need to provide harshly negative feedback, we trust players to reach for success and we want them to feel some reward simply in making the effort. In fact many players will try wrong solutions solely for the purpose of seeing what happens. This encourages them to push the boundaries of their understanding and expand their potential for learning. That said, we never give false positive feedback and design responses so players can easily distinguish between full and partial success.

Players build scaffolding for future learning. *Labyrinth* is not courseware and we do not expect players to 'cover' the curriculum while playing. Rather we have created mechanisms whereby players can engage with some of the big ideas of mathematics while remaining playful. Because the game fosters deep, repeated engagement with these ideas, we expect that players will have begun to master them even before they encounter the concepts in school. We will say more about this shortly.

Avoiding time pressure enables collaboration and conversation. Playing against a clock, and the time pressure that comes with it, often makes for an exciting game, but there are several good reasons to avoid time pressure as a factor in game activities. When there is time pressure, players have a hard time collaborating, as the more aggressive or confident player will want to seize the mouse and control the game. Remove that pressure and players become willing to discuss each move before it is made. The need to discuss and justify decisions will sharpen players' thinking and enable them to both teach and learn in the course of the gameplay. If students can play collaboratively and discuss their ideas, it is usually possible for teachers to observe their gameplay and acquire greater understanding of their thinking. When immersed in time-sensitive gameplay, players can be annoyed by observers' questions, but when playing in a more relaxed mode, they are usually proud to discuss their strategies and show off their accomplishments.

There are nevertheless ways to replicate the excitement that the game clock brings. If games are designed so that players must achieve certain goals within a limited number of moves, the excitement mounts with every move the player makes. Learning to solve problems efficiently and with the minimum number of moves may be a better analogue to real-life problem-solving than is the need to simply think fast.

Design principles: structure

A game is more than a collection of individual activities. The game's larger structure determines the patterns by which players will engage in individual activities. The game's system of scoring and rewards will have a powerful effect on how players progress through its landscape and how they define their own personal goals. While many different game structures can make for a pleasurable game, there are certain key elements that will, we believe, enhance learning.

Players make multiple passages through each challenge. In *Labyrinth's*, winning is achieved by accumulating points, represented as 'credits' which are a kind of currency. These points can be earned by replaying the same puzzle several times, something that remains entertaining, as the solution differs every time a puzzle is played. Indeed, we do not expect players to solve the puzzle the first time they encounter it and so they will have to engage with the puzzle repeatedly. While repetition is necessary for increasing one's score, there is a pedagogical purpose as well. It has been our observation that players are usually on the edge of comprehension when they master a puzzle for the first time. By giving them incentives to solve a puzzle several times, we expect them to solidify their understanding and to build a more robust scaffolding of the puzzle's embedded ideas. In *Labyrinth* we require a player to solve a puzzle three times before we credit them with 'beating' it, at which time the game invites them to engage with a harder version of the same puzzle, one that will introduce new complexities and further deepen their understanding.

Offer partial reward for partial success. Players accumulate points just for trying to solve puzzles. Not only does this provide incentive for continued effort, but also it reflects the fact that for many difficult challenges, the very process of trying to solve the problem is as important as finally getting the right answer. Not all the struggles in students' intellectual lives will be winnable, but they should begin to experience the pleasure of simply trying.

Nurture emerging ideas. Labyrinth puzzles are designed to reflect concepts, such as proportionality or coordinate systems. Our own observation is that players do not understand these concepts all at once, but actually grope towards understanding in stages. For example, we have seen students begin to recognize correspondence between the first coordinate in a pair and its position on the X-axis without yet understanding that the other coordinate represents a position on the Y-axis. The big 'a-ha' moment when a student finally sees the whole system is preceded by a long period in which the idea emerges bit by bit. This is an additional reason for encouraging repeat engagement with a challenge and for offering partial rewards.

Offer clear incentives for more success. While we do offer rewards for simply trying, the rewards for full success are clearly denoted. We start with the assumption that all players are, at the heart of the matter, really competing with themselves. They play to achieve mastery, that is to improve on their own initial efforts. While this goal is fundamentally an intrinsic one, enjoyment of the game increases if its reward structure mirrors the players' goals. Rewards should therefore be significant when the player makes significant progress.

Avoid Brick Walls. Many games do not allow players to pass through specific points until they have mastered particular challenges. The game designers probably think that they are enforcing a pedagogically valid sequence of learning, but these 'brick walls' often lead to discouragement and to players abandoning the game. They also fail to take into account different learning styles, and the kind of emergent ideas that we discuss above, and allow for in our design. *Labyrinth* allows players to advance on many different fronts at the same time. If one path is blocked by a difficult challenge, the player is free to take a break and try a different path. Indeed the game can be won without completely mastering any one puzzle. We trust players to rise to the challenges we put before them, but we know that in order to remain playful, they must have maximal control over the way they meet those challenges.

Allow more than one way to win. We have explained why games should reward partial success, and avoid brick walls. In the same spirit, we enable players to bring their game to a satisfying ending without requiring that every player accomplish exactly the same goals. One player might master every puzzle and march quickly and directly to the game's conclusion. Another player might struggle and fail to fully beat every puzzle, but this player can nevertheless achieve a win state through the gradual accumulation of points. In keeping with the principle of offering clear incentives for greater success, the first player will earn a much higher score and may achieve other markers, for example bonus points, reflective of that achievement. In order to get a win without total mastery, less accomplished players will have to spend significantly more time, but their persistence will be rewarded and the repetition increases the likelihood that core ideas will eventually be mastered. We assume that players will recognize the difference between the multiple forms of victory and that they can decide whether to try again for a higher score.

Design principles: narrative

Many good games have little or no formal narrative, for example Chess, Tetris, and the absence of narrative does not necessarily say anything about a game's worth. Nevertheless, it is also clear that many games, including the majority of computer games, do have a narrative component, and that players are very much drawn to the characters and plots of games. It is therefore important to examine what narrative features might make a game.

The game world should embody the subject matter. It is not sufficient to simply create a compelling narrative into which you insert quizzes about unrelated content. Rather the game world should engage players' imagination with the very themes and ideas that animate the learning goals. For example, the *Education Arcade* is currently designing a language learning game. Since learning a language is about gaining entry to a world that is otherwise off limits, this game's story will involve characters starting as outsiders and gaining status as they master the game's challenges. In the same vein, a game about history might involve players in examining past events, whether fictional or real. While this might be achieved through a strategy game, like *Civilization*, which focuses on the spread of actual historical empires, it might also be achieved through a narrative that takes the form of a murder mystery, with a detective protagonist examining documents and conflicting accounts of past events.

A science game might involve players in a world whose workings are mysterious and in need of decoding. *Labyrinth* is set in a factory where the player is required to engage with machines whose operation depends on the manipulations of quantities, magnitudes and rates of change.

The game world should allow players to explore their identity. Many games allow players to customize their avatar and in the process try on different identities. Some games even let players decide on whether they want their characters to be good or evil. These choices invite players to engage with the game in more imaginative and playful ways, and we believe this in turn will lead to more creative problem-solving in the course of gameplay. It also situates the game more authentically in students' emotional lives, where they are regularly experimenting with different aspects of self and personal identity. This kind of role playing can be particularly relevant to the study of literature, social studies and language, where empathy and the ability to imagine the lives of others are important.

Games should not patronize or flatter. Too many learning games patronize young players by trying too hard to be cute or nice. Big-eyed cartoon characters talk in overly demonstrative ways, much the way some adults over-articulate when talking to young children. Failing to recognize children's lives includes darkness as well as joy, these games present narratives with all the drama of a Sunday school picnic. Other games try to flatter children by presenting narratives about unrelentingly 'cool' kids who can do no wrong and who are likely to appear more cool to adults than to children. In fact, children live in a world whose rules are confusing and often arbitrary. They are still learning where to be brave and take risks, when to trust in others and what their own reserves are. Many of the commercial games children play engage with these issues through their narrative and there is no reason that learning games should not do the same.

Games can be non-gendered. The issue of gender in games is too complex to receive a proper treatment here, but it is at least worth pointing out that there are alternatives to games that are perceived of as male, such as games about personal combat, espionage and warfare, and those rare attempts to create games that are explicitly female, such as games about girls socializing, clothing design or cute fantasy worlds. We will side-step the question as to whether these highly gendered games have their place, and simply observe that there is vast room to manoeuvre between these extremes. Our own work proceeds from an assumption that young people do not display uniformly 'gendered' attitudes towards games or education. *Labyrinth* for example blends themes that might be perceived of as female, such as saving small animals, and male such as gross and slimy monsters, but its underlying theme is about persistence and creative problem-solving. It blends the pro-social theme of teaming up with others to protect the world with moments of individual heroism. Players are free to imagine their avatars as male or female and the monsters they encounter appear to play roles within the factory totally without regard to gender. Great literature rarely occupies spaces that are explicitly male or female and there is no reason why our game narratives should be any more narrowly gendered.

Integration of play and the classroom

At the outset of this chapter, we discussed the ways in which the worlds of play and the classroom were at odds and we enumerated the impediments to the adoption of meaningful game experiences in the school day. Though we have tried to argue that players learn best from games that remain playful, we have said little about how these games might be used in school. We did hint at some possibilities in our discussion of *Labyrinth* but that now bears amplification.

Allow the game to be played outside of school. Although *Labyrinth's* Flash-based web delivery is well-suited to school computers, we actually hope that the game will largely be played outside of school. We want students to under-take the game with the four freedoms of play intact. If most of the gameplay occurs outside of the classroom, teachers do not need to commit scarce class-room time to technologies that, in their eyes, remain unproven. On the other hand, assigning it to students may be a satisfactory alternative to other forms of homework, though students should not be graded on their gameplay if we want them to play freely.

Use games as preparation for formal learning. We have mentioned that *Labyrinth* is not courseware focusing on the minutiae of standard curricula but rather it engages with the big ideas of mathematics. We do not expect students to play the game and immediately score higher on standard assessments. But we do expect students who play it to be armed with new mathematical concepts and models, understanding we hope teachers will be able to build upon. We hope that the game will be assigned to students at the start of the academic year, or even the summer before, and that teachers will be able to reference the game experience throughout the year.

Make minimal demands upon teachers' technical knowledge. Teachers can launch *Labyrinth* in their classrooms simply by filling out a single web-based form. After that, all they need to do to get started is to pass on to students the URL and login information that the game provides. Most middle-school students should know how to login to a web site and most of them will be comfortable entering game environments without instructions. Since students will be teamed with classmates in the game, those few who are less fluent with games should be able to get help from their team-mates. Teachers do not initially need to know how to play the game, though of course they will receive plenty of supporting material to help them do so. Since, students can be up and running without instruction, teachers can catch up on the game gradually and at their leisure.

Let the students demonstrate expertise. The world of computer games is one in which many students already feel confident. A teacher might easily encourage the students to play the game and a week or two later ask a student for help in getting started. It can be wonderfully empowering for a student to be invited to instruct the teacher and to display authentic mastery.

Use games as thought starters and visualization tools. While we do not expect *Labyrinth* to be played extensively in class, we do give teachers tools to bring it into the classroom in a targeted way. Even a teacher who has not played much of the game has the means to bring up any individual puzzle on a classroom computer and we provide materials that relate each puzzle to standard curricula. Imagine a teacher telling their class, 'I know we've never discussed variables before, but I also know that you are all pretty good at working with them. Do you remember when you played the Vending Machine puzzle?' At this point the teacher projects the puzzle on the classroom screen and asks the students to talk about the strategies they used to solve the puzzle. Instead of treating each new topic as another area in which students are neophytes, the teacher can leverage the students' authentic achievements within the game, treating them as accomplished math students and giving them the confidence to go deeper. Furthermore, the game employs imaginative ways of visualizing mathematical concepts and teachers as well as students may find these to be useful alternatives to the abstract forms in which these concepts are usually presented in textbooks.

Use games as pre-assessments. Labyrinth player data is stored on a central server and teachers can log on to see how far each student has advanced through the game, but also to read the team message boards where players will demonstrate their understanding through the questions they ask and the strategic help they give team-mates. While we would not endorse the use of this data for determining grades, we do think it can give the teacher powerful insights into students' thinking. Teachers can more carefully tailor their instruction when they know more about what topics the students have already mastered and where they are struggling. In our own work, we have seen kids who are not considered strong maths students, nevertheless display genuine ability in the context of a game. We would love it if teachers could use games to discover talents and insights that students do not otherwise display in the classroom.

Though *Labyrinth* was not designed for this purpose, we imagine that *games in the future might serve as powerful evaluation tools.* Games allow for a nice balance of open-endedness and well-defined situations for problem-solving which can establish a context for nuanced evaluation. A well-designed game can set before students' challenges that are once constrained, while allowing for flexible choices of action within those constraints. Rather than simply measure whether a student solved a problem with a 'correct' answer, games can actually reveal and record the decision-making strategies students employ. Using motivational structures and other design elements one can evaluate not only the outcome, but the process used along the way. This promising avenue will require greater collaboration between evaluators and designers in defining shared goals and framing meaningful measurements but through such efforts we might reasonably hope to develop more insightful evaluation tools than we currently have.

One step at a time

We have described above a use of learning games that preserves what is playful about games and one that has some reasonable chance of being adopted in schools, as it requires relatively little class time, and does not demand too much of teachers all at once. We are fully aware that there are still barriers to this model's widespread acceptance. Teachers must not only embrace the idea that learning occurs in games, but they must also give up a measure of control, trusting that students can make their way through games with minimal instruction. Also, there must be good materials to help teachers relate the learning in games to traditional academic disciplines.

On the other hand, this is an approach that does not require teachers to radically alter their classroom style or abandon existing curricula. It is one with which teachers can experiment, lightly at first, more thoroughly as they gain confidence.

While we share the desire for a radically transformed classroom in which students are allowed to more freely pursue their interests and develop their talents using a range of tools with or without technology, we know that vision has advanced little during two decades of computers in schools. We have either asked schools to embrace technological change wholesale or we have asked technologists to dumb-down their products to accommodate the classroom of today. Perhaps the time has come to further develop the marginal space where the two worlds of school and play meet. It may be a challenge, but what good game is not challenging?

References

Gee, J. P. (2003). *What Video Games Have to Teach Us About Literacy and Learning.* New York: Palgrave Macmillan.

Jenkins, H., Purushotma, R., Clinton, K., Weigel, M. and Robison, A. (2006). *Confronting the Challenges of Participatory Culture: Media Education for the 21st Century.* Chicago, IL: The MacArthur Foundation.

Jenkins, H. Camper, B., Chisholm, A., Grigsby, N., Klopfer, E., Osterweil, S., Perry, J., Tan, P., Weise, M. and Teo, C. (2009). From serious games to serious gaming. In U. Ritterfeld, M. Cody and P. Vorderer, eds. *Serious Games: Mechanisms and Effects.* London: Routledge, Taylor and Francis.

Neuman, S. and Celano, D. (2006). The knowledge gap: implications of levelling the playing field for low-income and middle-income children. *Reading Research Quarterly,* Vol. 41, No. 2, pp. 176–201.

Opie, P. and Opie, I. (1969). *Children's Games in Street and Playground.* Oxford: Oxford University Press.

Part 3
Praxis
Theory into Practice

Constructions of Games, Teachers and Young People in Formal Learning

8

Richard Sandford, Keri Facer and Ben Williamson

Chapter Outline

Introduction

In recent years the idea of using computer games to support learning has become increasingly visible in education. While games have long been thought of as having educational application (Botturi and Loh, 2009; Brewster, 2002; Haddon, 1992), and computer programs described as educational games have been on sale since home computers became widely affordable, the recent interest in the educational potential of computer games is distinctive for the way in which its rise parallels the contemporary acceptance that a 'twenty-first century world' demands a radically different approach to education, one that supports the acquisition of skills peculiar to knowledge economies in a 'network society' (Castells, 2000), and one that necessarily has new digital technology at its core. In this context, the technological advances represented by current game software and the hardware needed to run it are often represented as attractive examples of just this kind of new technology, and the conflicts between modern gaming practices and the expectations of 'traditional' teaching represented as standing for the difference between the old, traditional world and a new, digital society (Prensky, 2001).

For teachers, then, the domain of computer games is one that increasingly features in their professional discourse. The negative representation of computer games has become well-established over the last decade, with games characterized as encouraging violence, mindlessness and other anti-social behaviours, in much the same way as television and video technology were vilified in the preceding years (Palmer, 2006; Buckingham, 2002). However, more positive associations are being made through policy and research publications that emphasize the desirable qualities of many computer games for educators (e.g. the Consolarium – The Scottish Centre for Games Based and Emerging Technologies in Learning), and through more general publications that emphasize the growing economic contribution made by the games sector, as well as the increasing role it plays in peoples' cultural lives. It might be expected that teachers, as participants in society at large as well as in their professional roles, would hold a variety of beliefs about computer games, their relevance to education and the ways they might be used in an educational setting.

Two sets of surveys conducted for Futurelab explored these beliefs (reported in Sandford et al., 2006 and Williamson, 2009). One, conducted by Ipsos MORI as part of the 'Teaching with Games' research project over 2005 and 2006, asked teachers and students to report their use of games and their attitudes towards using games in education, while the second, carried out in 2009 by the National Foundation for Educational Research (NFER) for the report 'Computer games, schools and young people' (CGSYP: Williamson, 2009), addressed only teachers. Together they indicate that teachers hold a number of beliefs about the positive role games can play in education, yet significant proportions of teachers rarely, if ever, play games themselves, in contrast to the students interviewed. The data from these surveys will be discussed later in this chapter: for now, it is sufficient to note that these positive views of games use in learning contexts are unlikely, in most cases, to have been derived from personal experience of games use, given teachers' reported lack of first-hand experience, and so are more likely to be based on popular conceptions of gaming practices. These conceptions of the use of games in the wider world – who plays them, what place they should have in education, what sort of behaviour they promote – are likely to be an important part of any decisions teachers make to explore their use in formal educational settings: as such, it suggests that it is important to explore the ideas associated with games that teachers draw upon when exploring how to use games in schools.

At the same time, much academic and popular research in the field of game-based learning is located outside the school in the spaces of informal digital cultures. In this research, a dominant analytic paradigm has been socio-cultural psychology and situated learning which has been used to interrogate the relationships between game players, the tools they use and the communities of which they are a part (Gee, 2003; Steinkuhler, 2004; Shaffer, 2006). As such, the focus in this analysis has fundamentally been on 'learning' and on the children or young people doing that learning.

In these accounts, however, it is usually the learner and player who makes things happen: they are shaping and co-creating the world. Any reader looking for a traditional 'teacher' would find it hard to identify one in these accounts (and this is, of course, precisely the point of much of this research). For example, consider the following account from Gee of what makes games engaging:

> . . . from a learning perspective, what is important about video games is not inter-activity per se, but the fact that in many games players come to feel a sense of agency or ownership. In a video game, players make things happen; they don't just consume what the author (game designer) has placed before them. In good games, players feel that their actions and decisions – and not just the designer's actions and decisions – co-create the world they are in and shape the experiences they are having. Their choices matter. What they do matters. (Gee, 2003: 35)

When looking at how we might draw on such research to support learning in teacher-centred educational settings, then, we are dealing with a significant tension. In much of the research literature and practices of informal gaming a familiar 'adult/teacher identity' is absent from the dominant accounts (see Sandford and Williamson, 2005, for an overview). There is no traditional 'pedagogue' and no formal curriculum which a pedagogue is responsible for delivering. Researchers, designers and enthusiastic teachers interested in bringing games into school are therefore, to some degree, attempting to bring into a teacher-centred setting a set of practices developed outside education in which the teacher has no role. They are 'invisible'.

This invisibility is a natural challenge to teachers' notions of professional identity. Understanding the ways in which teachers respond to this challenge requires a sense of the ways in which this professional identity is constructed. Beijaard and colleagues in their 2004 review of literature addressing teachers' professional identity, suggest although there are many different conceptions of what constitutes a professional identity, there are a number of general features shared by all of them. Teacher's professional identity is not static but a continuous process, a reflexive and dynamic process of reflection and interpretation that lasts throughout a teachers' career. It is shaped and informed by the context in which they work, both their professional institution and the wider social setting in which they are situated. It may more properly be considered an aggregation of 'sub-identities', personal and professional, which cohere to a greater or lesser extent. And teachers themselves construct their own professional identity, indeed use the notion of a 'professional identity' to do so, rather than inhabiting one delineated by an external authority.

Carlgren (1999) suggests that external notions of what it means to be a teacher have more of a role to play in teacher's construction of professional identity, offering the notion of 'paradigmatic correctness', or adherence in teachers' practice to a dominant (perhaps theoretical) conception of what teaching ought to be. In this practice, we could observe that computer games and their use are as invisible as the pedagogue is in socio-cultural accounts of learning in informal games use. She addresses the tension between these established notions of what teaching is – primarily classroom-based, perhaps, supporting externally mandated curriculum objectives – and new demands on teachers that make redundant the sort of 'craft' knowledge, knowledge gathered solely through experience, that for many teachers defines their role: she suggests that these new demands, responses to wider social changes of the sort described above, extend teachers' role beyond the delivery of curriculum in a classroom to encompass the design of learning activities that are the product of reflection on fundamental curricular aims.

Kimber and colleagues (2002) address a notion of 'teacher-as-designer' more positively, suggesting that the tensions between contemporary pedagogic demands centred on the need to engage with new media practices and traditional, 'industrial-age' teaching practices arise through the threatening and insistent nature of demands for teachers to redefine their practice, and that teachers need not necessarily consider the student-centred pedagogies that arise from a consideration of current digital technology practices a challenge to their role and agency. Through recognizing the importance of the teacher in creating the environments in which students learn, their agency and central role can be re-affirmed.

In projects where we attempt to introduce computer games (both tools and practices) into schools, then, we are likely to observe tensions between teachers' existing notions of what it means to teach and the new demands placed on them through the use of a form of media from outside this domain. We might see, too, a challenge to the established relationships between teachers and young people a process of negotiation between their institutional relationships as learners and teachers, and their imaginary relationships as 'games players' and 'invisible adults'. It is this process of negotiation which produces the 'meaning' of the games that are played; technologies, in this case, computer games, are never simply 'technologies'

> . . . [they] are in fact embodiments, stabilisations and concretizations of existing social structures and cultural meanings . . . The promises and the pitfalls of certain technological forms are realized only through active and ongoing struggle over their creation, uptake and revision. New technologies go through what sociologists of technology have called a period of 'interpretive flexibility' during which it is still not clear which social actors will have a role in stabilizing the new technology's meaning and form. As time goes on and different social groups work to stabilize and contest the technology, we move into a period of closure and stabilization. (Itō, 2009: 11)

This chapter explores the ways in which teachers work to re-construct their professional identities in the face of the tensions described above, through a fresh look at data from two studies of classroom interactions which explored the use of 'gaming' software in school settings.

Overview of the two studies

As suggested above, the notion that informal learning can be supported through computer games has a long history, and resonates with a wider conception of young people as belonging to some kind of 'digital generation' whose learning must necessarily be supported through digital technologies, computer games being one such (Bennett et al., 2008; Prensky, 2001). The games most frequently discussed in this context have been for the most part commercially produced games designed for entertainment and readily bought from software retailers (e.g. Gee, 2003; Squire, 2003, Egenfeld-Nielsen, 2005), often referred to as 'commercial off-the-shelf games', or COTS, and a number of researchers have catalogued their use by teachers in schools (e.g. Kirriemuir, 2005; McFarlane *et al.,* 2002). However, by 2005, there had been no sustained examination of what happened when these games, designed for use in bedrooms and living rooms, were transplanted for use, by non-specialist teachers, with limited support, in mainstream curriculum contexts with pupils in classrooms. This was the focus of the Teaching with Games study.

In May 2005, 12 teachers and 4 schools were recruited to participate in a study exploring the potential use of computer games in mainstream curriculum contexts. Not in after-school clubs, not as treats for completion of other activity, not as ways of 'keeping smart kids occupied', but as a central component of teaching curriculum objectives. The project did not aim to evaluate the learning gains of the use of these games, but instead sought to build detailed case studies of the factors that informed how teachers appropriated these resources into their day-to-day activities. In particular, the project aimed to explore the ways in which teachers planned and implemented games-based learning in their respective curricular contexts.

The participating schools represented a variety of student intakes (both urban and rural, private and state) and levels of ICT use across the curriculum. They also represented diverse curriculum approaches curricula – some following subject-based curricula, others following 'thematic' and project-based curricula, others following a German curriculum, with less restricted afternoon lessons. Three games were selected for potential use by the teachers, based upon previous research into the games most likely to be of benefit and use in school settings (Sandford and Williamson, 2005). On this basis, *The Sims 2, Roller Coaster Tycoon 3* and *Knights of Honour* were chosen.

The teachers themselves ranged from science educators, to linguists, to specialists in developing personal skills and competencies, to curriculum innovators to ICT specialists. Five were experienced users of computer games, playing certain genres such as racing or strategy games regularly. Six used to play years ago but now played only occasionally, while the remainder had minimal or no experience with computer games (though one was well-used to programming environments). All were given copies of the games to play over the summer months prior to the start of the project, though not all found time to engage with the titles.

Central to the project was the sense that teachers would need to act as designers, responding to their specific professional context, creating new learning activities for their classes that they were confident would support students to meet their learning goals, rather than using a lesson plan developed externally. At the first meeting of the project team, the teachers chose which titles they would want to use in their specific subject areas. Over the following weeks, Futurelab researchers worked with the teachers, in groups and individually, communicating face-to-face and via email, to support them to become familiar with their chosen games, and to design learning activities that would allow them to mobilize their game in their lessons. Teachers were responsible for deciding which parts of the curriculum they wanted to address through the use of the game, the pedagogies and teaching approaches that would best support their learning aims, and planning the practical activities they would undertake with their students. Such lesson plans might focus on the use of the game, with students spending the majority of a lesson playing the game with a particular end in mind, or they might encompass other activities, with students responding to the game and their teachers' learning goals by (for example) writing newspaper articles, designing additions to a fairground in papier-mâché, or graphing the behaviour of their rollercoaster.

Teachers were free to change game titles, or indeed reject their use completely: in the event, two teachers ceased planning to use the game in their lessons, choosing instead to support their colleagues' work, and one changed the game used in their lessons. During this time, researchers also worked with school technicians and teachers to resolve the various technical issues involved in using these games, designed for private homes, in a school setting. Over the following term, the teachers implemented these plans over anything between 2 and 16 lessons in their classrooms.

In conjunction with these case studies, two national polls were carried out with Ipsos MORI, asking teachers and students about their use of computer games and their attitudes towards the use of such games in a school setting. In November 2005, a representative sample of 1,000 primary and secondary school teachers in England and Wales was surveyed by Ipsos MORI researchers using a questionnaire designed by Futurelab. This was followed in May 2006 by a similar survey of 2,334 children aged between 11 and 16 (topline data summaries of these two surveys are available at http://www.futurelab.org. uk/projects/teaching-with-games/research).

Two years later, Becta commissioned Futurelab to examine the use of games in formal education, as part of their research programme supporting the 'Harnessing Technology' policy strategy (A summary of the strategy can be found at http://publications.becta.org.uk/display.cfm?resID=37346). While the remit of the study included software written specifically for education as well as COTS games, the goal, like Teaching with Games, was to compare dominant ideas about game-based learning constructed through research literature with data on actual classroom practices, gathered in 2009 through in-depth interviews with teachers and students, and a representative survey of primary and secondary teachers. 10 teachers and 10 small groups of students from primary and secondary schools participated in semi-structured interviews with postgraduate researchers, exploring their use of games in the classroom, while a representative sample of 1,000 primary and secondary teachers completed a survey asking them about their experience using games and their attitudes towards using games to support learning. These findings were published in the report, 'Computer games, schools and young people' (Williamson, 2009). Participating teachers' previous experience of and enthusiasm for computer games, in personal and professional contexts, varied, with some committed players and others having little experience. The projects and approaches described were equally varied, treating the game as a core activity, a jumping-off point for further activities (creating related art, for example, or debating issues raised by the game).

There are important differences in methodology and research focus between the two studies. Quantitative data was collected through structured telephone interviews within Teaching with Games but through self-completed questionnaires within the CGSYP report. A more relevant distinction lies in the qualitative data generated in each case: in Teaching with Games, this was obtained through working with teachers new to using games in classrooms, while the CGSYP interviews were carried out with staff at schools known to have some prior involvement in using games to support learning. The CGSYP report was interrogating existing teaching practices that make use of games, while the Teaching with Games project examined the process of creating these sorts of teaching activities, with researchers actively supporting teachers in this. Teachers involved in Teaching with Games were, by default, engaged in the process of designing learning activities centred around a computer game, whereas those interviewed for the CGSYP report varied in their use of, and enthusiasm for, games-based learning. This difference in the experience of teachers in using games within their formal curriculum activities goes some way towards accounting for the differences in their attitudes towards such activity, and will illustrate one of the concerns of this chapter: that practical experience of, and engagement with, the ways in which young people use games enables teachers to design more rewarding game-based learning experiences.

Comparison of survey data

Despite these differences, these two studies offer insights into the ways teachers construct young people's game practices, their own professional identity, and the contribution these constructions make to the game-based learning activities they design. The surveys undertaken in each asked teachers to report the amount of time they personally spent playing computer games, whether they currently used or had previously used games in their classroom practice, their willingness to consider using games in their lessons in future, and the learning benefits if any) accrued through non-formal gameplay. While these surveys are not directly comparable, as noted earlier, there are some striking parallels:

- In 2006, nearly three-quarters (72 per cent) of primary and secondary teachers claimed never to play computer games, and just 9 per cent claimed to play every week. In 2009, fewer than half (42%) claimed never to play, and the proportion playing every week rose to 21 per cent.
- In 2006, 59 per cent of primary and secondary teachers would consider using games to support classroom learning. In 2009, again, this proportion remained at a similar level (60%).
- In 2006, 69 per cent of primary and secondary teachers reported that they had never used games in the classroom for educational purposes. In 2009, this proportion remained at a similar level, with 64 per cent claiming never to have used games in this way.
- Of these teachers who would consider using games in their classroom work, most (53% in 2006 and 44% in 2009) would do so because they thought games would engage or motivate their students.

The most striking change over the three years is the increase in the number of teachers claiming to play computer games, suggesting that teachers currently have much more contact with the games domain than was the case only four years ago. In the light of this, the comparative lack of change in the proportion of teachers who have never used games for teaching but would be happy to do so is interesting: it raises the possibility that teachers are basing their assessment of whether games would be a beneficial addition to their teaching practice on something other than their own experience. Popular constructions of children as gamers, the narratives of the 'imaginary child' suggested above, would be a plausible candidate for this.

The two studies highlight in particular one element of teachers' understanding of computer games: that they are believed to be motivating and engaging. Within the Teaching with Games survey, 53 per cent of teachers who would consider using computer games would do so because they understood them to be motivating. In the case studies and interviews discussed below, the ways in which this belief is characteristic of the ways in which participating teachers imagined students' relationship with computer games will be discussed further.

Exploring the case studies

The Teaching with Games study identified a range of factors that played a critical role in the appropriation of the computer games into the school setting. These included the existing technical infrastructure in the school, the extent to which the games 'themselves' could be disaggregated and used as separate components, and the institutional constraints within which teachers worked (the organization of time and space in schools, the availability of shared resources and so on). These are all discussed at length elsewhere – See Teaching with Games final report, at http://futurelab.org.uk/projects/teaching-with-games. Here, we examine the ways in which the tensions between teachers' existing notions of professional identity and the domain of games are visible in the different learning interactions and practices created by teachers in appropriating similar resources, and the negotiations between 'learner/teacher' and 'player/designer' that are undertaken with their students. In this light, of critical importance are the professional contexts of teachers' practice (the cultures of collaboration or knowledge sharing between teachers, the traditions of 'best practice' made evident in lesson planning and so forth), the individual teacher's personal experiences of gameplay and their personal and professional identities as teachers, as illustrated in the following vignettes and interview excerpts:

Teacher N

Teacher N was an experienced maths and physics teacher. In her initial interview she reported no gameplay other than Minesweeper. However, she was a very competent user of ICT and had created simulations that her students could use to observe ray motion in light. Her approach to using games was initially sceptical and she believed that while her students might be enthusiastic, they would gain only superficial understanding of concepts from gameplay.

Teacher N worked with RollerCoaster Tycoon 3 and used the sandbox area of the game (the element of the game which allows players to create new rollercoasters). The lessons were supported by a significant amount of preparation including a manual with reminders about how to play the game, worksheets to work through and 12 pre-prepared rollercoasters. Students were organised into pairs with one group of three.

The activities were constructed first to introduce the game, and second to draw students' attention to the factors that impacted the performance of a rollercoaster.

Students were asked to work through various individual factors in designing rollercoasters, including friction, launch speed and height, and were asked to draw graphs and work out relationships between these factors. In the final lesson they deduced the formula for kinetic energy. The amount of preparation done by Teacher N meant the lesson plans were followed as intended, including plenary sessions around a whiteboard at the front where the generated graphs were discussed. The focus solely on the 'sandbox' did mean, however, to some students that the fun was taken out of the game.

Teacher N conducted a pre-assessment of students' physics comprehension and game-play skills in the first of the double lessons and repeated this assessment at the end of the third double lesson. All the students had improved in physics though not as much in games skills. Teacher N was also pleased with the concentration and motivation displayed, reporting that students worked through their breaks and she was able to spend more time with individuals as the others were content to work in their teams.

Teacher A

Teacher A is an experienced teacher and had been responsible for authoring the new 'competency curriculum' for his school. While playing console games (particularly racing and fighting games) he had little or no interest, for his own entertainment, in the sorts of strategy games that were selected for the project. This teacher, at the first workshop, selected the Knights of Honour game for use as part of the competency curriculum with his Year 7 pupils. Through playing the game and talking with colleagues he focused his use of the game on three competencies: 'finding and using information', 'team work' and 'communication'. He set aside 16 lessons for the scheme of work he developed.

The first activity involved a plenary session introducing the game and objectives for the programme of work to students. They were then organized into self-selecting teams of four or five. The objective for the teams was to play Knights of Honour with the goal of conquering Europe. Teams were organized into distinct roles, with different children taking on the role of, for example, leader, 'driver', scribe or timekeeper. On completion of the game, Teacher A was to run a plenary session reflecting on the different skills the students had had to use in the game. Finally, students were asked to use the game as a resource alongside the internet and books in creating a presentation on medieval life. The students were expected to evaluate the efficacy and reliability of the game as an information resource against these more conventional tools.

In practice, the students took significantly longer to develop competency in playing the game than envisaged, a fact which led to time constraints within the lessons. As a result, the reflection stages planned by the teacher were often missed out. Despite this, the teacher reported high levels of engagement and motivation amongst the students and reflected that, should he use the resource again, he would have a better idea of the time issues involved and be better able to ensure that space for reflection and critical analysis was more systematically built into the activities.

What is clear from these accounts is that the teachers' learning designs are very different from the social systems that are understood to support games in non-formal education settings (what Gee describes as the 'Game' as opposed to the 'game' software: Gee, 2008). They attempt to create a new set of roles for both students and teachers which are absent from the practices described in informal gaming systems. At the same time, these learning designs are informed by teachers' expectations of their students, expectations that are directly influenced by popular conceptions of children as enthusiastic and expert players of all types of games.

Indeed, many of the teachers' learning designs can be characterized by the assumption that computer games would act as an intrinsically motivating device for students:

> . . . 'the main hook is that students want to use games'
>
> I'm a real believer in anything that can be used as a motivational tool, to engage, excite and motivate kids in the topic they're learning . . . it [computer game] would be exciting and up to date and would appeal to students, after all, a proportion, a fair proportion, have good hardware and software at home [transcripts from the study].

Above, we noted that over half of teachers who would consider using computer games would do so because they believed them to be 'motivating'. This last quote, however, foregrounds the extent to which 'motivation' to play games is assumed to be tied up in the hardware and software, in the technology 'itself' rather than in the cultures of gaming practices that surround them (Itō, 2008; MacKenzie and Wajcman, 1999).

At the outset of the project there was little critical analysis of what it might be about game software and game cultures that might make them motivating or engaging to young people. As a result, lesson plans were not structured to build on the factors identified by researchers as contributing to that motivation and engagement – namely, the capacity to get hands-on, the opportunity to exhibit agency, the opportunity to explore new identities (Gee, 2003). For example, one pair of teachers took the motivational qualities of games for granted in their lesson planning, yet designed their learning environment in such a way that the game was used like a video, bypassing the opportunity for students' hands-on and exploratory play. Where game-based software is considered intrinsically motivating, without an analysis of the different adult-child identities and practices that contribute to the engagement of gameplay, it is unlikely that these entertaining and engaging elements of games will translate into the classroom. Indeed, where the use of a game does seem linked with increased motivation, it may have more to do with the novelty of a different teaching approach than any intrinsic property of the game itself:

> I asked them how they thought [playing The Sims to learn competency skills] compared [to a standard lesson] and they all said they actually thought it was a better way of doing it and a more interesting way of doing it because it was a different way of doing things.

Many of the teachers also operated with an assumption that children would be expert games players:

> kids can do games
> I did have an expectation that they'd all be really good at it

All teachers, however, were comfortable with the possibility that their students might have a greater expertise in playing the game, with one commenting that he was 'used to saying to children, look, I'm not an expert in this'. In the early stages of lesson design, many teachers explicitly attempted to build new adult-child relationships in the classroom. For example, in five cases, the teachers used the skills of 'expert groups' of pupil game players, to build in-game resources prior to the lesson, or to mentor peers during the lesson. Noticeably, however, this did not usually involve the teacher taking on a new identity as a novice gamer. Teachers were for the most part content to absent themselves from gaming practice, leaving students to demonstrate the required expertise, with the exception of those few teachers who felt in possession of greater game-playing competence than students: these teachers drew on their personal identities as game players, mobilizing their game competence in service of their professional role. Perhaps, however, the similarity with an identity of 'learner' is too great a tension with existing conceptions of professional identity: expertise can only be demonstrated by students in the teachers' absence, to avoid too great a challenge to the teacher's usual expert role.

Teacher identity is maintained not only through pedagogic practice and student-staff relations, but through the assemblage of materials, institutional routines and practices that constitute the everyday experience of 'teaching'. In response to the novel task of incorporating gaming, we saw teachers beginning to articulate this novelty with existing legacy materials and practices, such as, for example, developing worksheets, setting up booklets for assessment and so forth:

> In the regular test paper many of them proved that they had understood the physics very well and achieved better results than in the test paper half a year ago. (Teacher N)

> [The students] haven't completed the booklet but you kind of know that they do know what they're talking about. But it's kind of like a proof thing that it would have taken them literally 5 minutes to go through the booklet. If they've got that much knowledge to gain, it would have taken them 5 minutes to literally go click click click click click click click click click 'There you go, there's your booklet, can I play the game now please?' (Teacher H)

Teachers designed and developed materials within existing professional networks of peers and colleagues, including, for a time, other teachers on the project:

> In preparation it was quite useful to talk about it [to other teachers in the project] and get certain ideas, but in the end we all did something completely different – one teacher was doing it more in design or something and the other one was creating parks, I used it in physics which nobody else really did – there was not much interaction after we had our ideas, as far as I know (Teacher N)

> Normally I develop schemes of work from existing activities which I know work well and I have an opportunity to trial lessons or incorporate lessons that I know work well. Also the work for this project was different as that I did all the work, thinking and planning on my own when normally other people are involved. (Teacher G)

And yet, the novelty of the activity, and the current lack of acceptance of gaming in schools, means that the development of new forms of professional practice was, for many of these teachers, an individual process in comparison with the more common collective design practices they were familiar with.

Teacher identity is fundamentally tied up with notions of expertise and knowledge, and the order of schooling is a process that structures inculturation into particular domains of knowledge, usually sequentially. The relationship between knowledge and both teacher and student identities in this project was complex. For example, the expectations of expertise on the part of students played themselves out in different ways in teachers' appropriation of the games in the classroom setting. For example, as evidenced in the vignette above, a common issue to arise was the need for teachers to allow significantly more time than they had expected to allow the students to develop competency in the game:

And I did kind of double the amount of time I was taking to do it and thinking right well it took me this long, it's going to take them twice as long. But instead it was taking them four times as long (Teacher B)

It was just really bizarre because even the kids that did play the game and said that they were very good at it, still made mistakes. And they made mistakes I didn't think they would make (Teacher H)

A significant challenge here, however, was the question of what counted as 'expertise' to students and teachers.

For example, both teachers and researchers' conceptions of 'games expertise' were, at the start of the project, more linear than students'. Teachers and researchers conceptualized students as being at different 'levels' of expertise (e.g. novice, beginner, intermediate, expert) and also to assume that within these levels of difficulty, similar tasks would be equivalent. This would make it safe to assume that if a student could do task X, she would also be able to do task Y if task Y was assumed to be of a similar level of difficulty. There seems to have been a further assumption, that tasks of a certain difficulty would be attempted only after tasks of lesser difficulty had already been mastered. As an ad hoc model of competency this seems to be underpinned by common sense. When tested as a working assumption with students, however, this model was inadequate to describe students' actual use of games. Students appeared not to draw the same distinctions between levels of difficulty within the game as teachers, displaying a confidence with some tasks assumed by teachers to be 'expert' (e.g. using cheats or working out how to import images) while still finding basic menu tasks difficult. To teachers, students seemed to have 'spikes' of expertise, rather than displaying the linear model that might be assumed to be commonsensical.

This may reflect a difference between teachers and students in their under-standings of the demands made on players by a game. The 'spikes' of expertise, apparent islands of competence in playing the game, might reflect a mis-diagnosis of the game on the part of the teacher rather than a genuinely erratic acquisition of skills on the part of the student. What seems hard to a teacher unfamiliar with game practices (e.g. using a cheat code to ensure unlimited resources for a character in the game) may seem so because the result of that action appears advanced: to the student who follows their friend's instructions, using this cheat is far easier than a more orthodox game task, such as exhibit-ing the fine control of their avatar that would make it unnecessary to use the code. The discrepancy would arise, then, not because there is a different model of expertise in operation – one that is not sequential or ordered by degrees of difficulty – but because the level of competency demanded by particular game tasks has not been understood by the teacher. The model of expertise used by teacher and student might be the same, but the ordering of game tasks by degree of difficulty may be different. If this were the case, these apparent 'spikes of expertise' would point to a need for the teacher to improve their understanding of how students play games, and how game designers intend games to be played.

On the other hand, this discrepancy between teacher expectations and the behaviour exhibited by students may reflect a genuine difference between the kind of expertise demanded by games and that privileged within a formal learning context. Perhaps expertise that is produced in relation to meaningful activity is specialized and collaborative, whereas expertise developed in relation to formalized knowledge acquisition is structured in a linear and sequential fashion. If so, the identity of the teacher in these sorts of knowledge environments would be fundamentally different from that they are used to playing.

Regardless of the true facts of the matter, the notion of these 'spikes' is useful in two ways: first, for describing how students' practice appeared to teachers, and second, in illustrating the tight focus on certain gaming practices many students appeared to display – rather than seeking to excel at the game as a whole, many students seemed to concentrate on one aspect of the game, such as resource management or strategy, at the expense of others. That this discrepancy exists at all is indicative of the ways in which teachers conceptualize games and young peoples' game practices have real impacts on the ways games are used in a classroom setting.

The following two cases taken from the CGSYP study support this, illustrating the differences that can exist between individual teachers' beliefs about games and young people, and the ways these can shape their design of learning experiences using games:

The enthusiastic secondary school teacher

An ICT teacher at a Northern Ireland secondary school is a keen games player, favouring online multiplayer role-playing games. The appeal for the teacher is the social aspect the games provide as well as the challenge of the problem solving required. Her students have varying degrees of gaming experience, with some playing a few hours each night, and others playing very infrequently only when bored. Motivations to play games include fun, competition and an opportunity to socialise with friends.

The teacher's appreciation of games outside the classroom has developed into an appreciation of their potential for education. The teacher is a strong advocate of games-based learning, and is extremely open to the integration of non-traditional applications into the formal classroom. She appreciates the numerous skills that games can encourage such as thinking skills, logical thinking, planning and team work.

This teacher also has experience with using games, such as The Sims, at a previous school, and of using games with pupils who have behavioural difficulties. The teacher felt that games were instrumental in engaging disengaged students, and resulted in improved learning outcomes, as demonstrated by the qualifications the pupils earned. In this school the teacher is currently trying to implement games-based learning further into the curriculum, and hopes to develop a programme in which pupils will author games and subsequently review each other's work. The teacher has already used the authoring tool of Caspian Learning's Thinking Worlds in this school, as part of an extra qualification offered to sixth form pupils. Her students were positive about using games for learning.

The cautious secondary school teacher

A teacher interviewed at a secondary school does not play games in her spare time, and thinks they could be a waste of time, feeling that computer game playing amongst children should be closely monitored. Boys in her class, though, say they enjoy the challenge of playing games as well as appreciating the opportunity to experience scenarios otherwise unavailable to them in real life. The school has some recent experience with games based learning, having recently trialled a citizenship game designed specifically for the Northern Ireland Curriculum, using Caspian Learning's Thinking Worlds. The teacher felt that the source of these games (CCEA – Council for the Curriculum, Examinations, and Assessment in Northern Ireland) encouraged her to try them, as she was confident that they would be educational resources. The games were trialled with a Year 10 class, which included pupils with learning and behavioural difficulties. The teacher commented on how initial excitement from the pupils was evident; however, she also noted how after a few weeks of playing the games, boredom was also evident once the pupils were very familiar with the content. The teacher has highlighted how games can address certain changes being implemented within the new ICT curriculum, with gaming technology addressing and facilitating some new curricular objectives, such as the role of exhibiting work, exploring and expressing ideas. Plus, she foresees that teachers working with the new curriculum will go beyond the use of multimedia and will soon extend to the development of websites and games. She warns, however, that there is a lack of experience, expertise and confidence amongst teachers with regards to gaming technology, highlighting how ongoing training is required for teachers implementing game-based learning.

These two accounts represent two clearly different experiences with and approaches to teaching with computer games. Where one teacher sees an opportunity for logical thinking and co-operative behaviour, the other sees reasons for concern and a need for adult control. However, within the accounts of both, there are elements that resonate with and extend the themes discussed in relation to the earlier material from the Teaching with Games project. These teachers, like those in the Teaching with Games project, both expected a degree of student motivation as an outcome from the use of games, with one employing them in order to engage hard to reach students, and the other recognizing that their initial use occasioned excitement among the class. Other teachers interviewed for the study demonstrated a similar expectation of a relationship between student motivation and computer games:

> the biggest thing is motivation really, because it's relevant to them, it's a big part of their lives, it's what they relate to (primary teacher, female).

> I've got this idea that sometimes teachers use computer games in class because it's a fun activity and it keeps the kids engaged (secondary teacher, male).

> It is noticeable that of the two teachers described earlier, the teacher with little direct experience of games and the perception that their use might have negative outcomes reported a drop in student engagement once the initial reaction had worn off, while the teacher with more personal engagement with the domain of computer games mentioned no such difficulty. While there is no way of being certain whether this reflects their students' actual level of engagement, this distinction between the two reports mirrors the experiences for teachers involved with Teaching with Games, where teachers having less familiarity with computer games did not necessarily see the high levels of engagement they expected.

Where these descriptions differ from the earlier study, however, is in the degree to which these teachers are aware of the place of games in their students' lives outside school. The games enthusiast recognizes that different children have different ways of engaging with games, rather than assuming a homogeneous relationship with computer games across the group. The less enthusiastic teacher has an idea of some of the elements that make games engaging for her pupils – they are challenging and offer experiences that would be inaccessible outside the game. There is an indication that these teachers have paid more attention to the social aspects of computer games, recognizing that they are part of the wider media ecology in which their students are situated (Ito, 2009; Buckingham, 2007; Sefton-Green, 2004). It may be that, unlike their colleagues in the Teaching with Games study, these teachers are seeing the motivation and engagement associated with games, not as intrinsic features of game software, but as a reflection of the place they occupy in many students' lives. Rather than constructing games practice as something other, a domain that excludes them as adults, there are indications here that these teachers feel entitled at least to interrogate the broad social narrative. In contrast to the teachers in the earlier vignettes, who rarely if at all recognized the ways in which games functioned in young people's lives, one secondary teacher acknowledges the wider social practices that arise around games:

> I would certainly challenge any idea that computer games are intrinsically non-social, because it seems to me that not just multiplayer games, but the way that kids get together around computers and play games, and the way they talk about games and share experiences is very pro-social and very socialising, and is probably for some children who would otherwise find it difficult to, to sort of establish strong social relationships and so on, can be quite a powerful thing. (secondary teacher, male)

While another makes a connection with another, older related discourse of play:

> when we were very young we used to go out and play in the street and play street games. And . . . it's no different, you learn from those, you learned how to team play . . . and those are all really valuable skills which are part of the revised curriculum, we're trying to teach them about self management and . . . games do that beautifully, and so we should use them (secondary teacher, female).

These extracts offer glimpses of an understanding that there is more to the use of games in classrooms than simply having the software used in lessons, that the place of the game in students' lives outside school is something to be understood if it is to be used well in a formal setting: to use Gee's term, they suggest a sensitivity to not just the game but the Game.

Discussion

It must be remembered that these teachers are currently in a minority: even if the three years that separate these investigations saw an increase in the number of teachers who play games themselves, the use of games in formal education is still far from mainstream today and both studies discussed here reveal a dominant popular discourse of games that makes visible concerns about the promotion of anti-social behaviour through playing games and their lack of relevance to curriculum aims, as well as reproducing beliefs about games' ability to enhance players' capacity for logical thought and their fine motor skills. These discourses are premised upon assumptions about games' power to engage young people, and young people's level of competence; and these assumptions subsequently informed teachers' design of game-centred learning activities. On examination, however, these assumptions were revealed in some cases to be erroneous. These beliefs, inherited not from direct experience of playing games but from participation in wider popular discourses, reveal something also of the ways in which teachers constructed their own professional identities: the common expectation that students would excel at these games brought with it the expectation that teachers would not, and few teachers in the early study felt a need to demonstrate competence with the game they selected. Being 'good at games' was not seen as part of being a teacher. In fact, defining oneself in opposition to games culture and gaming, was seen as a defining feature of teacher professional identity, even for some teachers who had volunteered to and were actively involved in introducing games into schools. Bringing games into school, then, may be more about 'doing it for the kids', than from a re-examination of the nature of professional identity aspired to in many of the arguments for learning from gaming informal education.

There are also a number of possible reasons why it may be difficult to draw on competence at playing games in constructing teachers' professional identity. The popular discourse of 'computer games' mentioned above strongly associates youth and gaming, building perhaps on earlier ideas of play and leisure and the construction of childhood as a time before adult responsibilities and obligations come into force. Notions of 'irresponsibility' also figure strongly in computer games discourses, in part due to the capacity of games to offer opportunities for activity that would, in real life, be reckless and wasteful, and in part through the sense that time spent playing computer games is time not spent fulfilling other obligations: there may also be a sense that time spent playing computer games is unhealthy and so contributes to a lack of personal responsibility. To what extent these various currents are found in computer games discourses in different contexts is not our current object: the point here is that social practices linked with immature and irresponsible behaviour are unlikely to be desirable parts of an identity centred around being adult and responsible.

But as has been noted above, some teachers had personal identities as game players that they drew on professionally in the design and implementation of learning activities. Clearly, being associated with games is not always so toxic as to prevent teachers from including this 'sub-identity' in the construction of their professional identities. In these cases, being a game player offered them the opportunity to demonstrate greater competence and expertise than their students (as well as supporting their relationship with students, allowing them to support students' use of the game during the lesson and offering other beneficial outcomes), two qualities which feature strongly in the construction of teacher identities by teachers, in their wider professional contexts and in popular constructions of teaching more generally. Demonstrating competence in games can offer some teachers a chance to reinforce their position as a figure of authority. This raises the possibility that what seem to be significant changes in teaching practice may in reality be reinforcing the same approaches to teaching that they were introduced to challenge: much of the enthusiasm for using games in education stems from the conviction that they can support the sort of moves towards a more collaborative approach to learning, centred around the learner and emphasizing the co-construction of knowledge within a learning group, that have been called for repeatedly in recent times. However, existing constructions of professional identity that embody more traditional ideas about the appropriate relationships between teachers (adults) and learners (young people) may still operate, and are unlikely to be removed by the sort of intervention described above.

The tensions between dominant constructions of teachers' professional identities and the new demands placed on them when making use of games in their classroom teaching seem clear, and bound up with popular notions of adulthood and childhood that work to separate the domains of 'teaching' and 'computer games'. However, as the comparison of data from the Teaching with Games and CSGYP work indicated, gaming is becoming a more mainstream activity, and in the short time separating the two surveys has become an activity in which a greater proportion of teachers participate. As gaming becomes a more mainstream activity in society and within education, these two domains of 'teaching' and 'games' are likely to be traversed more easily, and games' presence in a classroom may increasingly reflect shared membership of a common domain, rather than providing an opportunity to reinforce preconceived ideas about classroom roles, and generational and expert differences. Gaming may lose its function as a marker of distinction (Bourdieu, 1984).

In part, this more mainstream presence may be ascribed to the greater diversity of games and game genres available than in the past. While there may not be any fewer games of the sort that most readily conflict with the sorts of aims and values of educators, there are many more games than existed previously which present no particular challenge to a school's or parent's ethos, and game developers and publishers are now aware that many groups traditionally not considered part of the market for computer games – women, adults unwilling to commit large amounts of time to playing games, families – are keen to play, if appropriate titles are available. New hardware such as the Nintendo Wii and DS, controllers and peripherals that encourage physical action or support group play (dance mats, the Wii controller, specialist controllers such as that sold with Guitar Hero) and a boom in the 'casual' games sector (simple games with mechanics that are easy to comprehend) have all led to a change in tone and appeal among recently published titles. Even within the core games market there is an increased emphasis on communication between players and on collaborative action, as these titles become more complex and bandwidth becomes cheaper. These changes in games make it harder to characterize them as anti-social or likely to promote negative attitudes and behaviour: consequently it may be easier for educators to consider them as potential tools for their teaching practice and for parents to see them as a positive activity for young people.

This change in the nature of games and the way they are perceived may be happening in parallel with changes in the nature of teaching. While the current appetite for games within education to some extent might be seen to be driving some changes in policy and pedagogy, teaching is widely characterized as being in the midst of a long process of change, moving away from transmissive approaches in which knowledge is treated as discrete and quantifiable towards approaches that see knowledge considered as something to be actively constructed through interaction with tools and other learners. More recently, the boundaries of the education domain have been redefined by a series of policy initiatives and reports in the UK (the Children's Plan and the Byron Review (Byron, 2008), extended school opening hours, a more explicit role for teachers in supporting the work of social services, greater attention paid to food in schools and childhood obesity) that have asked schools and teachers to take more responsibility for aspects of students' wider lives – it might be that these general shifts in the priorities of educators make it easier for teachers and parents to recognize games' capacity to promote skills that map less readily to curricula organized by subjects or disciplines, such as understanding the consequences of action in a complex system, or functioning well within a group working towards a specific goal.

The most significant factor contributing to the increasing acceptance of computer games in the classroom is likely, however, to be the changing demographics of game players. In 2005, a BBC survey found the average age of a UK gamer to be 28, while in 2009 a US study found the majority of players to be aged between 35 and 55 (Weaver et al., 2009 – the BBC Audience Research survey was carried out on behalf of the New Media and Technology Division, and can be accessed at http://open.bbc.co.uk/newmediaresearch/files/BBC_ UK_Games_Research_2005.pdf). As the first generation to grow up with computer games continues, with subsequent generations, to age, it seems plausible to expect greater number of adults to be familiar with computer games, and for the popular construction of 'computer games' as being of primary interest to young people to slowly fade. This implies that teachers are more likely to feel a sense of ownership, belonging or entitlement around games, sharing with their students membership of a common domain. As a greater proportion of parents, too, are likely to have some engagement with computer games, young people will become more familiar with the idea of adults as participants in the practice of playing computer games, with it being easier perhaps for adults to be not 'adults' but 'players'.

Conclusion

The two studies examined here describe some of the ways in which the tensions between popular constructions of games, teachers' roles and their relationship with students play out when introducing computer games into formal learning settings. They illustrate the increasing familiarity and acceptance of games among educators as wider demographic and market factors shape the ways in which games are used and perceived; they highlight too the need for a greater understanding of the kinds of demands the use of these games make on teachers' practice, a more detailed articulation of the sorts of pedagogies that might both build on accounts of informal learning using these tools and be relevant to classroom teaching, and a way of reconciling the apparent tensions between traditional notions of teachers' professional identity and the need to engage with forms of digital media from outside institutional life.

One possible approach to this last issue of professional identity might be to support teachers to construct themselves as designers, as individuals able to exercise agency and to play a central role in their students' learning. This would be a response to the uncertainty around new forms of technology felt by many teachers unfamiliar with such digital tools, allowing them to treat the game as a learning tool and situate it as a part of a wider web of learning activities, enabling them to be present during learning rather than abdicating responsibility for demonstrating and assessing expertise to their students. However, for those concerned with investigating genuinely new forms of learning and making the most meaningful use of games as a learning tool this may on its own be insufficient. Many of the theoretical arguments for the use of games in school settings are motivated by a desire to change the relationships between student and teacher, to re-organize the classroom on a more equal principle and to afford students greater opportunity to contribute to the process of learning. Despite this focus, when using games in the classroom it is possible for existing notions of authority, adult expertise and so forth to remain unchallenged by teachers. For teachers to be able to interrogate their professional practice, they need to be given the opportunity to feel comfortable in a role as learner if they are to be able to truly make the most of the opportunities these outside technologies represent.

Acknowledgements

Thanks to Mary Ulicsak for contributing to the vignettes in this chapter.

References

Beijaard, D., Meijer, P. and Verloop, N. (2004). Reconsidering research on teachers' professional identity. *Teaching and Teacher Education*, Vol. 20, No. 2, pp. 107–28.

Bennett, S., Maton, K. and Kervin, L. (2008). The 'digital natives' debate: a critical review of the evidence. *British Journal of Educational Technology*, Vol. 39, No. 5, pp. 775–86.

Brewster, F. (2002). Using Tactical Decision Exercises to Study Tactics. *Combined Arms Center Military Review*, November–December.

Botturi, L. and Loh, C. S. (2009). Once upon a game: rediscovering the roots of games in education. In C. T. Miller, ed. *Games: Purpose and Potential in Education*. New York: Springer.

Bourdieu, P. (trans. Nice, R.). (1984). *Distinction: A Social Critique of the Judgement of Taste*. Cambridge, MA: Harvard University Press.

Buckingham, D. (2002). The Electronic Generation? Children and New Media. In L. Lievrouw and S. Livingstone, eds. *Handbook of New Media: Social Shaping and Consequences of ICTs*. Thousand Oaks, California: Sage.

Buckingham, D. (2007). *Beyond Technology: Children's Learning in the Age of Digital Culture*. London: Polity Press.

Byron, T. (2008). *Safer Children in a Digital World: The Report of the Byron Review*. Available at: http://www.dcsf.gov.uk/byronreview/ Last accessed 30.4.10.

Carlgren, I. (1999). Professionalism and teachers as designers. *Journal of Curriculum Studies*, Vol. 31, No. 1, pp. 43–56.

Castells, M. (2000). *The Rise of the Network Society*. Oxford, UK: Blackwell.

Children's Plan, The (2007). The Children's Plan. Available at: http://www.dcsf.gov.uk/childrensplan/. Last accessed 30.4.10.

Consolarium, The, (no date). Learning and Teaching Scotland, at http://www.ltscotland.org.uk/ictineducation/gamesbasedlearning/. Last accessed 30.4.10.

Gee, J. (2003). *What Videogames Have To Teach Us About Learning and Literacy*. London: Palgrave Macmillan.

Haddon, L. (1992). Explaining ICT Consumption: the case of the home computer. In R. Silverstone and E. Hirsch, eds. *Consuming Technologies: Media and Information in Domestic Spaces*. London: Routledge.

Itō, M. (2008). Education vs. entertainment: a cultural history of children's software. In K. Salen, ed. *The Ecology of Games: Connecting Youth, Games and Learning*. Cambridge, MA: MIT Press.

Itō, M. (2009). *Engineering Play: A Cultural History of Children's Software*. Cambridge: MIT Press.

Kimber, K., Pillay, H. and Richards, C. (2002). Reclaiming teacher agency in a student-centred digital world. *Asia Pacific Journal of Teacher Education*, Vol. 30, No. 2, pp. 155–67.

Kirriemuir, J. (2005). *Computer and Video Games in Curriculum-based Education*. London: Department for Education and Skills.

Mackenzie, D. and Wajcman, J. (1999). *The Social Shaping of Technology*. Milton Keynes: Open University Press.

McFarlane, A., Sparrowhawk, A. and Heald, Y. (2002). *Report on the Educational Use of Games*. Cambridge: TEEM.

Palmer, S. (2006). *Toxic Childhood: How The Modern World Is Damaging Our Children and What We Can Do About It*. New York: Orion.

Prensky, M. (2001). *Digital Game-Based Learning*. New York: McGraw-Hill.

Sandford, R. and Williamson, B. (2005). *Games and Learning: A Handbook*. Bristol, UK: Futurelab.

Sandford, R., Ulicsak, M., Facer, K. and Rudd, T. (2006). *Teaching with Games: Using Commercial Off-the-Shelf Computer Games in Formal Education*. Bristol, UK: Futurelab.

Sefton-Green, J. (2004). *Literature Review in Informal Learning with Technology outside School*. Bristol, UK: Futurelab.

Shaffer, D. W. (2006). Epistemic frames for epistemic games. *Computers and Education*, Vol. 46, No. 3, pp. 223–34.

Steinkuehler, C. (2004). Learning in massively multiplayer online games. In Y. B. Kafai, W. A. Sandoval, N. Enyedy, A. S. Nixon and F. Herrera, eds. *Proceedings of the Sixth International Conference of the Learning Sciences*, pp. (521–28). Mahwah, NJ: Erlbaum.

Weaver, J., Mays, D., Weaver, S., Kannenberg, W., Hopkins, G., Eroğlu, D. and Bernhardt, J. (2009). Health-risk correlates of video-game playing among adults. *American Journal of Preventative Medicine*, Vol. 37, No. 4, pp. 299–305.

Williamson, B. (2009). Computer games, schools and young people. Bristol, UK: Futurelab.

9 Games and Simulations in Informal Science Education

Kurt Squire and Nathan J. Patterson

Chapter Outline

Introduction

This chapter seeks to outline the possibilities and challenges that games and simulations pose for informal science education, learning outside the contexts of schools. Three crucial opportunities and related challenges shape the field:

(1) Informal science educators are largely free to pursue a variety of educational goals, from increasing ethnic diversity among scientists to increasing interest in science, technology, engineering and mathematics careers, to increasing scientific citizenship among the general populace. Further complicating the matter, informal science educators operate in environments ranging from unstructured settings, such as homes to highly structured workshops. This diversity in goals and context frees educational game designers to create

experiences that appeal to personalized, students' interests or span home, school or after-school contexts, and indeed requires them to do so. However, such diversity of goals, contexts and methods for reaching those goals makes a fragmented field.

(2) Much of research, theory and practical wisdom in informal science education occur outside the traditional domains of Science education. Some of the most complex forms of scientific thinking occur in commercial entertainment games with no overt educational goals at all. Further, edutainment games have far greater budgets, scope and polish than most educational games and simulations, frequently developed in research contexts. However, they may also lack coherent models of educational gameplay, privileging marketing or commercial goals over some educational values.

(3) Research methods appropriate to informal science education contexts are needed. Informal science educators, tasked with competing with all of the other potential 'out-of-school interests' have been deeply concerned with methods that enable them to improve designs, particularly in how to create quality materials, that is process goals, build and sustain learner, interest and engagement, support learners in forming identities affiliated with science and in creating lifelong interest in the field. There is a general desire to treat design seriously as its own field, rather than as a 'natural extension' of learning theory. The diversity of informal science educators' goals, methods and contexts puts it outside the purview of much of the contemporary discourse in educational research (see National Research Council, 2002). The key features of informal science education, such as interest-driven learning, voluntary participation, divergent learning outcomes and connections across contexts rather than isolating variables, run counter to the underlying logic of many predominant research designs, such as randomized controlled trials. Yet, research methods are needed that produce credible evidence for learning through experiences with games and simulations in informal contexts.

The chapter begins with a brief introduction of simulations and games in informal science education, seeking to connect the relatively disparate enterprises of research, theory and practical wisdom from education and entertainment games across a variety of contexts. It provides a short history that frames the paper and attempts to clarify ambiguities between games and simulations. Next, it examines the research and theory on learning in structured informal learning environments, for example workshops, after-school programmes, some museum workshops, providing a framework for contrasting these structured informal learning environments with more formalized learning environments, such as school. Next, it reviews research on relatively unstructured learning environments, such as home or online experiences, focusing specifically on the research on learning across these contexts. Finally, it concludes by briefly offering some thoughts on the opportunities and challenges for informal science education with games.

Recently, there has been a re-awakened interest among educators in video games and their associated technologies for education. A wave of science-based learning games, including *Whyville, WolfQuest, Fold.it, Resilient Planet, Nobel Prize games, River City, Evolution, Pontifex, Mind Rover, Immune Attack, MeChem, Sharkrunners, Quest Atlantis, Supercharged, Mad City Mystery* and *Star Logo NG* are all designed to support science learning in formal or informal contexts. Some of these come from academia but many were also created in entertainment or commercial contexts and have not been researched. A challenge in conceptualizing the field is how to balance the need for theory-driven research with research responsive to the innovations occurring outside academic contexts.

Although dozens of games and simulations have been developed for informal science education, there is still a paucity of research on them. The wave of educational games released in the 1980s and early 1990s largely ran counter to prevailing educational concerns and thus were not researched extensively. The most robust programme of research around this era of games was the *Fifth Dimension* Project (Brown et al., 2002; Cole et al., 2006; Ito, 2003). The *Fifth Dimension* is a role-playing meta-game based around existing commercial off-the-shelf computer games. Ito (2003) describes the games of this era as falling into three genres: edutainment, entertainment and authoring games. Ito writes,

> The genre of 'edutainment' was founded by progressive educational reformers pursuing equity in learning, but has gradually been overtaken by more competitive and achievement idioms in its commercialization. The genre of 'entertainment' is dominated by visual culture, produced by entertainment industries in alliance with children's peer culture. The genre of 'authoring' grows out of a constructivist approach to learning and hacker subcultures and becomes a tool for children to create their own virtual worlds and challenge the authority of adults (Ito, 2003, p. iv).

Fifth Dimension research emphasizes the centrality of context in determining how participants appropriated such software. Different encompassing institutions, from libraries to schools, implant their own participant structures upon the software influencing its appropriation. Children's own voices and goals co-constitute how the games are (or are not) appropriated as tools as well, as they may place their own cultural framings of video games, toys or other cultural categories upon games (Ito, 2003). Papert's (1987) research on *LOGO* makes similar claims reminding educators that it is impossible to research *LOGO*, but rather, one always researches *LOGO* implemented for particular reasons in specific contexts.

Ito describes how the edutainment and educational games of this generation largely drifted away from the educational values of their original designers. Indeed educators have criticized much of this generation of software for its failure to integrate content and gameplay, poor production values and generally 'dumbing down' for educational audiences (Jenkins et al., 2004; Holland, Squire et al., 2004; Papert, 1998; Ito, 2003; Squire, 2006). A new generation of games built on learning sciences principles and contemporary developments in the commercial video games industry seeks to re-insert such complex problem-solving back into games. Indeed, a host of new games, many of which are actually quite good by most accounts, now suggest the potential for creating immersive learning experiences in which core gameplay is tied to academic practices in science (Gee, 2003, 2005, 2007; Klopfer, 2008; Shaffer, 2006; Squire, 2006).

What are games and simulations?

Before going further, it is worth considering what is meant by games and simulations and giving bounds to the scope of the inquiry. The differences in text-book definitions between games and simulations are pretty simple. Games are sets of rules that are temporarily adopted for the purposes of entertainment. While playing *Monopoly* we all agree to assign a value to take turns rolling dice and moving pieces, trading *Monopoly* money and so on. *Monopoly* is also instructive in that it is a blend of written and 'house' rules. Most people write their own rules to achieve various ends, such as speeding play (see Salen and Zimmerman, 2003).

Simulations, in contrast, are generally defined as representing one symbol system through another. This definition is simple enough when it comes to weather or health care simulations, but what about a case like *Monopoly*? *Monopoly* is a game in that it has rules that players adhere to for enjoyment, but also a simulation in that it could be regarded as taking the real estate market and remediating by a set of materials, such as dice, squares and player symbols. Critics might note that *Monopoly* does not seem like a particularly good real-estate simulation, and in fact they

⇨

What are games and simulations?—Cont'd

might be right, depending on what *Monopoly* was purported to be a simulation of and for what purpose. If someone wanted to predict the next 12 months of real-estate values in Southern California following the sub-prime crash, *Monopoly* would not be especially useful. On the other hand, if you wanted to show an eight-year-old the basic idea of how monopolies stifle competition, you could imagine how that might work.

The more consequential difference between games and simulations for many is who developed them, that is do the developers come from the game community or the simulation community, and then for what purposes they are deployed, rather than being static properties of the media themselves (see Sawyer, 2006; Squire, 2006). Many simulation developers come from military, health and science backgrounds, and place a premium on representing systems with accuracy (sometimes for legal reasons), beginning with a realistic simulation and then scaling backwards. Game designers in contrast tend to focus on the player's experience of the media, and 'cheat', by intentionally reducing model accuracy in order to achieve these goals. Prensky (2000) describes how the military simulation developers were 'blown away' when they played the entertainment versions of the military flight simulators. The entertainment developers 'cut corners' in aspects of the simulation that players never experience, enabling them to gain much better performance in areas that they do experience. Observers of both industries have noted how these differences in orientations to development have led to different development tools, programming practices and ultimately products (Prensky, 2000; Sawyer, 2006).

The existing research on contemporary games in informal science education settings spans completely unstructured contexts, such as homes; and semi-constrained contexts, such as after-school clubs or museum workshops. The unique concerns of informal science educators have not been properly addressed, perhaps because most game-based research is produced by educators working in formal classroom education settings. The needs of informal science educators, such as developing interest in science or building affiliations with science identities, have often taken a backseat to academic concerns. Further, the unique opportunities for informal science institutions to pursue local place-based education or scientific citizenship through games have not been explored extensively. As a result, this review draws upon edutainment, education and authored games where appropriate in terms of understanding the challenges and opportunities to science educators.

Simulations and games in science education

Science educators offer a way out of the dilemma between 'games and simulations' by distinguishing between idea and predictive simulations (Edmonds et al., 2005). The difference is straightforward: is the simulation designed to predict the future vs. is it designed to illustrate key relationships? Predictive simulations are most often used for planning, either in social policy, for example what is the fate of social security under current conditions? or the natural sciences, such as weather prediction, for example will it rain tomorrow? In contrast, educators, and many scientists, are generally looking for insights into a particular idea. Instructional designers make similar distinctions between high-fidelity and low-fidelity simulations and maintain that low-fidelity simulations are often most desirable for learning. High-fidelity simulations are typically computationally expensive and potentially confusing to newcomers.

Resilient Planet

Resilient Planet is a scientific role playing game developed by Filament Games for classroom use, but it is also a free download available via the National Geographic Website. One can easily imagine how it might be tied to a museum installation or issue of local importance.

In *Resilient Planet*, players are scientists investigating a decrease in monk seals in a marine reserve in Northwest Hawaii. They drive an underwater vehicle tracking, photographing and counting sharks. They also tag seals, pump sharks' stomachs to investigate their diets and place cameras on seals to 'observe the world as a seal' might.

Back at the lab, players use their data to construct arguments about scientific phenomena. Through series of arguments, they expand their notions of scientific phenomenon, argumentation and the nature of scientific inquiry.

As an example of the issues in predictive vs. idea simulations, *Resilient Planet* originally included a 'realistic' ecology of predators and prey in which the species reacted to the player and one another in realistic ways. After weeks of experimentation, the game designers deduced that they could create an ecosystem that functioned 'good enough', by stripping out the simulation and simply scripting events (White, 2006). Stripping out the simulated components enabled them to focus instead on the player experience.

As such, simulations used for teaching – idea simulations – have an entirely different set of 'success criteria'. Idea simulations are often valued for their elegance and explanatory power with a relatively few number of variables (see Carpenter et al., 2008). For example, the classic Lotka-Volterra equations, which are the basis for many predator prey models, show how a system with too many predators eventually results in a reduction in prey. When too many prey die then predators begin dying as well. The reduction in predators then creates, in turn, an overabundance of prey. Then, the prey dies off as it over-feeds and the predator population to rebound. These fluctuations continue, and Lotka-Volterra shows how such fluctuations result in spikes in both pred-ator and prey populations enabling ecologists to make sense of their observa-tions in the world.

Modelling and gaming social practices

When viewed as social practices, there are key differences in modelling, or model building, and gaming as modes of inquiry. Modelling involves the recursive process of observing phenomenon and building representations to illustrate those core ideas, also called abductive inquiry, see Peirce (1877/1986). Models, such as Lotka-Volterra, are constructed by scientists. Scientists engage in cycles of data collection, model building and model testing. In contrast, games are generally constructed by experts trying to communicate ideas to novices. Educational games seek to teach the player the model's rules and emergent properties through playing them (Gee, 2003; Squire, 2005). However, this mode of learning by which players learn is also abductive, in that they hold models about how the world works, and then are forced to amend those understandings as they encounter new experiences of them.

Although these two processes are distinct enough to keep separate, para-digms of game-based learning often deliberately try to blur them. Games, such as *GameStar Mechanic*, or game design curricula in which students design local games, seek to create series of tight, integrated loops of playing and designing games (Games, 2008; Mathews et al., 2009). This learning-through-gaming model that integrates gameplay and creation seeks to capitalize on the agency provided by game authoring packages, while also guiding the learner in a way most open-ended approaches do not. As such, it seeks to respond to recent critiques of constructivist and inquiry-based pedagogical approaches that note the difficulties educators have in immersing students in complex, open-ended tasks before they develop robust understandings in domains (Kirschner et al., 1996).

Research results on these more recursive play-design styles of games are still emerging and evidence is needed before we will know to what extent it addresses this dilemma. This said, games offer one model for teaching learners the requisite knowledge, skills and attitudes in a manner that prepares them for more open-ended tasks (Shaffer et al., 2005). The learning 'cycle' in games involves recursive experiences of developing goals, observing phenomena, hypothesizing how they might act within the system to achieve those goals, observing the results and then repeating iteratively (Aldrich, 2003; Ito, 2003; Salen et al., 2002; Squire, 2006). Studies of *Sims* and *Civilization* players have shown that as the players learn the rules of the system, they can use editing tools to change those underlying rules to explore ideas or match their play style (Squire, 2008; Hayes et al., forthcoming). Indeed, as they become literate with game creation tools, they can use them to create their own modifications or indeed their own games (Games, 2008; Hayes et al., forthcoming; Squire, 2007).

Structured informal learning environments

Informal science education contexts are different and unique, particularly for those most familiar with the more formalized, regulated nature of schooling, in that they are free to operate in widely diverse contexts. Whereas schools must respond to a variety of local and national political needs, pressures and concerns, informal science educators have significant freedom in how they pursue goals germane to institutional interests. In designing local games for learning with informal science education partners, Squire and colleagues (2007) found educational goals, ranging from instilling a sense of civic ownership over local lakes, to fostering environmental ethics. Common goals of science educators range from increasing the diversity in science to promoting national science literacy (Miller, 1998; NAS, 2009). There are many factors known to increase such interest in science, including curiosity in topics, such as dinosaurs to hobbies, such as radios, model airplanes, or video gaming, to experiences of natural places, such as a lake, to relationships with loved ones (Azevedo, 2006; Crowley et al., 2002; Feynman, 1985; Horwitz, 1996).

Building games that leverage such ideas and mechanics is a natural route for designers of games in informal settings to pursue.

Sorting out the needs of organizations that span from local ecology groups to national associations of scientists can be difficult, but the National Research Council's (2009) report Learning Science in Informal Environments makes a strong case for six key facets of informal science education (see Table 9.1, below). These six facets apply to all science education contexts but the report emphasizes the unique capacity informal science education has to: (1) increase interest in science, and (2) encourage affiliation with science as an enterprise, for example building identities in science. Of course, any media, from books to lectures, may address these facets in any number of ways. Moreover, given the history of educational media research (see Clark, 2003), researching games in conjunction with other media is a better approach than comparing them or examining them in isolation. The NRC (2009) report emphasizes the importance of media as a tool for informal science education used to achieve various goals and as a context for studying science. Scientists have reported that experience with diverse media, ranging from science-fiction novels to *Legos* to *Logo*, was instrumental in their decisions to pursue careers in science, and already there are reports of games driving students to computer science (Jenkins, 2004; Kafai et al., 2008).

Table 9.1 Facets of Informal Science Education and Ways Addressed in Resilient Planet

Facets of Informal Science Education	Ways Addressed in Resilient Planet
1. Experience excitement, interesting, and motivation to learn about natural and physical phenomena.	Resilient Planet leverages an intrinsically interesting aspects of science, the allure of underwater exploration.
2. Generate, understand and use concepts, explanations, arguments, models and facts related to science.	Players construct arguments about the causes of various phenomena, such as the monk seal population reduction or the health of the ecosystem.
3. Manipulate, test, explore, predict, question, observe and make sense of the natural and physical world.	Players use cameras and vehicles to observe phenomena, and then compare the data they gather with that predicted by models.
4. Reflect on science as a way of knowing; on scientific processes, concepts and institutions; and on their own learning.	The game includes multiple types of investigations enabling students to experience or compare different types of investigations.
5. Participate in scientific activities and practices using scientific tools and concepts.	Players are given access to authentic tools that they use to conduct procedures such as biodiversity surveys.
6. Affiliate with the enterprise of science, developing an identity as someone who knows about, uses and contributes to science.	In order to appeal to Students' interests, players assume roles as one of four different types of scientists.

The learning principles of games, as identified by Gee (2003) and others, suggest that games may be particularly well-suited for developing skills, knowledge, attitudes and identities (see also Shaffer, 2006). To illustrate, consider how *Resilient Planet* (produced by National Geographic and Filament Games) embodies these facets.

Games, such as *Resilient Planet*, suggest the great potential for using games in informal science education contexts. However, like many educational games it was designed to be used in schools. As such, it is only a few hours long, is relatively linear, and by design eliminated some features, such as the chance to freely explore the world, that one might want in an educational game. One might imagine how a game designed for informal science would include more open-ended gameplay, more collaborative problems and better ties outward from the game experience towards scientific communities of practice.

In fact, the research on informal science educational contexts emphasizes the unique different opportunities and constraints they face (NRC, 2009). Table 9.2, below, compares some of these key factors as they pertain to games. These comparisons along particular dimensions, such as how time is structured are not intended to put informal settings 'in response' to formal settings; informal settings may be be every bit as important as formal settings in people's attitudes towards and experience of science (Barron, 2006; Crowley et al., 1992; NRC, 2009). Also, there are evident differences in how formal educational institutions are structured; Milwaukee, WI, alone has over 40 charter schools with a smörgasbord of constraints. Although they cannot rely on compulsory attendance laws to require participation, informal science educators generally have more freedom in the topics they pursue, how they pursue them and in the extent to which they need to serve all audiences. As a result, informal science educational institutions feature a diversity of programmes, educational approaches and learning outcomes.

Table 9.2 Comparison of Attributes of Informal and Formal Educational Settings

	Informal Settings	Formal Settings
Time Structure	Flexible	Rigid
Participation	Voluntary	Compulsory
Educational Goals	Emergent	Largely Defined
Age Grouping	Flexible	Largely Age Divided
Degree of Authenticity	Potentially High	Generally low
Uniformity of Outcomes	Little	High
Disciplinary Boundaries	Flexible	Fixed

As an example of these potential opportunities and pitfalls, DeVane and Colleagues (2009a) describe their attempts to build systemic ecological-economic thinking among *Civilization* game players in an after-school gaming club. This curriculum aimed to tie together ecological, economic and political concerns around a gaming series based on global sustainability (Brown, 1992; Diamond, 2005; Durga, forthcoming). Such a curriculum may be difficult to implement in schools that teach biology but not ecology and that do not link either biology or ecology to economics on political science. DeVane and colleagues adapted *Civilization* to consider just these issues, particularly food shortages, agricultural policy, trade relations and environmental concerns, reporting that participants developed a type of systemic thinking across geo-political systems (see Durga, in press). Thus, pursuing this kind of educational goal may be much more feasible in informal settings.

At the same time, as a voluntary after-school option, participants chose it over playing basketball, cooking or scouts. Moreover, many students resisted taking pre- or post-tests, particularly if they 'smelled like school', making assessment difficult – a phenomenon also reported elsewhere in the literature (see Hayes et al., 2009; Steinkuehler et al., forthcoming). As a result, informal educators are much more concerned with building and sustaining student interest than most formal educators (NRC, 2009). In fact, informal science educators have the unique opportunity to pursue goals difficult in formalized settings.

Informal settings also enable opportunities for students to develop highly individualized interests and pursuits. Researchers investigating analogous programmes in informal information technology settings find students developing deep interest and expertise in areas ranging from computer programming to historical modelling (Bruckman et al., 2002; Resnick et al., 1998; Squire, 2008). These communities – like games culture in general – are built on a valuing of expertise (Squire, 2008b). One's background or credentials matter less than one's ability to meet and at times push the boundaries of community norms. Figure 9.1 depicts the trajectory that gameplayers undergo when becoming expert designers in Apolyton University, an online 'college' of *Civilization* players. Those programmes that involve lengthy participation (upwards of 100 hours) report players developing personalized and idiosyncratic skills that arise from an intersection among the participants' interests, the affordances of the game and the pathways made available within the game-playing community (Bruckman et al., 2002; DeVane et al., 2009b; Resnick et al., 1998).

Even in its most 'structured' settings, the qualities of informal science education, such as participant-driven learning goals, divergent learning outcomes,

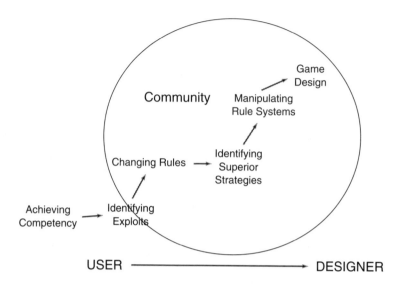

Figure 9.1 Trajectories of experience from user to designer among gamers

flexible participation models and emphasis on developing interest, frequently run counter to the assumptions of many modern statistical methods, such as uniformity of learning outcomes, treatment fidelity, pre-specification of learning objectives and isolation of variables. As a result, educators working in informal settings have frequently preferred case studies or other methods that enable them to gain longitudinal data, understand the role of the participant in defining the learning experience and examine how participants' identities are shaped beyond the learning experience. Certainly, experiments are still possible in such environments, but the importance of user choice in activities still creates challenges as it is, for example, difficult to administer a uniform task to multiple participants and expect meaningful results. One immediate direction researchers may pursue to understand the patterns of behaviour, across broader numbers of participants, is through methods, such as non-parametric statistics. However, the underlying logical problems of 'user-defined learning goals' or uniformity of treatment still needs to be addressed.

'Unstructured' informal learning environments

In their ethnography of youth media producers, Ito and colleagues (2008) describe a similar process of 'hanging out', 'messing around' and 'geeking out'.

This trajectory enables participants to enter media production cultures in non-threatening ways and provides multiple pathways towards developing expertise. Currently, educators are exploring potentials for designing informal learning spaces based on these principles, literally mapping out informal learning centres so that spaces, such as the downtown library in Chicago are designed to promote these three activities, for example hanging out, messing around, geeking out and the interchanges between them. This vision matches well with that of Squire (2006) and others, but as of yet, few educators have designed games for science built on this model of scientific literacy.

However, design-based researchers have begun to map out how to mesh forms of scientific thinking with gameplay, avoiding many of previous problems with science games that involved game-play mechanics non-congruent, or even counter to the ways of thinking encouraged in science (Klopfer, 2008; Schaller, 2009; Squire et al., 2007). Because informal science educators must compete with all the other demands on youth like athletics, video games and television, they need to have sophisticated models of what constitutes academically engaging gameplay. Design, which is at times given a backseat to other forms of inquiry within educational research, is of utmost importance in a context in which a poorly designed artefact fails to attract any research subjects. With a new generation of educational games now released on the market, for example *Fold.it, Resilient Planet, WolfQuest*, opportunities exist for educators to study these designs and effects on players more formally.

Some of the most compelling research on the potential of games to support deep scientific thinking occurs completely outside the 'designs' of educators. For example, Steinkuehler and Duncan (2008) examined participation in *World of Warcraft* (WoW) forums to examine what kinds of thinking take place in that context. Such forums are of particular interest to educators as they are where participants try to make sense of the game as a model, indeed games like *World of Warcraft* are large simulated models that players puzzle through. Steinkuehler and Duncan (2008) find that contrary to some expectations, the overwhelming activity in these forums was social knowledge construction (86 per cent). This knowledge construction involved citing evidence, gathering evidence and building original mathematical models to argue ideas. These models can be quite complex, involving several variables, coefficients and modifiers.

The example of *World of Warcraft* suggests the potential for games to support large, multi-aged and diverse bodies of learners in pursuing complex pursuits. Although not every *World of Warcraft* forum participant necessarily 'builds their own model' in an attempt to reverse engineer the game world, *World of Warcraft* forums function to model a type of discourse congruent with those of scientific argumentation. Steinkuehler and Duncan remind us that this sort of 'reverse engineering' is a form of scientific inquiry, for example abductive reasoning, see Peirce, (1877/1936). However, because game worlds are intentionally programmed by designers and operate according to built-in mathematical rules, there is a potential pitfall in that its rules are inherent simplifications of reality. At the same time, the practice of knowing by modelling and then judging what works is similar in games and in many sciences.

Further, this line of research reminds educators of the importance of looking beyond learning from any particular game to the study how learning occurs through gaming. Effective models of educational gaming may be created by designing compelling, multi-layered challenges and designing spaces for coordination and argumentation; see also *I Love Bees*, a game about distributed intelligence (McGonigal, 2007), such spaces recruit players from multiple ability levels and diverse backgrounds, creating numerous opportunities for formal and informal apprenticeship.

Learning findings in games- and simulations-based informal learning environments

These examples show some of the ways that scientific thinking is naturally supported by games and suggest how games may be particularly well-suited for informal learning environments. Scholars of different paradigms of education have begun to provide explanations for the learning potential of games and simulations in informal learning environments. These studies have considered participatory simulations, epistemic games, role playing games for citizenship, targeted games and investigative role playing games in multiplayer virtual environments (Barab et al., 2005; Colella, 2000; Nelsonet al., 2007; Games-to-Teach Team, 2003; Klopfer, 2008; Klopfer, Yoon et al., 2005; Shaffer, 2006; Squire, 2006; Squire, 2007). These explanations tend to emphasize the interactive nature of games, particularly how they function as worlds for players to inhabit and explore rather than traditional stories to be interpreted. Design research on educational games emphasizes that games operate by an experiential logic; players are immersed in problem-solving situations in which they adopt particular perspectives within simulated systems. Although there is relatively little evidence about the efficacy of games of this type, most notably *Immune Attack!, WolfQuest, Whyville* and *Resilient Planet*, emerging research findings suggest there is great potential for the use of games for learning in informal science education. Of particular interest in this regard are research findings about products, such as *Whyville* or 'augmented reality games for learning', which are used at homes and in museums. Here we present findings from this emerging research.

Learning gains

Learning gains in science have been identified using epistemic games in structured, workshop-like settings. Across a number of studies, David Shaffer's group has found positive gains in knowledge, skills and attitudes through participating in their epistemic games in intensive summer programmes as measured by traditional tests, clinical interviews and concept maps (see Shaffer, 2006). In epistemic games, players assume the roles of engineers, designers, planners or journalists in an intensive multi-week summer programme. Although not computer or video games *per se*, epistemic games are built around role playing, and frequently involve digital authoring tools, such as *Soda Constructor*. Most recently, Shaffer and colleagues have begun doing network analysis of participants' actions in order to capture knowledge *in situ*, a potentially useful method for science educators interested in teaching processes, such as investigation, argumentation and design (see Rupp et al., in press).

Conceptual change and changes in scientific inquiry

Eric Klopfer (2008) and colleagues (see Colella, 1998) have used participatory simulations to teach about biology, virology, immunology, epidemiology and scientific methods in a variety of formal and informal secondary school contexts. In participatory simulation games, players are participants in a system in which they might pass virtual diseases or bear offspring with particular genetic characteristics. The games are tuned to include latency in diseases or recessive genes so that players must conduct their own investigations to determine the causes of the outbreaks. Using concept maps, interviews and survey instruments Klopfer has shown conceptual changes in how participants think about diseases and how they prioritize steps in conducting investigations.

Somewhat similarly, but on a bigger scale, in 2005, several hundred thousand of the 1.2 million users of *Whyville* contracted *Why-Pox*. *Whyville* is centred around science-themed mini-games and involves a virtual community consisting mostly of 8–16 year-olds. *Why-Pox* was a virtual epidemic launched in the community to study how the community responded to a virtual epidemic, a little like Klopfer's *participatory* diseases but spread out over hundreds of thousands of people. *Why-Pox* rampaged through the community, affecting Whyvillians with a small rash and bumps. Foley and La Torre (2004) found that this was quite engaging for many participants, with at least 1,000 participants entering the *Whyville* 'Center for Disease Control' website to learn about diseases and participate in online discussions, all in a voluntary context.

In their study of *Whyville* in a classroom scenario, Yasmin Kafai and colleagues (in press) studied how students experienced the events. They studied conceptual change among *Whyville* players and found positive changes in going from pre-biological towards biological causal models for understanding the events. Kafai also found changes in type 2 vocabulary, that is, vocabulary, such as 'contamination', that is not 'everyday' but also not entirely scientific, such as 'E.coli'. Type 2 vocabulary has been shown to be critically important for struggling readers' success in school (see Beck et al., 2002).

Interestingly, Squire (2009) also reported positive changes in type 2 scientific vocabulary among augmented reality game players. As players read and interpret documents they develop understandings of type 2 vocabulary. Through the course of the unit, they regularly use these terms in discussions, reports and presentations as they role play as scientists. Students also gain proto-experiences of 'authentic', as opposed to contrived, investigative experiences, something critically important to science educators for communicating dispositions aligned with those of science. Although this study reported findings in classroom settings, this general pedagogical model of location-based games also has worked in museum and after-school settings (Klopfer, 2008; Squire et al., 2007).

Event-driven learning

In reflecting upon the *Why-Pox* outbreak, Kafai and colleagues (in press) show how shared virtual experiences of such events can create shared experience, which can be the basis of shared communal membership, engagement and learning, such as they are in *World of Warcraft*, which experienced a similar outbreak, which *Why-Pox* was modelled after. Although other informal science structures, such as robotics or programming competitions are also event driven, *Why-Pox* was unique in that it mobilized hundreds of thousands of youth in authentic inquiry in real-time to identify the cause of and to minimize the impact of a disease that was personally meaningful to them. This is the type of event and learning process that educators might want to exploit further. In informal learning environments where timescales are flexible, participation is voluntary and multiple forms of participation can be used to integrate different ability levels, from long-term sustained participation to develop deep expertise to short-term experiences to raise interest, event-driven learning appears particularly useful.

Distributed mentorship

Across these studies, even in studies that are entirely outside of school, researchers examined the impact of instructors and noted the importance of mentorship in learning. Nulty and Shaffer compared students with and without mentoring, and found in post-tests that students receiving mentorship performed much better than those not being mentored. Similarly, Kafai noted the importance of mentors in their study.

Many informal science educators hope that virtual worlds, such as *Whyville*, *River City* or *Quest Atlantis* may distribute teaching across the community, as in *World of Warcraft*, so that there are no 'teachers' *per se*, but rather, a network of peers and mentors who coach one another. The *Why-Pox* example suggests that such mentoring can happen in spontaneously forming organizations and at least in this instantiation, mentors were critical for producing conceptual change. Knowing that certain participant structures, such as 'grouping mechanics', foster the collaborative problem-solving known to be critical to learning in Massively Mulitiplayer Games, one can imagine their value in informal science education environments. However, to date those design features have not been sufficiently explored (Steinkuehler, 2005).

Role/Expertise differentiation

A key opportunity for informal science education is to create contexts for collective participation without identical learning outcomes for each student (Collins et al., 2009). Informal science learning contexts can support the co-construction of learning goals between learners and designers. Learners can, and should, have significant opportunities to pursue interests, develop unique identities as consumers and producers of information and media and develop unique identities as 'professionals' in domains.

Research suggests that role playing games are a good tool and context for creating such learning experiences. Shaffer's work, for example, emphasizes the active nature of role play in such settings, as people integrate knowledge, skills, attitudes and identity under an epistemic frame. As players confront these increasingly challenging situations, they embark upon trajectories from novices to experts. Notably, there is frequently no one model 'expert' within a given game community but multiple ways that one can perform 'being an expert' (Steinkuehler, 2006). In their most advanced forms, games frequently include authorship opportunities for players with learning trajectories often leading towards legitimate participation in social relations beyond the game context.

Science as science civic literacy

Today's global future requires an ever better public understanding of science. Today's key social and scientific issues, such as climate change, gene therapy, pandemics or personalized medicine, require an informed populace capable of understanding scientific advancements as they develop, as opposed to learning 'all they need to know' in school. Yet, scientific civic literacy rates in the USA struggle to reach 20 per cent (Miller et al., 1997). Miller (1998) articulated a framework of 'scientific civic literacy' that may be particularly useful for informal science educators seeking to design games around key problems, like pandemics, that mobilize a citizenry towards action. Scientific civic literacy, according to Miller, requires:

1. An understanding of critical scientific concepts and constructs, such as ecosystems, the molecule, or DNA;
2. An understanding of the nature and process of scientific inquiry;
3. A pattern of regular information consumption; and
4. A disposition towards taking action to make change in one's lifestyle as necessary (adapted from Miller, 1998).

Many of the games described herein address these same goals. However, as a field, perhaps we have been too occupied with the notion of creating 'professional scientists' rather than developing scientific civic literacy in our populace. Offering models of citizens who have 'a disposition toward taking action to make change in one's lifestyle' may be more productive and beneficial than promoting scientific careers alone.

There is reason to hope that media can address this challenge. In a recent survey of scientific civic literacy, the consumption of informal science materials, such as science magazines, television programmes, books, science websites or museums, trailed only the completion of an undergraduate science course as a predictor of scientific civic literacy (Miller, 2001/2002). The participatory nature of games, which are hypothesized to create dispositions towards taking action in the world (see Thomas et al., 2007) may be particularly well suited to fostering this disposition.

Participants' goal-driven learning: whose goals?

A key opportunity for games-based researchers, and challenge for educators most familiar with formal educational situations, is that informal learning environments, like games, ultimately are fueled by interest or passion-driven learning. Informal science educators, like game designers, have the task of designing enticing learning experiences in which learners are compelled to learn more. The key difference may be best summarized by Klopfer's (2008) description of scientific mystery games at museums in which parents and student pairs paid money to attend game-based learning workshops. How many students would pay to go to biology class? A trick for game designers is to create learning experiences that leverage learners' interests and goals, address the needs of the umbrella institution and respond to the concerns of science educators more broadly. Thus, whereas the development of student interests and identities is not a primary goal for schools, this may be crucial to informal science education.

Next steps: where to go from here

In 1956, Bell Labs Science films released *Our Mr. Sun*, an educational film about the importance of the Sun for life on Earth. Written and directed by Frank Capra, this was the first of nine films that paired Bell Labs scientists with Hollywood talent, including the likes of Mr. Capra, Walt Disney, Jack Warner, Mel Blanc and Sterling Holloway. The films, designed for primetime television, were an unqualified success. They were shown on television, then used in classrooms for over thirty years and now are sold on DVD for home and school use. The producers behind the series dubbed it, 'Operation Frontal

Lobe' to describe the power of media for supporting public understanding in science both in and out of schools (Jenkins et al., 2003). Created in response to Sputnik, this series was but one example of many academic-industry partnerships designed to bolster science education in the USA.

If science educators hope to play a leading role in the development of games-based learning, rather than leaving it to the commercial enterprises then new models of educational media development are needed. We need models that take seriously the challenge of identifying intrinsically interesting aspects of games, the ways that games motivate learners and how these can be integrated with science education goals. Creating compelling media of this sort demands partnerships among education, academics and the media, in order to leverage the resources such games require. These assets are not simply financial, professional knowledge about production processes and access to market research and distribution channels are needed. As Ito describes, the 1990s were ultimately marked by many educators being left out the conversation about educational games mostly because they ended up researching internet-based learning.

Given the fast-paced nature of scientific discoveries, a goal for game designers in informal science education may be to not look at 'standardized' curricula that has gone through the lengthy state adoption processes, but rather, to take fresh approaches to the challenge of ensuring that our populace is capable of making good decisions about our futures, all the while taking lessons from curricula designed for formal settings. Free of many of the constraints experienced by school curriculum designers, informal educators have the opportunity to partner with scientists to create materials of direct and immediate interest to broad publics, effectively 'bypassing' the unnecessary steps of federal, state and schools bureaucracies. One can imagine learning systems like *Whyville* aimed at educating a populace about contemporary issues in science, including the nature of science as an enterprise rather than simply 're-teaching' school-based content in new ways. As recent political discussions suggest, the future of our democracy could depend on it.

References

Aldrich, C. (2003). *Simulations and the Future of Learning: An Innovative (and Perhaps Revolutionary) Approach to E-Learning*. US: Pfeiffer & Co.

Azevedo, F. S. (2005, Fall). Serious Play: A Comparative Study of Learning and Engagement in Hobby Practices. PhD Dissertation in Education. University of California: Berkeley.

Bagley, E. and Shaffer, D. W. (2009). When people get in the way: promoting civic thinking through epistemic gameplay. *International Journal of Gaming and Computer-mediated Simulations,* No. 1, pp. 36–52.

Barab, S., Dodge, T., Thomas, M. K., Jackson, C. and Tuzun, H. (2007). Our designs and the social agendas they carry. *Journal of the Learning Sciences,* Vol. 16, No. 2, pp 263–305.

Barab, S., Thomas, M., Dodge, T., Carteaux, R. and Tuzun, H. (2005). Making learning fun: Quest Atlantis, a game without guns. *Educational Technology Research and Development,* Vol. 53, No. 1, pp. 86–107.

Barab, S. A., Sadler, T. D., Heiselt, C., Hickey, D. and Zuiker, S. (2007). Relating narrative, inquiry, and inscriptions: supporting consequential play. *Journal of Science Education and Technology,* Vol. 16, No. 1, pp. 59–82.

Barab, S., Zuiker, S., Warren, S., Hickey, D., Ingram-Goble, A., Kwon, E. J. and Kouper, I. (2007). Situationally embodied curriculum: relating formalisms and contexts. *Science Education,* Vol. 91, No. 5, pp. 750–82.

Barron, B., Martin, C. K. and Roberts, E. (2006). Sparking self-sustained learning: report on a design experiment to build technological fluency and bridge divides. *International Journal of Technology Design in Education,* Vol. 17, pp. 75–105.

Bridge Builder (2000). Chronic Logic. Microsoft Windows, Mac OS X, Linux. http://www.chroniclogic. com. Last accessed 9 April 2010.

Brown, K. and Cole, M. (2002). Cultural historical activity theory and the expansion of opportunities for learning after school. In G. Wells and G. Claxton, eds. *Learning for Life in the 21st Century: Sociocultural Perspectives on the Future of Education,* pp. 225–38. Oxford, England: Blackwell.

Brown, L. R. (1992). The new world order. In A. Tripathi and V. Bhatt, eds. *Changing Environmental Ideologies.* New Delhi: Ashish Publishing House, pp. 19–35.

Bruckman, A., Jensen, C. and DeBonte, A. (2002). Gender and programming achievement in a CSCL environment. Computer Support for Collaborative Learning: Foundations for A CSCL Community (CSCL 2002 Proceedings), pp. 119–27. Carpenter, S. R., Armbrust, V., Arzberger, P., Chapin, T., Elser, J., Hackett, E. and Ives, T. (2008). The Future of Synthesis in Ecology and Environmental Sciences. Madison, WI. University of Wisconsin, Madison. Retrieved from limnology.wisc.edu/ media/Report_Synthesis_v10_FINAL.pdf Last accessed: 29 July 2010.

Chinn, C. A. and Malhotra, B. A. (2002). Epistemologically authentic inquiry in schools: a theoretical framework for evaluating inquiry tasks. *Science Education,* Vol. 86, No. 2, pp. 175–218.

Cole, M. The Distributed Literacy Consortium (2006). *The Fifth Dimension: An After-School Program Built on Diversity.* New York: Russell Sage Foundation.

Colella, V. (2000). Participatory simulations: building collaborative understanding through immersive dynamic modeling. *The Journal of Learning Sciences,* Vol. 9, No. 4, pp. 471–500.

Collins, A. and Halverson, R. (2009). *Rethinking Education in the Age of Technology: The Digital Revolution and the School.* New York: Teachers College Press.

Crowley, K. and Jacobs, M. (2002). Building islands of expertise in everyday family activity. In G. Leinhardt, K. Crowley and K. Knutson, eds. Learning conversations in museums, pp. 333–56. Mahwah, NJ: Lawrence Erlbaum Associates.

Diamond, J. (2005). *Guns, Germs and Steel: The Fates of Human Societies*. New York: Norton.

Edmonds, B. and Hales, D. (2005). Computational simulation as theoretical experiment. *The Journal of Mathematical Sociology*, 29(3): 209–232.

Evolution. (1999). Discovery Channel Networks.

Evolution. (1999). Discovery Channel Networks. CD-ROM, Windows 95.

Evolution. (2007). Free World Group. Adobe Flash. http://www.freeworldgroup.com. Last accessed 9 April 2010.

Not the same game as the one for Discovery Channel:

Evolution. (2007). Free World Group. Adobe Flash. http://www.freeworldgroup.com. Last accessed 9 April 2010.

Feynman, R. P., Leighton, R. and Hutchings, E. (1997). 'Surely you're joking, Mr. Feynman!': adventures of a curious character. New York: WW Norton & Company.

Fold.It. (2008). University of Washington Departments of Computer Science & Engineering and Biochemistry. Microsoft Windows, Mac OS X, Linux. http://fold.it/portal/. Last accessed 9 April 2010.

Foley, B. J. and La Torre, D. (2004). Who has Why-Pox: a case study of informal science education on the Net. In *Proceedings of the 6th International Conference on Learning Sciences*, pp. 598–598. Santa Monica, California: International Society of the Learning Sciences.

Games, I. (2008). Three Dialogs: a framework for the analysis and assessment of twenty-first-century literacy practices, and its use in the context of game design within Gamestar Mechanic. *E-Learning*, Vol. 5, No. 4, pp. 396–417.

Games-to-Teach Team. (n.d.). Design principles of next-generation digital gaming for education. *Educational Technology*, Vol. 43, No. 5, pp. 17–33.

Games-to-Teach Research Team (2003). Design principles of next-generation digital gaming for education. *Educational Technology*, Vol. 43, No. 5, pp. 17–33.

Gee, J. P. (2003). *What Video Games Have to Teach Us About Learning and Literacy* (1st ed.). New York: Palgrave Macmillan.

Gee, J. P. (2007). *Good Video Games and Good Learning: Collected Essays on Video Games, Learning and Literacy* (New Literacies and Digital Epistemologies). New York: Peter Lang Pub Inc.

Hayes, E. and Gee, J. P. (2009). Not just a dollhouse: what The Sims 2 can teach us about women's IT learning. *E-Learning*, Vol. 17, No. 1, pp. 60–69.

Hayes, E. and Gee, J. P. (forthcoming). The Sims challenges & game design literacies. Invited article for a special E-learning issue on Gaming Literacies.

Holland, W., Jenkins, H. and Squire, K. (2003). Theory by design. In M. J. P. Wolf and B. Perron, eds. *Video Game Theory Reader*, pp. 25–46. London: Routledge.

Horwitz, W. A. (1996). Developmental origins of environmental ethics: the life experiences of activists. *Ethics & Behavior*, Vol. 6, No. 1, pp. 29–53.

Immune Attack (2008). Federation of American Scientists. Microsoft Windows. http://fas.org/immuneattack/ . Last accessed 9 April 2010.

Ito, M. (2003). Engineering Play. PhD Dissertation. Palo Alto, CA: Stanford University.

Ito, M., Horst, H., Bittanti, M., Boyd, D., Herr-Stephenson, B., Lange, P. G. and Pascoe, C. (2008). *Living and Learning with New Media: Summary of Findings from the Digital Youth Project.* Chicago, IL: The John D. and Catherine T. MacArthur Foundation.

Jenkins, H., Klopfer, E., Squire, K. and Tan, P. (2003). Entering the education arcade. *Computers in Entertainment,* Vol. 1, No. 1, pp. 1–11.

Kafai, Y. B., Feldon, D., Fields, D., Giang, M. and Quintero, M. (2007). Life in the times of Whypox: a virtual epidemic as a community event. In *Communities and Technologies: Proceedings of the Third Communities and Technologies Conference,* Michigan State University, pp. 171–90. New York: Springer.

Kafai, Y., Sun, J., Heeter, C. and Denner, J., eds. (2008). *Beyond Barbie and Mortal Kombat: New Perspectives on Gender and Gaming,* Boston, MA: The MIT Press.

Kirschner, P. A., Sweller, J. and Clark, R. E. (2006). Why minimal guidance during instruction does not work: an analysis of the failure of constructivist, discovery, problem-based, experiential, and inquiry-based teaching. *Educational Psychologist,* Vol. 41, No. 2, pp. 5–86.

Klopfer, E. (2007). Blurring Lines with Mobile Learning Games. *Educational Technology Magazine: The Magazine for Managers of Change in Education,* Vol. 47, No. 3, p. 4.

Klopfer, E. (2008). *Augmented Learning: Research and Design of Mobile Educational Games.* Massachusetts & London: The MIT Press.

Klopfer, E. and Osterweil, S. (in press). The boom and bust and boom of educational Games. *Transactions in Edutainment.* Berlin: Springer.

Klopfer, E., Roque, R., Huang, W., Wendel, D. and Scheintaub, H. (2009). The Simulation Cycle: combining games, simulations, engineering and science using StarLogo TNG. *E-Learning and Digital Media,* Vol. 6, No. 1, pp. 71–96.

Klopfer, E.Y., Yoon, S. and Perry, J. (2005). Using palm technology in Participatory Simulations of complex systems: a new take on ubiquitous and accessible mobile computing. *Journal of Science Education and Technology,* Vol. 14, No. 3, pp. 285–98.

Lemke, J. L. (1990). *Talking Science: Language, Learning, and Values.* Norwood, NJ: Ablex Publishing Corporation.

LOGO, (n.d.). Epistemology and Learning Group, MIT Media Lab.

LOGO, (1967). Feurzeig, W. and Papert, S. MIT Artificial Intelligence Laboratory.

Mad City Mystery. (2005). Local Games Lab. Mobile Devices. http://lgl.gameslearningsociety.org/games.php. Last accessed 9 April 2010.

McGonigal, J. (2007). Why I love bees: a case study in collective intelligence gaming. *The John D. and Catherine T. MacArthur Foundation Series on Digital Media and Learning,* 199–227. Retrieved 04–29–2010 from http://www.mitpressjournals.org/doi/abs/10.1162/dmal.9780262693646.199

MeCHeM. HAGames. Adobe Flash. http://www.hagames.com. Last accessed 9 April 2010.

Miller, J. D. (1998). The measurement of civic scientific literacy. *Public Understanding of Science,* Vol. 7, No. 3, pp. 203–23.

Miller, J. D. (2001). The acquisition and retention of scientific information by American adults. In J. Falk, ed. *Free-choice Science Education: How We Learn Science Outside of School.* New York: Teachers College Press, pp. 93–114.

Miller, J. D. (2002). Civic scientific literacy: a necessity in the 21st century. *FAS Public Interest Reports*, Vol. 55, No. 1, pp. 3–6.

Miller, J. D. and Falk, J. (2001). The acquisition and retention of scientific information by American adults. In *Free-Choice Science Education: How We Learn Science Outside of School*, pp. 93–114. New York: Teachers College Press.

Miller, J., Pardo, R. and Niwa, F. (1997). *Public Perceptions of Science and Technology: A Comparative Study of the European Union, the United States, Japan, and Canada*. Madrid: BBV Foundation Press.

MindRover: The Europa Project. (1999). CogniToy. Microsoft Windows, Linux.

Monopoly. (n.d.). Parker Brothers and Waddingtons.

Nash, P. and Shaffer, D. (2008). Player-mentor interactions in an epistemic game: a preliminary analysis. Presented at the International Conference of the Learning Sciences (ICLS). Utrecht, Netherlands.

National Research Council. (2002), *Scientific Research in Education*. In R. Shavelson and L. Towne, eds. Washington DC: National Academy Press.

Nelson, B., Ketelhut, D., Clarke, J., Dieterle, E., Dede, C. and Erlandson, B. (2007). Robust design strategies for scaling educational innovations. In B. Shelton and D. Wiley, eds. *The Design and Use of Simulation Computer Games in Education*, pp. 209–231. Rotterdam, The Netherlands: Sense Publishers.

Nobel Prize (2001–2009). Nobel Web AB. Adobe Flash. http://nobelprize.org/educational_games/. Last accessed 9 April 2010.

Nulty, A. and Shaffer, D. (2008). Digital Zoo: the effects of mentoring on young engineers. Presented at the International Conference of the Learning Sciences (ICLS), Utrecht, Netherlands.

Operation: Resilient Planet. (2008). National Geographic & Filament Games. Microsoft Windows, Mac OS X. http://www.jason.org. Last accessed 9 April 2010.

Papert, S. (1987). Information technology and education: computer criticism vs. technocentric thinking. *Educational Researcher*, Vol. 16, No. 1, p. 22.

Papert, S. (1998). Does easy do it? Children, games, and learning. *Game Developer*, Vol. 5, No. 6, p. 88.

Peirce, C. (n.d.). The Fixation of belief. In N. Houser and C. Kloesel, eds. *The Essential Peirce* (Vol. 1). Bloomington, IN: Indiana University Press.

Pontifex I and II. (2004–2008), Chronic Logic.

Prensky, M. (2001). Digital Game-based Learning. New York: McGraw-Hill.

Quest Atlantis (2001). Indiana University Center for Research on Learning and Technology. Microsoft Windows, Mac OS X. http://atlantis.crlt.indiana.edu/. Last accessed 9 April 2010.

Resnick, M., Rusk, N. and Cooke, S. (1998). The Computer Clubhouse: Technological fluency in the inner city. In D. Schön, B. Sanyal and W. Mitchell, eds. *High Technology and Low-Income Communities*. Cambridge, MA: MIT Press.

Rosenbaum, E., Klopfer, E. and Perry, J. (2007). On location learning: authentic applied science with networked augmented realities. *Journal of Science Education and Technology*, Vol. 16, No. 1, pp. 31–45.

Rupp, A. A., Gushta, M., Mislevy, R. J. and Shaffer, D. W. (2010). Evidence-centered design of epistemic games: measurement principles for complex learning environments. *Journal of Technology, Learning, and Assessment*, Vol. 8, No. 4. Retrieved 04–29–2010 from http://www.jtla.org.

Preferred citation (by journal):

If you want pages it's actually the whole issue, so pp. 1–47.

Salen, K. and Zimmerman, E. (2003). *Rules of Play: Game Design Fundamentals.* Massachusetts: MIT Press.

Sawyer, B. (2006, March). Games and more games. Military simulation and training magazine, *International Defense and Training Journal,* Vol. 3, pp. 20–22.

Schaller, D. T., Goldman, K. H., Spickelmier, G., Allison-Bunnell, S. and Koepfler, J. (2009). Learning in the wild: what wolfquest taught developers and game players. In *Museums and the Web: Proceedings.* Toronto: Archives & Museum Informatics.

Schaller, D. T., Goldman, K. H., Spickelmier, G., Allison-Bunnell, S. and Koepfler, J. (2009). Learning in the wild: what Wolfquest taught developers and game players. J. Trant and D. Bearman, eds. *Museums and the Web 2009: Proceedings. Toronto: Archives & Museum Informatics.*

Shaffer, D. W. (2006). *How Computer Games Help Children Learn.* New York: Palgrave Macmillan.

Shaffer, D. W. and Gee, J. P. (2005). Before Every Child Is Left Behind: How Epistemic Games Can Solve the Coming Crisis in Education. WCER Working Paper No. 2005–7. Wisconsin Center for Education Research, Madison, WI: 18.

SharkRunners (2007). Discovery Channel. Adobe Flash. http://dsc.discovery.com/convergence/ sharkweek/shark-runners/shark-runners.html. Last accessed 9 April 2010.

SodaConstructor (2000). Soda Creative Ltd. Java. http://sodaplay.com/creators/soda/items/constructor. Last accessed 9 April 2010.

Squire, K. (2006). From content to context: video games as designed experiences. *Educational Researcher,* Vol. 35, No. 8, pp. 19–29.

Squire, K. and Jenkins, H. (2004). Harnessing the power of games in education. *Insight,* Vol. 3, No.1, pp. 5–33.

Squire, K. D. and Jan, M. (2007). Mad City Mystery: developing scientific argumentation skills with a place-based augmented reality game on handheld computers. *Journal of Science Education and Technology,* Vol. 16, No. 1, pp. 5–29.

Squire, K. D., DeVane, B. and Durga, S. (2008). Designing centers of expertise for academic learning through video games. *Theory into Practice,* Vol. 47, No. 3, pp. 240–51.

StarLogo TNG. July (2008). MIT Scheller Teacher Education Program. Microsoft Windows, Mac OS X. http://education.mit.edu/drupal/starlogo-tng. Last accessed 9 April 2010.

Steinkuehler, C. Virtual worlds, learning, & the new pop cosmopolitanism. *Teachers College Record,* Date Published: 17 November 2006. http://www.tcrecord.org ID Number: 12843, Date Accessed: 4/29/2010.

Steinkuehler, C. and Duncan, S. (2008). Scientific habits of mind in virtual worlds. *Journal of Science Education and Technology,* Vol. 17, No. 6, pp. 530–43.

Steinkuehler, C. and King, B. (n.d.). Digital literacies for the disengaged: creating after school contexts to support boys' game-based literacy skills. Manuscript in preparation for 'On the Horizon', University of Wisconsin – Madison.

Steinkuehler, C. A. (2006). Massively multiplayer online video gaming as participation in a discourse. Mind, Culture, and Activity, Vol. 13, No. 1, pp. 38–52. Supercharged! The Education Arcade. http:// educationarcade.org/supercharged. Last accessed 9 April 2010.

The River City Project (2002). Harvard University, Arizona State University, Active Worlds. Microsoft Windows. http://muve.gse.harvard.edu/rivercityproject/. Last accessed 9 April 2010.

Thomas, D. and Brown, J. S. (2007). The play of imagination: extending the literary mind. *Games and Culture*, 2(2): 149.

White, D. (2006). Resilient Planet. Master's Thesis. Madison, WI: University of Wisconsin – Madison.

Whyville (1999). Numedon. Java. http://whyville.net/smmk/nice. Last accessed 9 April 2010.

Wolfquest (2008). Eduweb. Microsoft Windows, Mac OS X. http://www.wolfquest.org/. Last accessed 9 April 2010.

World of Warcraft (2004). Blizzard Entertainment. Microsoft Windows, Mac OS X. http://www.worldofwarcraft.com/index.xml. Last accessed 9 April 2010.

Yoon, S. and Klopfer, E. (2006). Feedback (F) Fueling Adaptation (A) Network Growth (N) and Self-Organization (S): A Complex Systems Design and Evaluation Approach to Professional Development. *Journal of Science Education and Technology,*Vol. 15, Nos 5–6, pp. 353–66.

From Master to Games-master: Managing Disequilibrium and Scaffolding in Simulation-based Learning

10

Karen Barton and Patricia McKellar

Chapter Outline

Learning the law through computers, games and simulations

The use of paper-based simulations and games has been evident for many years in legal education. The most common forms of simulations are frequently of a fairly short duration, such as tutorial-based activities, mostly involving role play and revolving around mock trials, debates, interviews or similar types of activities. Arguably the best-known form of simulation is the use of the 'moot court', not to be confused with mock trials, which has been employed extensively for many years at all levels of legal education throughout the world, and has been widely reported as an effective means of teaching substantive law as well as advocacy, legal argument and other essential legal skills. There are many examples of the use of moot courts as a pedagogic method within legal education and it has almost grown into a sub-discipline in its own right (Rachid and Knerr, 2000; Knerr and Sommerman, 2000; Ringel, 2004). In a number of other disciplines, where the primary aim is not the study of law, legal situations or problems lend themselves well as the basis of simulations or games to teach English language skills (Eck, 1999; Jung and Levitin, 2002; Dixon, 2002), social sciences (Martin, 1979) and citizenship (Hollins, 1980). In most of these examples, the main premise of the simulation appears to be based on the common perception of the lawyer as advocate, performing oral argument and is generally expressed in a form of extended role play of one sort or another. Authors report high levels of engagement, motivation and spontaneity as some of the reasons why this form of learning is apparently so successful. While most of these simulations tend to be classroom- or paper-based, in recent years more sophisticated forms of simulations that harness technology to greater effect have started to appear in legal education. Some of these new approaches have extended the nature of the traditional legal educational simulation, as described above, and shifted the emphasis away from an historically adversarial and court-room bound notion of simulation to that, for example, of the *legal transaction* (Bradlow and Finkelstein, 2007). This concept is one that we shall return to later.

Other forms of what we might term more traditional computer-based learning (CBL) or computer-aided instruction (CAI) have also appeared in legal education from time to time with mixed results. In some cases these have taken the form of computer-based 'games' structured on the type of rule-governed architecture underpinned by Artificial Intelligence (AI) techniques (Bench-Capon et al., 1998) which, at first glance, are ideally suited to teaching skills such as legal argument. More commonly, computer-mediated conferencing, discussion forums and email have been used, sometimes with an element of role play, as a tool to facilitate debate and discussion in place of, or to supplement, tutorials. A summary of work carried out in this area prior to 1997 and a description of one particular approach is provided in Widdison and Schulte (1998); and an early version of a more sophisticated role play negotiation using email and a discussion forum is described in Blackie and Maharg (1998). Self-contained CBL tutorials published via CD-Rom or the Web have also been developed for subjects, such as employment law, medical law and negligence (Migdal and Cartwright, 1997 and 1998). The largest-scale development of such an approach in the UK was undertaken by the Law Courseware Consortium in 1991 to produce law courseware in six different legal subjects and one 'service' course in law for non-law students. The resulting courseware,

IOLIS, has been in use for a significant period of time in law schools across the UK and has been developed over time, extending content and improving functionality. The software was based on a Socratic dialogue of question, answer and feedback and comprehensive reviews of this project, for example in Moodie (1997), Widdison (1995) and Paliwala (1998), demonstrate that it was successful in many respects, not least in its adoption rates throughout UK law schools. Evaluations have pointed to the fact that learning objectives were adequately met using these methods and the system succeeded in its aims to teach substantive law effectively (Moodie, 1997). In a discipline, such as law, where traditional lectures and seminars based on legal texts and the written word form the main foundation of the curriculum, this was a significant step forward in the integration of technology, law and legal education.

However, where the paper-based simulations mentioned earlier claim to capture students' imagination and raise their motivation, if only for a very limited time and purpose, many traditional CBL systems that have been developed are often based on instructivist principles with the result that they tend to be content-focused, linear, solitary and, possibly in the eyes of the students, more functional than fun. This inevitably leads to the issue of engagement in learning, which is an issue not merely for law and legal education, but for every discipline.

The research base on this issue is considerable. Turkle's (1995) work highlights the development of virtual personae as a powerful motivator for the degree of engagement or participation in online worlds. Gee (2007), for example, looks towards a time when the 'line between education and entertainment is truly erased'. Perhaps in this world the best aspects of gameplay and instructional design can be harnessed to provide a uniquely engaging educational experience. This debate has been circulating for some time as educationalists try to capture the essence of good games design and transform this into an educational paradigm. Barab and colleagues (1995), for example, talk about 'learning as play' as opposed to 'learning as work' within the school environment and question whether it is possible to 'combine the framework of gaming, with the content and inquiry-based pedagogy of school' and 'harness the best potential of entertainment as a foray into more meaningful and engaged learning' (Barab et al., 1995, p. 15). Barab's subsequent work with others, and in particular on the *Quest Atlantis* (QA) project is based on the premise of making learning fun within an immersive environment and basing academic activities on a combination of learning, playing and helping (Barab et al., 2005). However, even proponents of games-based learning question the value of simply grafting so-called edutainment games, such as *Sim City* or *Civilization* onto the curriculum and warn against overlooking several important issues in the general enthusiasm for educational gaming. Squire (2002), for example, notes in an early paper that, '[t]he research on games and simulations in education cautions against over exuberance about the potential of digital games to transform education.' His clear message is that 'there needs to be a close match among desired learning outcomes, available computer and supporting human resources, learner characteristics, such as familiarity with games conventions, "educational" game-play and potential supplementary learning experiences' (Squire, 2002, 6).

In this chapter, we will present some of the lessons we have learned through our experiences in designing and working with computer-based simulations in legal education over a period of almost ten years. Among other things, our experience has confirmed for us that we 'need an active teacher designing tools around the games that come to constitute a curriculum' (Gee, 2003, 216). However, our experience has also taught us that while, on the surface, this may appear to be a fairly obvious statement, achieving it is not as straightforward as first appears, and there are many issues that need to be addressed when considering this approach. In describing and reflecting on our practices, we will therefore attempt to explore whether Gee's vision of truly capturing the learning potential of games and simulations is a viable proposition. We will then go on to discuss what these changes might mean for teachers if they are to implement these new models of learning.

The Civil Court Action: a brief history

In the beginning . . .

The first iteration of our computer-based simulation, *The Virtual Court Action,* was developed in 1997 and was designed for use in a first-year undergraduate module in Civil Procedure as part of a BA in Law programme (Barton and McKellar, 1998). Recognizing the limitations of the existing rather traditional teaching and learning strategies adopted in the module we wanted to provide a more active form of learning that would engage the students in a way that was both meaningful and practical. For us, the obvious solution was to involve the students in a form of extended role play where they would take part in their own hypothetical court action on behalf of a fictional client, providing them with a sense of responsibility and legal decision-making in a situation where their actions would have direct consequences on the final outcome for their client. The idea of the 'legal transaction' or 'narrative of the case' was central to this concept. In addition, because civil court actions are adversarial in nature, students would require to be paired up in some way so that they were responsible for either raising the prosecution or defence of the action. The pivotal role of the court in the progress of the action was also critical. All of these elements required to be considered and accommodated effectively in the project design. Students would therefore learn *about* civil procedure by *enacting* civil procedure in a controlled and supported way through experiential learning and problem-solving rather than the more traditional, didactic approach that had been the prominent pedagogic model up to that point.

Although initially we considered a paper-based version of our idea, we disregarded it as impractical for a number of reasons including concerns regarding administration, practicality, monitoring and assessment of students – both formative and summative. The implementation of our design concept was therefore based around the innovative use of document assembly software to facilitate the drafting of the complex court documents, that require to be lodged within the normal progress of a civil court action, and the use of email as the communication medium between all parties in the action, including the court. The rationale behind this approach was based partly on pragmatic considerations and partly on pedagogic principles. First of all the students involved, level one undergraduates, came with very limited prior experience or practice in legal drafting skills or, indeed, a sound understanding of basic legal principles. Requiring them to draft complex legal documents at this stage in their learning without providing significant levels of scaffolding and support was likely to be counter-productive. We reasoned that the level of cognitive overload this would induce would far exceed the ability of the students to complete the task successfully and affect motivation and confidence. In addition, it was likely to shift the focus of the module away from developing an understanding of procedural law to an over-emphasis on form and content.

From a more practical viewpoint, the technology and resources we had at our disposal were such that any bespoke software development was completely out of the question. We could envisage, however, that the innovative use of the document assembly software integrated within our overall concept of the simulated court action would provide a context-rich learning environment that would meet our needs. We therefore developed the project concept around these ideas and drafted templates and other support materials in order to bring these ideas to fruition. The project was highly successful and, in this form, ran for a period of five years from 1997 until 2002 and ceased only due to the relocation of the authors to other institutions or departments.

A new era

In 2005, the opportunity arose to develop the *Virtual Court Action* and re-launch it in a new form and with new objectives. However, there were a significant number of differences between our initial concept and resulting implementation of the project and the circumstances that were presented at that time. The student cohort was now postgraduates who had already gained a law degree and were about to embark on the professional education and training phase of their personal development in the Diploma in Legal Practice Course at Glasgow Graduate School of Law (GGSL). Concerns about students' level of legal knowledge and basic drafting skills were a much less significant factor. In fact, we reasoned, providing this cohort of students with the same degree and type of support that was required for first-year undergraduates within the context of a simulated court action would potentially render the project too trivial and less realistic at this level, resulting in low engagement and limited learning. For the same reason that we decided to take a particular approach to the project design for level one students we opted to alter that design to suit the postgraduate level students. Primarily that involved dispensing with the document assembly aspect of the initial approach.

It is also worth considering how the wider context of the Diploma course influenced our design. Within the Diploma Civil Court Practice module students practised advocacy and written pleadings, as well as the formal court procedure. The traditional teaching and learning methods had dictated that court procedure was taught in weekly lectures while advocacy and drafting skills were practised in small group sessions. There was little harmony between the two elements that were also assessed separately. These students were also engaged in a much more vocationally oriented programme of study and the concept of 'transactional learning' (Maharg, 2004) was central to large elements of the course design and philosophy. In the Diploma programme, the students were allocated into 'firms' of four students for the duration of the course and carried out a number of simulated legal transactions under the supervision of tutors within a safe and controlled environment. Technology had also moved on rapidly. Based on similar ideas that had influenced the design of our original *Virtual Court Action*, a virtual learning environment had been implemented by a small team of developers at GGSL to enhance

Transactional Learning. Against the backdrop of a virtual town called *Ardcalloch*, students were now also provided with a rich context for these transactions that enhanced the authenticity of the learning environment far beyond the initial modest scope of our *Virtual Court Action*. Our goal, with what now became known as the *Civil Court Action* within the *Ardcalloch* Transactional Learning environment, was to find a way of developing a learning tool which would allow students to actively understand legal procedure in addition to practising legal skills required in the court process.

The development of the project and its implementation is described in greater detail elsewhere (Barton and McKellar, 2007). Briefly it involved students in their firms raising or defending an action on behalf of a client who had provided a statement and ancillary documentation in support of their case, progressing the case up to a particular point in the procedure. Students were required to initiate the correct procedure, as well as correspond with their client and other relevant parties, including the opposing firm of students in the transaction, within the virtual environment of Ardcalloch.

A look to the future

The virtual town of Ardcalloch, and the concept of Transactional Learning has been documented over the last decade (e.g. Maharg, 2004; Barton and Maharg, 2007; Barton and McKellar, 2007). Maharg (2007) maps its history and discusses the theoretical and practical synergy between technology, curriculum and learning. Part 3 of the book describes the history of Transactional Learning in detail and provides an in-depth case study summarizing the results of much of the action research that has taken place in the use of technology and simulation-based learning in the Diploma in Legal Practice at Glasgow Graduate School of Law. In 2006, the initiatives at GGSL obtained joint funding from the Joint Information Systems Committee (JISC) and the UK Centre for Legal Education (UKCLE) to design and build an, open-source Transactional Learning environment using gaming technologies and mobile learning technologies. The technology and design involved large-scale implementation in a range of professional disciplines to be used by students, staff and administrators across three Faculties within the University of Strathclyde, as well as incorporating projects from UK Law Schools. The *SIMulated Professional Learning Environment* (SIMPLE) that was created as a result enables students to engage in authentic simulations of professional transactions and has been designed to be used as a teaching, learning and assessment environment.

The SIMPLE project addressed two fundamental sets of issues in the use of simulation. First, the project sought to consider the design and implementation of an online professional learning environment that can be used in a wide variety of professions. The model for the 2D simulation described above which was developed at GGSL could clearly be translated into a variety of professional disciplines, particularly those where a set of processes or procedures with multiple respondents or parties were involved. The project has created an environment where academics can create their own simulation *blueprint* using a suite of tools. The blueprint is then deployed in the SIMPLE platform, hosted on an institutional or external server and can be accessed by staff and students.

The project also addressed the educational, organizational and management issues that arose from the large-scale implementation of such an environment, in particular those of:

- social presence, collaborative learning and the emergence of learning;
- use of simulation spaces in a complex organization, and the relation between simulation spaces and other learning spaces on a course, including paper-based and online resources, face-to-face classes, other teaching and course administration;
- authenticity in the design of simulation tasks and effective assessment of professional learning.

While we will not attempt to discuss the wider issues arising from this extended project, it is useful at least to mention them here as a context for the *Civil Court Action* (CCA), which was reconstructed to become one of the transactions the students undertake within the SIMPLE environment along with a number of others – the purchase and sale of a property, the winding up of the estate of a deceased person and a personal injury negotiation. The environment is supported along with other SIMPLE simulations from other disciplines and institution through the SIMPLE community (http://simple-community.org).

The Civil Court Action: game or simulation?

In discussing the *Civil Court Action* over the years, we have variously described it as a form of computer-based learning, computer-based training or a Transactional Learning project, and our perspective has been based primarily on our viewpoint as educational developers. Interestingly, however, in our initial aims, along with 'active learning' and 'context-rich learning environments', we referred to the term 'simulation' to describe our approach to its design (Barton and McKellar, 1998). We used the word to describe the abstracted and guided representation of the process that we wanted to model and that the students would require to follow in order to learn about civil procedure. In more recent literature reviews where the characteristic of games or simulations have been defined or discussed, others have attempted to identify the essential attributes of games and simulations in a more precise way. Sauvé and colleagues (2007, 248), for example, propose six attributes that distinguish an *educational game*, namely, 'player or players, conflict, rules, predetermined goal of the game, its artificial nature . . . [and] the pedagogic nature.' Taken together, this forms their definition of an educational game as 'a fictional fantasy or artificial situation in which players, put in conflict with one another or against other forces, are governed by rules that structure their actions in order to meet learning objectives and a goal determined by the game' (Sauvé et al., 2007, 251). In contrast they define an *educational simulation* as 'a simplified, dynamic and precise representation of reality defined as a system' (Sauvé et al., 2007, 252) exhibiting a different set of attributes which they identify as 'a model of reality defined as a system; a dynamic model; a simplified model; a model that has fidelity, accuracy and validity . . . [and] should address directly the learning outcomes' (Sauvé et al., 2007, 251). They go on to distinguish a third concept, namely that of a *simulation game* which occurs when 'one or more players participate in a simulation and interact with its various components, [upon which] the notion of a winner and loser is introduced' (Sauvé et al., 2007, 253).

By these definitions, we can see various aspects of the *Civil Court Action* reflected in each one: players, rules, fictional fantasy, model of reality, etc. However, while at first glance, it would appear to fit more closely into the 'simulation game' category, the concept of 'winner and loser' had a slightly different meaning, or at least emphasis, in our implementation. In order to be successful as a learning design, students must recognize that, while they are involved in an adversarial situation, 'winning' in a traditional sense is not the main goal of the simulation. Crucially, they need to appreciate that they will not be *assessed* on whether they win the case for their client or not: in this type of situation there must always be one 'loser', and that single outcome cannot be relied upon solely in a high stakes assessment. Instead, students need to demonstrate a deep understanding of legal process, client care and professional ethics and actively progress the transaction to the complete satisfaction of their client and of the court. However, this concept of competition and winning is clearly a motivating factor in games design and one that we wanted to retain in some form. These conflicting factors highlight two issues in our design. First of all, the transaction must be sufficiently open-ended so that each side has a reasonable starting position upon which to build a good case for their client and hence enable them to feel they have a chance of winning. We therefore designed the transactions and associated resources carefully in order to provide realistic fact patterns that did not point towards any obvious foregone conclusions or favour one side over the other. Second, the reactions of the 'virtual characters' within the simulation, in the form of the client and court personnel, among others, allow one side to emerge legitimately as the 'losers' in the transaction without jeopardizing the outcome of their assessment or final grade. By granting consent or signalling approval at key stages in the simulation, the virtual characters provide feedback that validates the course of action taken by the firm. Effectively, what might be considered a 'defeat' within the simulation can still indicate success in the course assessment.

The concept of virtual characters and their role within the transaction is therefore central to our notion of the simulation and reminiscent of a particular genre of computer-based games where players interact with avatars and other fictional characters in order to solve problems and hence progress in the game. There are many examples of this form of 'adventure' game from early examples such as *Adventure* and *King's Quest* to more recent examples such as *The Apprentice* (see also http://www.adventuregamers.com/ for a comprehensive list of titles plus reviews of adventure games). Other, broader definitions of computer-based simulations and games might therefore fit our model more closely. Van Eck (2007), for example, regards the term 'game' as being too narrow to describe the variety of genres which exist in the world of digital games-based learning (DGBL). In his taxonomy of game types, reproduced from an earlier work, he lists 'simulations' as one of these forms of game and defines it as a '[s]imulation of processes, events or phenomenon' with the '[e]mphasis on realistic representation' (Van Eck, 2007, 274). He then goes on to identify four pedagogic principles inherent in all digital games:

- play theory, cycles of learning, and engagement;
- problem-based learning; situated cognition and learning;
- question asking, cognitive disequilibrium; and
- scaffolding. (Van Eck, 2007, 275)

According to these definitions and principles, we would certainly have described the *Civil Court Action* as a simulation in the broader sense of a form of digital game.

Although his proposals are based on the notion of designing an *adventure game* which he sees as providing the 'greatest potential for addressing all levels of the learning taxonomy' (Van Eck, 2007, 276) the ideas that he brings together from across a number of disciplines are pertinent to other forms of games and simulations. He also highlights Piaget's theory of cognitive disequilibrium and Vygotsky's zone of proximal development and scaffolding as two key principles in the design of successful digital games. He proposes that, '[t]he extent to which games foil expectations (create cognitive disequilibrium) without exceeding the capacity of the player to succeed (going beyond the zone of proximal development), determines to a large extent whether they are engaging' (Van Eck, 2007, 287). In our experience, this is certainly one of the biggest challenges we have been faced with as educational designers when attempting to use simulations as learning tools; and at various stages in the development of our project we have had to hold both concepts in creative tension in order to create a simulation that was both educationally valid as well as stimulating. For example, in our earliest iteration of the project we needed to provide the students with assistance to draft complex court documents, since requiring them to draft these would have far exceeded their capacity to do so. Hence we devised scaffolding in the form of highly structured templates with extensive additional guidance within a document assembly system in order to facilitate this aspect of the simulation and allow students to make progress through the transaction. Conversely, providing this level of scaffolding for the postgraduate Diploma students would have rendered this element of the simulation too trivial and hence un-engaging. Interestingly, taking this notion further, what we have found is that there are occasions in learning when disequilibrium, in itself a negative, is actually quite positive. And there are times when scaffolding can negatively affect learning. The subtlety of good design therefore lies in knowing when to do something (scaffold) or create an absence (disequilibrium). In fact, the one may depend on the other like binary code.

Prensky (2001) also discusses the question of whether simulations are games. He provides some definitions of simulations but concludes that they are not 'in and of themselves, games'. He argues that although the use of simulations in training and education are useful, particularly in providing a platform for 'what-if' experimentation and a means of practicing in safety, it is not the fidelity of simulations that determine their effectiveness as learning tools, but the extent to which they actually engage the learner: 'low fidelity or high, all simulations can be made into games' (Prensky, 2001). While one of the main purposes of simulations is to replicate a situation or process or place; reality, he warns, 'can lead to boredom, which then actually *reduces* learning' (emphasis in original). Interestingly, Prensky contends that 'just because something is a simulation does not mean it's engaging, and [...] a simulation game, to be effective does not necessarily have to be a totally realistic portrayal of the situation or job'. What Prensky is referring to here is the concept of situated cognition and the idea that learning is more powerful when it takes place in meaningful contexts rather than in a more formal, instructional setting. The situation is therefore the key and that does not necessarily mean the absolute replication of some form of reality, or the fidelity of the simulation *per se*, but rather the activities, context and culture associated with that representation of reality (Brown et al., 1989). The best type of simulations, he claims, exhibit many of the motivational and formal structural elements of games including a goal, rules and competition and 'keep pulling you to continue to the end in spite of yourself' learning 'stealthily' rather than directly. From an educational design perspective this means paying heed to the idea of cognitive apprentice-ship, based on authentic tasks and ill-defined problems that results in learners engaging in a process, which allows them to construct and negotiate their own meaning through engagement with apprentice-like situations. This is exactly the type of approach we tried to take when designing the *Civil Court Action*. Students were not expected to know exactly how to raise or defend a civil court action at the outset, but would learn this through trial and experimentation, making use of congruent feedback from the virtual characters they interacted with to enable them to learn and hence progress. So, while certain aspects of the simulation did not completely mirror reality, for example the actual court timescales, the core activities students carried out, the style documents they were provided with and the interactions they engaged in provided a true reflec-tion of the context and culture of the world of a trainee solicitor.

Learning by design: an iterative process

As we have outlined, the *Civil Court Action* has been in use and evolved over a period of time and perhaps one of the reasons for its longevity has been our ability to extend the project's scope over that duration, introducing one new element in each year of the project or altering particular elements of its implementation in some way. Facilitating this annual innovation has required significant consideration of pedagogic, technical, capacity, resource and support issues. With hindsight, while it might have been possible to introduce some elements earlier, the authors and students have gained more by the incremental approach. Over the five years to 2009, we have extended the length of time over which the students progress the action, introduced more client information which requires the students to undertake further investigation and more complex procedural steps and, most recently, we piloted a real-time procedural court hearing before a judge in one of the inferior courts in Scotland (titled a sheriff). Each of these steps has entailed detailed planning to ensure smooth transitions between stages and resources.

One example will suffice. Due to the nature of procedure in the Scottish court system, we were able to design a case scenario which, if the correct procedure were followed, allowed the firms to progress the transactions up to but not including the first mandatory court hearing without the necessity for a formal court hearing prior to that date. Occasionally we had to 'manage' the court action to ensure that no actual appearance in front of the court was required. This was usually facilitated through the actions of the client who usually instructed *against* her agent's advice – the authors played all clients in the simulation – to avoid the student firm taking the action down an undesirable route. For instance, a firm suggested that a counterclaim against the opposing side would be appropriate but the client – played by the authors in their roles at tutor managers – declined to authorize this, thus ensuring that the attendant court appearances for this alternative procedure were not necessary. However it had long been one of our goals to extend the simulation of document exchange into the arena of court advocacy and we designed a pilot court appearance to be included in the simulation for the year 2007/08. Eight firms were selected to progress their actions to the mandatory court hearing which occurs approximately two months after commencement, and although each member of the firm would be involved in preparation for the hearing, only one member would orally present the case.

This hearing – the Options Hearing – takes place once the pleadings have been adjusted between the parties and, after hearing the agents for the parties, the judge will decide what happens next. We had imagined that the hearing would be short, rather formal and predictable. We could not expect that all the students, or indeed entire firms, would take part as this was an extra, non-assessed part of their course but, following the hearings, it was clear that all who had participated in any way had gained significantly from the experience. Three ways in which games can motivate players have been identified by Malone (1981) as fantasy, challenge and curiosity. Amory and colleagues (1998) also cite curiosity as a frequent motive when playing a game. The students in the pilot were fulfilling a desire expressed in feedback from our students in previous years that they want to complete the action – or at least find out 'what happens next'. It appeared that they were so involved or caught up in the 'game' that they want to keep going to discover the eventual outcome, rather than stop simply because it would not gain them any additional bonus in the form of more marks. As a result of the success of this pilot we have since amended the tutorial programme to include a mandatory Options Hearing for all students as the culmination of the simulation.

Our students' engagement with the simulation suggests aspects that can be likened to 'flow', first addressed as such by Csikszentmihalyi (1990), a key factor that reveals why people play games. However, while our students are not necessarily immersed in the simulation to the exclusion of all else, the quality of experience they were having kept them motivated to continue with the transaction. In addition a number of Csikszentmihalyi's nine elements that characterize the 'flow' were present, for example clear goals, a balance between challenges and skills, action and awareness merged, self-consciousness disappears, sense of time distorted, the activity becomes autotelic and there was a sense that the students were clearly absorbed in the progress of the transaction beyond that which was required. There has been considerable discussion as to how the 'flow' can be harnessed and how it might make the player more open to 'receiving, comprehending and using educational based content and skills' (Csikszentmihalyi, 1990). The 2004 Futurelab Review suggests that rather than producing games which on the surface appear similar to 'fun' activities or even hide or disguise the educational content within the game, 'it might be argued that we should understand the deep structures of the gameplay experience that contributes to "flow" and build these into environments designed to support learning' (Kirriemuir and McFarlane, 2004).

Within the *Civil Court Action* simulation we have endeavoured to make the procedure more realistic with authentic tasks and use of actual document templates, relevant websites etc. While this encourages engagement and immersion in the virtual world, simulations can rarely replicate every aspect of real life. For instance in our court action we have had to alter time limits to accommodate the university semester system to avoid the action taking on the real life time limits, which might allow a case to take some years to complete.

This intervention does not assist with the 'flow' but, as we have observed previously, if managed appropriately and with adequate explanation or support this will not detract significantly from the learning.

Our observations on what we have learned

The experience of designing a large-scale simulation such as the *Civil Court Action* has given us new insight into some of the issues we struggled to understand initially and allowed us to place these in the context of a wider heuristic of simulations and games as an educational paradigm. We will attempt to articulate some of these reflections and illustrate them through specific examples drawn from this first-hand experience.

1. *Our initial objectives were far exceeded – emerging outcomes led the way for us*
   Each time we introduced a new aspect to the project, we were concerned that students would find the workload too onerous or fail to meet the learning objectives we had set. In reality, the opposite was often the case. For example, we have observed that some students get really engaged by the simulation and become quite engrossed in the narrative and their role. They go down every possible avenue and are frustrated if the routes are closed off to them. In a scenario involving a disputed property transaction, a firm wrote to the Ardcalloch town council, the Keeper of the Registers and the harbour-master requesting information under the Freedom of Information Act 2000. This was far beyond what we, but interestingly not our students, expected, and made us realize what efforts the students would be willing to make on behalf of their client with very little prompting on our part, and how far we could stretch them in future. In this instance as the FOI Act allows an organization 21 days to produce the documentation, we were able to reply to the request in such terms and hence delay production until after the life of the project. There have been other situations, however, when we have been forced to draft further documentation while the project has been underway, for example the client in one scenario was asked to produce newspaper notices of a planning application, which we then had to create in authentic format. The issue for us in this situation is that we have to be one step ahead in order to respond appropriately and congruently with such requests, which makes post-project discussion as to which resources and documents should be made available for the fictional characters within the simulation very important. We are considering, for example, if we need to further develop the town's newspaper, the *Ardcalloch News*, so that students can search for appropriate notices and advertisements which they may use in their court actions. Additionally we have found that students can learn much

more than we had originally planned for. Although we designed the simulations so that they would follow a particular 'standard' path, in reality the students could effectively branch off this path at various points because of the actions they or their opponents might take. In previous work we have described our simulation designs in terms of a spectrum 'open-field' and 'closed-field' approaches (Barton and Maharg, 2007). These branches are akin to Gee's (2007) *Multiple Routes* as well as *Probing* learning principles, and provide opportunities for students to learn about aspects of procedure that we had not intentionally designed into the simulation: an example of learning stealthily as Prensky would put it.

2. *Our roles as teachers and course designers changed fundamentally*

Integrating an online simulation like the *Civil Court Action* into a course or programme of study requires us to re-think our role as teachers. The main factor we have observed is that we became much less visible as the facilitators of students' learning although, perhaps surprisingly, we were able to carry out this role more effectively. Because we took on the roles of the fictional characters within the simulation, it was obvious exactly when the students encountered problems or could not understand substantive or procedural issues – more so than in traditional classroom settings. We could then respond to them in character in a way that helped them overcome their problem or correct their mistake, while maintaining the flow of the simulation. Sometimes, this meant directing them to other sources of information or asking them to clarify an issue. A simple but common example of this arose when some firms, in requesting a warrant from the court early on in the procedure, omitted the crucial element of payment. Rather than giving them formal feedback about court fees, these firms would receive a letter from the court stating that the warrant could not be issued at this point and directing them to the Court Website where details about payment and the relevant forms were displayed. This practical and experiential approach to learning was one that we had to adjust to ourselves. It is difficult at times to resist the temptation to slip out of character within the simulation and revert to a more familiar tutor role, especially when we can see potential problems looming ahead. Allowing students to make mistakes and finding ways to help them recover from this within the parameters of the simulation is always a challenge and a learning experience for us, as much as it is for the students. Importantly too, it is a valuable means of providing feed forward in order, simply, to keep the students on track or, more interestingly, to provide them with alternative ways to deepen their understanding. We can draw an interesting comparison here with Gee's concept of *Material Intelligence Principle* (Gee, 2007, 106–08; 110, and 224).

3. *Robust pedagogic design was the most important element of the process*

One of the most interesting aspects we have observed is that students appear to be less concerned with the fidelity or look and feel of the simulation platform, but tend to get upset or frustrated when the educational construct of the simulation breaks down. This could occasionally happen when, for example, the release of a particular piece of critical information, timed to occur at a particular point in the transaction appears to be out of step with the students' individual progress through the simulation, or when incomplete or partial feedback is provided that does not allow the students to move forward in the simulation in a meaningful sense. This is a perfect example of Gee's *Explicit Information on Demand and Just-in-time Principle* breaking down (Gee, 2007, 27 and 226), and also goes back to the notions of cognitive apprenticeship, disequilibrium and scaffolding discussed earlier. Providing scaffolding at the wrong time in the transaction is counter-productive, causing a particular type of cognitive disequilibrium that destroys the authenticity of the simulation and hence reduces engagement. This bears interesting comparisons with Gee's *Regime of Competence* principle where, 'the learner gets ample opportunity to operate within, but at the outer edge of his or her resources, so that at those points things are felt as a challenge but not "undoable" ' (Gee, 2007, 68 and 223). As educational designers, therefore, we must pay particular attention to the underlying learning objectives and ensure that we design our simulations to reflect these in a challenging but achievable way. For example, students find the completion of tasks that are not true to the narrative of the simulation pointless and confusing and the feedback they receive must be timely and authentic otherwise students feel they are proceeding *in vacuo*.

4. *What we were doing required a redesign/reconfiguration of the curriculum to accommodate the new learning and assessment methods*

Merging of the simulation environment with more traditional teaching and learning methods needs to be carefully considered. Sometimes this may mean a re-structuring of the course. For us, at a basic level this initially meant realigning the tutorials so that the students had the opportunity to practise particular aspects of drafting or reinforce particular aspects of procedure before the point at which they would have to carry this out within the simulation. Sometimes this resulted in unexpected outcomes and we found students acted in the simulation in accordance with tutorial discussion or focus. For example, a topic of discussion in one tutorial is the issue of 'counter claim' and although we have designed our simulations so that a counterclaim should not be required, inevitably some students attempt to take this course of action, although as discussed above, we are able to divert them from this route by responding in character as the client and instruct them not to take this action. In terms of assessment, previous summative assessments were also replaced by the completion of particular tasks within the project: a drafting assessment, for example, was dropped since students would now require demonstration of more extensive drafting skills throughout the whole duration of the simulation.

Timings of the tutorials within the weekly timetable were also important. Although students could discuss the court action whenever they wanted within their 'firms' they tended to meet before or after their tutorial in Civil Procedure which in our timetable occurred on a Thursday or Friday afternoon. These days often coincided with project deadlines, which meant that if students were submitting documents at this time there was very little time left to resubmit should that be necessary. At the beginning of the project some students also tended to submit then forget that the document may need resubmission before the deadline. They were treating this like an 'ordinary' piece of coursework where they are graded but progression in the module is not dependent on the outcome. Very quickly students realized that this project had a series of submission deadlines, which like the real world, had to be followed up and immediate steps taken to ensure that the document was acceptable. Arguably the longer the students are immersed in the simulation and undertaking authentic tasks, the more effective the learning. As students progressed through the simulation and became more caught up in the roles, the case, the characters and the virtual town, the more they saw the assessments as a step in the procedure rather than a formal piece of coursework. It became part of the flow of the transaction and was not longer seen as something that was submitted and forgotten about until it was returned at the end of the project. It became, in effect, an integral step in the progression of their client's case. This was facilitated through our attempts to make the assessment points natural places where documents would require to be 'checked' by either the Court or a Senior Partner, who would 'send' the assessment feedback directly to the firm.

At the points where we extended the project in some way, this also meant a re-configuration of the curriculum, and this was not always achieved without problems. For example, we always knew that extending the action to include a formal court hearing was going to be difficult. This was because of sheer numbers involved (272 students in 68 firms) but also because it would be difficult to assess. How could we ensure there was parity of assessment? If this aspect of the simulation was not going to be assessed would the students engage with it? Would some students in the firm complain that they were left to do all the work? In the end, our pilot court hearings far exceeded what we expected in terms of student learning, even with no summative assessment. However to be pedagogically effective, when we decided to extend the scope to provide all students with the opportunity to take part in a hearing, we recognized we needed to use the time as a formative assessment point in order to provide the students with completion of the feedback loop and allow them to reflect on their progress. In order to accommodate this, the tutorial programme for session 2008/09 was altered to accommodate the options hearing as a formal tutorial session.

5. *The most effective forms of learning are resource- and time-intensive*
The project requires a considerable investment of time in terms of the initial design and planning stage, but the day-to-day management can also be time-consuming. It is a common misconception that once created, the simulation will run itself. This can be true up to a point, as most routine tasks can be automated, assessment and the provision of feedback can be streamlined and there will be periods where little or no tutor input is required. Familiarity with the application has meant that each year we as tutors have become more proficient in dealing effectively with the project. In addition, we have a fluency with the scenarios which means we no longer have to continually check factual details which are requested by the firms

and we have an acquired awareness of how to respond to follow the story from both sides or where we have to 'create' new facts or documents to deal with a novel situation. Our experience has taught us, however, that to be most effective, and at crucial points, this project requires regular management. At any point, and for a whole variety of reasons, students may become 'stuck' in the simulation and require input from tutors in order to move forward. So like the binary analogy discussed earlier, 'stuckness' can be a positive experience when procedures are designed to catch students. This requires a proactive approach from tutors in order to avoid student drift or disengagement. The rolling programme of enhancement also has meant that the authors have been continually engaged with the project, although the dual role of management feeding back into design improvements has been beneficial.

6. *Innovation takes time and tenacity*

Even with fairly modest changes, we found that each new step took longer to develop than originally envisaged. For example, when producing supplementary resources and information for each scenario, we had to ensure that this would result in an equitable workload for each side of the transaction. Small changes in one area can lead to unexpected consequences further down the line, and we needed to work through the simulation each time we introduced a change, to ensure that there were no hidden pitfalls that we had not anticipated. This also applied to providing additional unplanned, information 'on the fly' as the simulation progressed, for example horse race results, newspaper articles, planning documents, and ensuring that these were as authentic as possible in terms of look and feel, but more importantly within the context of the narrative of the simulation.

7. *We often did not manage to get it right first time*

While we always attempted to plan the simulations in great detail and account for every eventuality, we frequently found that we had not considered as many issues as we perhaps should have at the initial stages. On the first run of the simulation at GGSL, for instance, we set the date for the Options Hearing, and therefore the completion of the project at that stage, too close to the end of the project. Although we had good justification for setting this end-point, in terms of alignment with the tutorial programme, had it been planned well in advance and had we made sure the students were well aware of this from the outset students would not have struggled to meet the deadline, because they were still ingathering information and exchanging adjustments to their pleadings, up to and beyond the deadline. We had underestimated just how engaged the students would become with this aspect of the simulation, how challenging it was for them to actually carry out the tasks involved and how time-consuming this particular part of the procedure was for them as a result. Again, an iterative approach to the design ensured that this sort of situation could be avoided in the future.

It is also clear that we cannot rely on students reading the project instruction documentation. We provide guides, FAQs and a discussion forum together with information in module handbooks, but each year there has been a minority of students who profess to have been perplexed by what was happening in the project and what they were meant to be doing. One of the reasons for this, we believe, is the location of these resources outside the simulation environment. The result is that they are viewed as part of the traditional learning environment and because the students have to break out of the simulation in order to access them, they can be misunderstood, ignored or forgotten. Perhaps we need to learn lessons from other games designers, and especially as Gee discusses, look at how we can better integrate these additional resources and texts into the 'appreciative systems' associated with our simulation (Gee, 2007, 97). His idea of the *Text Principle* certainly points to an approach that endorses this more integrated approach where text and embodied experiences are more closely linked (Gee, 2007, 106).

8. *We always learned something new from each iteration of the project*
As alluded to previously, because of the nature of this type of simulation, and even although we attempted to constrain it in certain ways, students would take the project in ways we had not expected. In one case a firm sought to arrest, that is suspend in a bank account, the funds of the defender in the action. This was a legitimate course of action but one that we could not permit in terms of the set-up of our simulation. While we could send replies from the various financial institutions effectively intimating that the individual had no funds lodged with them, we knew that this was at best a deviation and had detracted from the authenticity of the simulation. Over the years we have found students' inventiveness astonishing, and for us, continually responding to this and inventing new ways to deal with the unexpected has been both a challenge and an inspiration.

9. *We will always want to try to do something more than the current technology we have available will allow us to do*
One of the consequences of working with online simulations is a new-found appreciation of the potential of technology to enhance learning and recognition of ways in which other technologies might be employed to improve what we do. This includes the inclusion of email or text-alerts for tutors to the integration of voice, video, 3-D avatars etc. We are aware that there are many other ways in which we can improve the authenticity and engagement of our simulation. However, we know from previous experiences of integrating even simple technological changes, that above all else the educational integrity of the simulation must remain the priority and cannot be sacrificed in any way for the sake of technological trends or fashions.

10. *Student study routines are changing.*
We need to develop a more decentralized, individualized approach to learning that facilitates mobility and participation in our learning design. Traditionally, within the context of our simulations, a lot of the 'external' and perhaps more traditional input from tutors comes in the form of tutorials, discussion forums that sit alongside the project and formal feedback at assessment points. However, we are aware that the students we interact with today are different from those of ten years ago in terms of their familiarity with technology and their expectations of online

learning environments. With increasing ability to access, manipulate and sort information, students will need different support structures. They are already collaborating and accessing information in different ways, most notably through mobile phones. As noted earlier our simulation has allowed us to give instant feedback without interrupting the flow of the scenario with the student able to progress and build on what has gone before. It seems inevitable that the next challenge for us will be to understand this shifting trend and attempt to incorporate this in our approach to the design of our simulations and our curricula.

11. *The 'easier' the simulation, the less the students value it*

As discussed previously, engagement is crucial to the success of the simulation and finding the balance between challenging and over-stretching students is always the most difficult aspect to achieve in the design. We have to admit that, we have tended to underestimate their abilities. Our experience has reinforced for us that students will always ask for more. Where we try to ensure the students are not over-burdened in terms of work-load within the simulation, students often complain that the project was not taken far enough. In our yearly evaluations of the project, this has been a common theme, and in the most recent iteration of the project, those students who were not part of the options hearing pilot felt cheated that they did not get to the hearing stage. However, we have had to balance our own and the students' enthusiasm to progress too quickly. Inappropriately hasty introduction of technology to the classroom can be counter-productive and we have deliberately restricted ourselves to taking our simulation forward in small stages each year, with each stage being carefully planned and designed before implementation. This organic approach has ensured that we have been able to cope with the tangential routes some of our students have taken, the unexpected issues they have raised and effective management of a large number of virtual firms.

12. *Students' feedback pushes us to stretch our ideas, too, and students discover things we had not considered*

Following on from the point above we have found that, far from finding the simulation a chore, the students want to see more of this type of learning within their programme of study. They also frequently suggest ways that this particular simulation could be integrated with others that they complete as part of their overall course. For example, prior to commencing the *Civil Court Action* the students complete a personal injury negotiation which reaches a negotiated settlement. Students suggested that this scenario should be carried forward to the *Civil Court Action* with the virtual firms continuing to represent the same virtual client as if no settlement had been obtained. This ties in nicely with Gee's principle of *Transfer*. It is certainly clear to us that far greater benefits can be obtained by taking a wider curricular rather than modular approach to this form of learning. If we accept Gee's proposition that when 'previous experience is . . . recruited and transformed, giving rise to newer experiences that can be used and transformed in the future' (Gee, 2007, 127) then we need to consider how we can introduce opportunities for students to trigger 'transfer'. With careful curriculum planning we can therefore incorporate problems at later stages and in different contexts that require students to go through this process of adapting and transforming previous learning.

The simulation has also affected ways we align this with the webcast lecture programme that supports the subject by giving information about law and civil process. For example, student firms acting for the defender client could consider whether or not to lodge a counterclaim against the pursuer client. In terms of the legal action, although this was competent, we did not want students to go down this route. Although some students discussed this through email with their client, others proceeded to lodge the counterclaim documentation with no reference to formal instructions. This would have significant implications for the client in the progress of the action- not least of all on court expenses. While the students had been given full instructions on the procedure for counterclaims in the lecture programme, it was clear there was a gap in terms of ethical and client care issues that required to be addressed.

Conclusions

In an academic setting, learning the law through the use of online games and simulations is still relatively rare. However, we know from our experiences of designing and implementing educational simulations to help students learn about the practice of law that this type of approach can have positive and far-reaching effects. Nor need simulation be treated as secondary to the more common clinical experience (i.e. dealing with real clients and their cases) that students can obtain in a number of law schools. Though highly authentic and situated in real practice, one of the problems in using real cases, from law clinics as the basis for learning in a professional discipline like legal practice is that even we, as experts, have no idea how they eventually play out. What might start off looking like a simple conveyancing transaction, for example, may eventually turn into a complicated legal claim and take the learner into areas and domains of learning that are well beyond their competence levels and counter-productive to useful learning. The use of simulations, on the other hand, allows us to create 'fruitful patterns and generalizations . . . that allow the learner to make real progress in the domain and that can serve as the correct basis or good guides for more complicated patterns and generalizations' (Gee, 2007, 138). In order to maximize these advantages we must, therefore, pay particular heed to the development of authentic tasks and ill-defined problems that result in learners constructing and negotiating their own meaning through engagement with apprentice-like situations. This brings with it a new set of challenges in both curriculum design and academic practice which involves leveraging certain aspects of games design that enhance the learning potential of this approach. In particular, we have found that the dual aspects of cognitive disequilibrium and scaffolding are key and that the subtlety of good simulation design lies in knowing when to do something (scaffold) or create an absence (disequilibrium). The relationship between these two factors not only affects the authenticity of the simulation but determines to a large extent student engagement and so the learning potential of this approach. In addition, a basic understanding, or at least appreciation, of Gee's 36 learning principles built into good video game design provides a reasonable starting point from which to consider how we might go about designing a good educational experience. This is not to say that we deliberately sought to incorporate all of these principles into the design of our simulation, but rather we recognize those that are pertinent to the educational objectives we wish to achieve given the characteristics of our simulation as we have described it.

At this point we must return to the question we posed for ourselves at the start of this chapter: has what we have described come anywhere near Gee's visualization of truly capturing the learning potential of games and simulations? Perhaps the best way to answer that question is to view it from another angle: have we managed to capture the engagement potential of games and simulations in our learning design? We would like to think that we were at least some way towards achieving that, and would argue, in fact, that is precisely what we should be trying to do. Rather than trying to fit educational objectives around a game concept or design, we should be trying to integrate the best aspects of games and simulations into our educational models. Like Barab and colleagues' notion of *conceptual play spaces* we have sought to 'layer in curricular tasks, reflective moments and pedagogical elements to support academic learning' (Barab et al., 2008). We have a vast wealth of educational research and established theoretical models to draw on for support and if, in order to facilitate learning, we find an approach that stimulates, engages and motivates learners to do better then we should try to find ways to incorporate this into our thinking. However, this means also revisiting our roles as teachers: simulation requires re-thinking roles, responsibilities and employments in Higher Education. One of the most profound changes we have experienced through developing and using educational simulations is the shift in our role from what we would term 'master' to 'games-master'. By this we mean we are no longer concerned with purely designing a curriculum and filling it with information that will be consumed by students in an organized and tightly managed fashion. Instead, we enter into a relationship with the students where we take on roles within in their virtual world, sometimes as player and sometimes mentor, engaging in an exchange of moves and responses to their progress through the simulation, facilitating their learning. We need to be responsive and agile, understand when the students are stuck and when they can afford to be pushed, respond by providing clues, feedback or reward when appropriate, and above all achieve this within the construct of the simulation in a way that maintains the authenticity and retains engagement. In other words, we need to be prepared to enter into our own zone of proximal development, experience some cognitive disequilibrium and join in the game ourselves. If we do not truly try to understand and engage with the whole process, then why should we expect our students to do so? We would suggest that is the biggest challenge for all of us and one that we certainly had not anticipated when we first developed the idea of our simulation ten years ago.

References

Amory, A., Naicker, K., Vincent, J. and Adams, C. (1998). Computer Games as a Learning Resource, *Proceedings of ED-MEDIA 98 & ED-TELECOM 98*. In T. Ottmann and I. Tomek, eds. Association for the Advancement of Computing in Education, Charlottesville, pp. 50–55.

Barab, S., Arici, A. and Jackson, C. (1995). Eat Your Vegetables and Do Your Homework: a design-based investigation of enjoyment and meaning in learning, *Educational Technology*, Vol. 65, No. 1, pp. 15–21.

Barab, S., Dodge, T. and Ingram-Goble, A. (2008). Conceptual play spaces and transactive engagement: a 21st century pedagogy, http://inkido.indiana.edu/research/onlinemanu/papers/acad_play.pdf Accessed 8 October 2008).

Barab, S., Thomas, M., Dodge, T., Carteaux, R. and Tuzun, H. (2005). Making learning fun: Quest Atlantis, a game without guns, *ETR&D*, Vol. 53, No. 1, pp. 86–107.

Barton, K. and Maharg, P. (2007). E-simulations in the wild: interdisciplinary research, design and implementation of simulation environments in legal education, in D. Gibson, C. Aldrich and M. Prensky, eds. *Games and Simulations in Online Learning: Research and Development Frameworks*, Hershey, PA: Information Science Publishing.

Barton, K. and McKellar, P. (1998). The Virtual Court Action: procedural facilitation in law, *ALT-J*, Vol. 6, No. 1, pp. 87–94.

Barton, K. and McKellar, P. (2007). Transactional Learning: Ardcalloch Sheriff Court is open for business, *Journal of Information, Law and Technology*, No.1, Special Issue on Law Education and Technology.http://www2.warwick.ac.uk/fac/soc/law/elj/jilt/2007_1/barton_mckellar. Accessed 25.4.10.

Bench-Capon, T. J. M., Leng, P. H. and Staniford G. (1998). A Computer supported environment for the teaching of legal argument, *Journal of Law and Information Technology*, No. 3 http://www2.warwick.ac.uk/fac/soc/law/elj/jilt/1998_3/bench.

Blackie, J. and Maharg, P. (1998). The Delict Game, *Proceedings of the Thirteenth BILETA Conference*.

Bradlow, D. and Finkelstein, J. G. (2007). Training law students to be international transactional lawyers – using and extended simulation to educate law students about business transactions. *Pepperdine Journal of Business, Entrepreneurship & the Law*, Vol. 1, pp. 67–87.

Brown, J. S., Collins, A. and Duguid, P. (1989). Situated cognition and the culture of learning, *Educational Research*, Vol. 18, No. 1, pp. 32–42.

Csikszentmihalyi, M. (1990). *Flow: The Psychology of Optimal Experience*. New York: Harper & Row.

Dixon, R. J. (2002). Toward greater authenticity: a case for divergent simulations, *Simulation & Gaming*, Vol. 33, No. 3, pp. 360–66.

Ecke, P. (1999). Trial for Pinchetot: a simulation/game on justice and human rights. *Simulation & Gaming*, Vol. 30, No. 2, pp. 231–37.

Gee, J. P. (2007). *What Video Games Have to Teach us about Learning and Literacy.* New York: Palgrave MacMillan.

Hollins, E. R. (1980). Simulation review: trial lawyer, the jurisprudence game (1977). *Simulation & Games*, Vol. 11, No. 3, pp. 378–79.

Jung, C. S. Y. and Levitin, H. (2002). Using a simulation in an ESL classroom: a descriptive analysis. *Simulation & Gaming*, Vol. 33, No. 3, pp. 367–75.

Kirriemuir, J. and McFarlane, A. (2004). *Literature Review in Games and Learning.* Futurelab series, Bristol: Futurelab.

Knerr, C. R. and Sommerman, A. B. (2000). Undergraduate Appellate Simulation in American Colleges and Universities. *Report Prepared for Presentation at the Annual Meeting of the Southwestern Political Science Association*, Galveston, Texas.

Maharg, P. (2004). Virtual communities on the web: transactional learning and teaching. In Vedder, A., ed. *Aan het Werk met ICT in het Academisch Onderwijs – RechtenOnline*, Rotterdam: Wolf Legal Publishers.

Maharg, P. (2007). *Transforming Legal Education: Learning and Teaching the Law in the Early Twenty-first Century.* Hampshire, UK: Ashgate.

Malone, T. (1981). Toward a theory of intrinsically motivating instruction. *Cognitive Science*, No. 4, pp. 333–69.

Martin, D. S. (1979). Five simulation games in the social sciences. *Simulation & Games*, Vol. 10, No. 3, pp. 331–49.

Migdal S. and Cartwright M. (1997). *Pure electronic delivery of law modules – dream or reality? Journal of Information Law and Technology (JILT)* 1997 (2). Available at http://www2.warwick.ac.uk/fac/soc/law/elj/jilt/1997_2/migdal/. Last accessed 4.5.10.

Migdal, S. and Cartwright, M. (1998). Information technology in the legal curriculum – reaction and realities. *Proceedings of the 13*th *Annual BILETA Conference* (Dublin).

Moodie, P. (1997). Law courseware and Iolis: assessing the present and constructing the future. *The Journal of Information, Law and Technology (JILT)*, 1997 (1). Available at http://www2.warwick.ac.uk/fac/soc/law/elj/jilt/1997_1/moodie/. Last accessed 4.5.10.

Paliwala, A. (1998). Co-operative development of CAL materials: a case study of IOLIS, The *Journal of Information Law and Technology (JILT)* 1998 (3). Available at http://www2.warwick.ac.uk/fac/soc/law/elj/jilt/1998_3/paliwala/. Last accessed 4.5.10.

Prensky, M. (2001). *Digital Games-Based Learning.* New York: McGraw-Hill.

Rachid, M. and Knerr, C. R. (2000). A brief history of Moot Court: Britain and U.S. *Report Prepared for Presentation at the Annual Meeting of the Southwestern Political Science Association,* Galveston, Texas.

Ringel, L. S. (2004). Designing a Moot Court; What to Do, What Not to Do, and Suggestions for How to Do It. *Political Science and Politics,* Vol. 37, pp. 459–65.

Sauvé, L., Renaud, L., Kaufman, D. and Marquis, J. S. (2007). Distinguishing between games and simulations: a systematic review. *Educational Technology & Society,* Vol. 10, No. 3, pp. 247–56.

Squire, K. (2002). Cultural framing of computer/video games. *International Journal of Computer Game Research,* Vol. 2, No. 1. Available at http://www.gamestudies.org/0102/squire/. Last accessed 4.5.10.

Turkle, S. (1995). *Life on the Screen: Identity in the Age of the Internet.* New York: Simon & Schuster.

Van Eck, R. (2007). Building artificially intelligent learning games. In D. Gibson, C. Aldrich and M. Prensky, eds. *Games and Simulation in Online Learning: Research and Development Frameworks,* Hershey, Pennsylvania: Information Science Publishing.

Widdison, R. (1995). Law courseware: Big Bang or Damp Squib? *Web Journal of Current Legal Issues* No. 4. *Available at* http://webjcli.ncl.ac.uk/articles4/widdis4.html. *Last accessed 4.5.10.*

Widdison, R. and Schulte, R. (1998). Quarts into Pint Pots? Electronic law tutorials revisited. *Journal of Information, Law and Technology,* No. 1. Available at http://www2.warwick.ac.uk/fac/soc/law/elj/jilt/1998_1/widdison1/. Last accessed 4.5.10.

Designing Serious Games for Cultural Heritage Purposes

Francesco Bellotti, Riccardo Berta, Alessandro De Gloria,
Giulia Panizza, Matteo Pellegrino and Ludovica Primavera

Chapter Outline

Introduction

Cultural Heritage is of interest to many groups of people, as it concretely represents our background and roots, allowing us to share this with others. Knowing our heritage has important educational and cultural value, and provides a means to better understanding reality and our individual identity. Cultural heritage is also an expression of aesthetics. Exploring and understanding it is a meaningful challenge and an important experience for personal growth and enjoyment. In addition, it is the focus for many business interests, as witnessed by the increasing interest in cultural events and the growth of cultural tourism.

Serious Games (Gee, 2003; Prensky, 2003) can provide useful synergies for the promotion and exploitation of cultural heritage. On the one hand, game technologies are appealing to a wide audience, allowing flexible interactions over distance and time. On the other hand, cultural heritage artefacts can represent a compelling context for adventures and explorations. Moreover, Serious Games represent an opportunity for learning in their ability to engage users, and have the capacity to embed high-quality contextualized information for players. Finally, Serious Games can embed Web 2.0 technologies and tools such as forums, interactive maps, travel recommender and booking systems, instant communication support and conversational digital agents (Conrady, 2007). In this way they can support social networking, community building and collaboration.

Virtual Worlds are already popular among videogamers and wide user communities have already been established around famous Massive Multiplayer Online Games (MMOGs), such as *World of Warcraft*. It is likely that technologies and tools developed for videogames will be used in other application fields. In particular, we expect that next generation websites will feature virtual environments able to provide the user with a more compelling and engaging experience (Brutzman and Daly, 2007).

We are exploring these opportunities and challenges in the context of the 'Travel in Europe' (TiE) project (http://www.tieproject.eu/), which has developed an interactive multimedia platform as an innovative means for the promotion and dissemination of European artistic and cultural heritage (Bellotti et al., 2010). The TiE platform enables multiplayer online Serious Games in which users move in a faithfully reconstructed Virtual Reality environment with live educational and entertainment experiences, interacting among each other, with virtual characters and with virtual representations of the artistic and cultural heritage.

In the TiE project, Serious Games exploit the concept of travel, which is an engaging invitation to knowledge acquisition, and which also exploits geographic contextualization. The 3D reconstructions are of contemporary European cities, in which users are challenged to explore and discover local history, art and customs.

The game relies on the construction of knowledge through the exploration of urban spaces and the manipulation (through the TiE tasks/mini-games) of virtual representations of heritage artefacts. This pedagogical approach is considered as important in order to involve users who may be relatively uninterested in cultural activities but who, on the other hand, are fond of videogames, one of the most popular media nowadays and not only among younger learners.

From a business point of view, the platform intends to meet the ever-growing demand for advanced interactive systems capable of promoting heritage on a significant scale, for example through the internet, but which also retains roots in the local topography and culture. In particular, the platform aims at meeting three major needs from cultural and tourist stakeholders:

- Promotion of a territory. The system can be thought of as an evolution of the current advertising of resorts/regions on TV/magazines/journals.
- Support for geographic- and context-based knowledge acquisition. The exploration of the Virtual World is not purely virtual, but is strictly connected with the real world. The approach intends to support knowledge acquisition and experience and analysis of heritage realia and its history.
- The resulting environments and users' virtual travels are not intended as a substitute for visits to real places. The virtual is used as an invitation to visit the real, as in current TV promos that stimulate the user's desire to visit real places. It should also stimulate users to develop and exploit an effective method to plan ahead for their travels, e.g. by showing the importance of adequate preparation, the aesthetic and affective experiences they may have, together with the realia that can be experienced.This is very useful for regions and destinations that, for various reasons, are not yet popular.

Based on these principles, the TiE platform aims at enabling new kinds of interaction that link a territory with its history and resources. This means using a 3D map and a reconstruction of a territory, for example a city, a region, as the reference system for a pleasant virtual visit of the place, joining contemporary and historical features. This is very similar to a real visit, where the tourist goes through a city, and learns about it and its history, for example by visiting museums. During the exploration, the user can obtain more in-depth information and/or live contextualized experiences, for example videos, games, quizzes, that are embedded in the environment.

This chapter is organized as follows: the next section provides a background on Serious Games for education, while the next presents the conceptual framework proposed for Serious Games devoted to the cultural heritage. Subsequent sections go into the detail of implementation. In the process we discuss the notion of tasks as educational units; our Authoring Toolkit, and a sample implementation of a TiE Serious Game (a treasure hunt across European cities of art). We then summarize the results of a preliminary evaluation, and come to conclusions regarding the work completed to date and future research lines.

Background

Today, with the increasing availability of high-performance PCs and wide-band connections, education can make use of strategies and methodologies typical of video games in order to engage the current generation of learners described as 'digital natives' (Bennett et al., 2008), who 'have become disengaged with traditional instruction. They require multiple streams of information, prefer inductive reasoning, want frequent and quick interactions with content and have exceptional visual literacy skills – characteristics that are all matched well with Digital Game Based Learning' (Van Eck, 2006; Oblinger and Oblinger, 2005; Prensky, 2005).

Serious Virtual Worlds – a specialization of Virtual Worlds (VWs) that are used in training/learning settings (de Freitas, 2008; Prasolova-Førland, 2008) are capturing attention in the education research and practice community, as they offer a unique opportunity for immersive learning (Brown and Hobbs, 2008). The interest is shown by special issues dedicated to the topic by important international journals on education – for example the 'Learning and Teaching in Immersive Virtual Worlds' special issue of the *Association for Learning Technology Journal* (Bell et al., 2008) and the *British Journal of Educational Technology* special issue on the use in higher education of three-dimensional multi-user virtual environments (3-D MUVEs) (Salmon et al., 2009). Concerning cultural heritage and Serious Games, a workshop has been hosted annually for several years (SeGaCH, – International Workshop on Serious Games and Cultural Heritage).

The functionality of a Serious Virtual World should significantly enhance the user's experience of the environment, for example by supporting orientation, providing more detailed information, etc., and should be well integrated in the Serious Games /Virtual Worlds logic and aesthetic. It should not appear as tedious educational add-ons, for the overall environment should be pleasant and stimulating. Some of such functionality has already been presented in the literature and in commercial games and Virtual Worlds. Examples include: *Crystal Island* (Rowe et al., 2007), a narrative-centred learning environment in the domain of microbiology and genetics; *SeaGame* (Bellotti et al., 2009a), which promotes safe behaviours in sea-related activities; *Immune*

Attack (Kelly et al., 2007), a realistic 3D depiction of biological structures to teach Immunology; *JDoc* (Sliney and Murphy, 2008), a junior doctor medical simulator and *OceanQuest* (Parker et al., 2005), which teaches about the biological ecosystem of the ocean floor.

Providing the player with a 'sense of place – typically by the use of photorealistic 3D models, weather effects, surround audio, graspable virtual objects, natural lighting effects, etc. – is important to support the credibility of the learning topic (Cartelli, 2006). In such environments, players can explore the context, acquire information and manipulate objects, practising skills and constructing knowledge (Papert, 1993) in a natural way (Fullerton et al., 2004). Accurate contextualization in realistic 3D settings favours situated learning (Slater et al., 2009). If the player really feels the 'sense of place', his navigation inside the Serious Virtual World is more effective and the information provided more credible. Serious Games and Serious Virtual Worlds thus represent a great opportunity for learning, and it is important that they embed a lot of high-quality contextualized information so that players can learn from their exploration of the world and its realia. A significant issue concerns the risk that players get lost in the knowledge space of the simulated environment. It is known that the difficulty of navigating Virtual Worlds can impede conceptual learning (Whitelock, 1999). Thus, it is important that exploration and information extraction be well supported (Whitelock and Jelfs, 2005). This requires a meaningful, compelling plot and proper guidance, for example through spatial landmarks (Burigat and Chittaro, 2007) in order to guide players through their chosen knowledge paths or – in a more constructivist approach – effectively support them in their free exploration. Moreover, information/notions have to be embedded in the virtual environment by domain-expert authors who are typically not skilled in computer game design. There is thus a need to develop new methodologies and tools to help domain-experts produce content in a simple and effective way.

In particular, there is a need to identify frameworks and models to support content creation for learning in Virtual Worlds (de Freitas, 2009a; Dickey, 2003). The literature already includes proposals for producing guides for tutors about the use of VWs for teaching, like the MyPlan project's final report that contains guidelines for the creation of learning pathways in a lifelong learning context (de Freitas, 2009b). Another field involves supporting the author through graphical tools in the definition of the behaviour of 3D objects as a combination of basic behaviours (Pellens et al., 2008). There are also several case studies of games of various genres for example role playing, real-time strategy, developed ad hoc for teaching purposes (Kelly, 2007). Higher-level tools are needed to support the design from the domain-expert point of view. Approaches in this direction are based on ontologies, in order to move the authoring work from the graphics domain, which is typical of commercial game design, to the cultural domain (Bille et al., 2004; Vanacken et al., 2007). We argue that suitable methodologies are needed for specifying contents to overcome the current practices that are based on ad hoc design (Tutenel et al., 2008).

A conceptual framework for the use of Serious Games in cultural heritage settings

When designing a Serious Game, it is important to consider the expected impact on the users. There are two main issues in this regard. The first is related to entertainment value and enjoyment of use. Serious Games have to be exciting, in order to appeal to a wide audience, including users who are not keen on pursuing cultural activities. The second is related to education: we expect that interaction with cultural heritage improves knowledge and skills, for example the ability to observe pictures, to recognize artistic styles, to understand art/history texts and to make connections between historical events for users.

As a genre Serious Games are well-suited to engaging the learner and encouraging active construction of meaning and development of skills (Gee, 2005). However, a concern is emerging that 'we are just beginning to understand when and how games promote learning, and why' (Johnson, 2005). In particular, there is a need for scientific and engineering methods for the construction of games not only as more realistic simulations of the physical world, but also as a means for providing effective learning experiences (Greitzer et al., 2007). Thus, also in the field of cultural heritage it is necessary to find appropriate ways to enhance the player's educational experience.

Research on cognitive processing – how information is stored, retrieved and represented, (e.g. Atkinson and Shiffrin, 1968; Tulving, 1972) – stresses the importance of helping students to develop well-connected knowledge structures representing relationships among facts and concepts. When the knowledge structure of a topic is well-connected, new information is more readily acquired, since the cognitive load is low (Greitzer et al., 2007). There is a class of Serious Games – the Sand Box Serious Games (SBSGs), with a counterpart also in successful pure entertainment games such as *Grand Theft Auto* and *Oblivion* (Squire, 2008) that tends to support players in building such a knowledge structure. In rough terms, the model consists of:

- a concrete spatial organization – the Virtual World (VW) of the game that the player has to explore, and where knowledge is distributed;
- contextualized tasks, that are distributed in the VW. Tasks are simple challenge/trial activities that embody units of knowledge that can be discovered and accessed by players in order to construct meaning, build long-term memory and/or deepen their understanding of specific item.

This structure is quite simple and schematic. But it represents a format that is very scalable and flexible in terms of content that can be cost-effectively developed by authors, not least when employing a User Generated Content (UGC) perspective (Anderson, 2006). In such Serious Games, players/learners are challenged with tasks that they have to overcome in order to advance in the Virtual World exploration and compete with other players. There is strong motivation for a player to perform better. The simple, easy-to-understand gameplay structure consists of one or more environment-exploration missions within which are sequences of tasks that pose little cognitive overload to the player who can then effectively focus on the game's contents and its interactions. This is further strengthened by the fact that interactions consist of simple templates, for example quizzes, mini-games, conversations with Virtual Humans. Thus, a player can deal with different content that exploits a limited set of interaction modalities, with which he or she can soon acquire familiarity. Moreover, this modular structure offers the possibility of dynamically selecting the most appropriate task sequence based on the player's profile. Of course, it is fundamental that the settings of 3D objects and topographies are similar to those in the real world, in order for the game to be appealing to a wide audience.

From the pedagogical point of view, our work relies upon the Task Based Learning (TBL) theory (Willis, 1996; Willis and Willis, 1996), the theory that has been applied to language teaching (Ellis, 2003), and that highlights the importance of concrete, focused activities to construct knowledge and develop skills. Tasks are activities characterized by an ability to engage the learner's interest, a primary focus on meaning, a need to be completed, an outcome in terms of which the success is judged and a clear relationship with real-world activities (Willis, 1996). The educational relevance of contextualizing mini-games in Serious Games has already been argued in the literature (Frazer et al., 2007), and Bellotti et al. (2010) has shown that embedded quizzes/mini-games are perceived by players as elements that enhance a first person's exploration of a serious game. This allows for better engagement and tests ability levels, giving the learner satisfaction levels similar to video games.

Two issues are fundamental when designing tasks. One is their content. The other one is their delivery strategy, that is, when, where and how they become available or are assigned to the player. In serious applications, this last aspect is key for supporting effective knowledge-building and is usually tackled through author-scripted levels and missions, which can be costly and difficult to scale.

Our proposed framework aims to exploit a large availability of simple units of content, produced according to the UGC trend (Anderson, 2006), as indicated above. Content can be embodied in instances of simple task models, such as mini-games (Bellotti et al., 2008; Bellotti et al., 2010), quizzes, visiting a limited Virtual World zone, interactions with 3D objects or Conversational Virtual Humans that have knowledge about a game area (geographic or conceptual). Tasks are then semantically annotated by the domain-expert pedagogical authors, for example art historians or archaeologists, and then stored in a common repository, so that they can be properly employed in Virtual World environments, for example a city, an archaeological park, etc. A game designer can then select tasks from the repository and make them available for missions inside the Task Pool (TP) of his new Serious Game. The designer also specifies the requirements for the task delivery strategy, that is the criteria according to which tasks are selected from the TP and presented to players in runtime, according to his educational and entertainment objectives. The strategy will be managed in runtime by the Serious Game engine, which performs the gameplay task sequencing based on the author specification.

We do not expect that this approach based on the player's interaction with matching tasks contextualized in a meaningful exploration environment can give an experience comparable to games involving ad hoc authored, compelling narratives. However, the approach provides interesting features, such as:

- Exploration of a space, for example the city constructed as a labyrinth for pursuing cultural activities (Bellotti et al., 2009b), that can be easily differentiated across game sessions. Competition/ collaboration challenges may strongly motivate players to the game and spur knowledge acquisition.

- Domain-independence. The game is domain independent, and can be applied to several different contexts. For instance, a Virtual World with urban landscapes could be employed to teach electronics, foreign languages, cultural heritage. The Virtual World can be continuously enriched with new tasks (also exploiting UGC), without need to change the code.

We have implemented this concept into a concrete operational framework driving the reconstruction of each place, for example a city or several areas inside a city, in the following way. The 3D model is completely geo-referenced. The ground is elevated from a local 3D vectorial map and so, the placement of the buildings in the model is precise. This also allows exploiting synergies with various Geographic Information Systems (GISs). This last point is very important in the current scenario, where the combination of the powers of Web 2.0 technologies for user-generated content with open GIS APIs, for example Google Maps and Microsoft Virtual Earth have made it easier than ever to implement location-based services (Christansen et al., 2007). Some of these services are becoming ever more popular. As a basic implementation, the TiE models now integrate a 2D map interface where the position of the player is shown in real-time on the corresponding real city map.

In each area within the game, a few Point-of-Interests (PoIs) are implemented. These buildings are rigorously reconstructed to a high level of detail. We use this approach for culturally meaningful buildings, for instance, a cathedral, a theatre or a Renaissance palace.

The textures for other places are built dynamically by the TiE system using a statistical template-based algorithm. Since several zones within a city are typically characterized by relatively homogeneous building styles, we exploit a statistical description of the architectonic parameters and build the buildings' virtual models accordingly, using a limited set of parametric building models and textures that are instances of the architectonic features representative of that area. We have implemented this concept through the Style Area (SA) algorithm.

In this way, on the one hand the effort to cover extended urban areas is reasonably manageable. On the other hand, the reconstructed environment allows users live experiences that are visually similar to a real visit to a city, where a visitor typically perceives the feeling of being in a precise place but usually does not perceive/remember the particulars of each distinct building. We refer to this approach as based on an architectonic-style likelihood principle.

Embedding tasks in virtual environments

Task typologies and samples

Tasks are simple, short games that focus players' attention on a particular item that they may find during their free exploration of the Virtual World. Sample tasks are inspired from well-known simple game models, such as *Puzzle*, *MemoryGame*, *FindTheWrongDetails*. The idea, in fact, is that they should be immediate to play, so that the player can focus on the contents rather than on learning how to play. In order to provide consistent and homogeneous interaction modalities that can be quickly and easily learned by the player and then used several times, we have defined a library of task templates. Every task in the Serious Game /Virtual World is an instance of one of such template. We broadly divide task templates into three categories, according to the cognitive skills that they mostly involve (see Table 11.1).

Table 11.2 describes some of the implemented task templates.

A fundamental feature of task templates is that they are parametric. Every task instance is described by an XML configuration file that specifies the values of the parametric features of the instance. The configuration file is prepared by the author through a Graphic User Interface (GUI). Parameters involve contents, that is text, images, difficulty levels, timing that is timing

Table 11.1 Task template categories

Category	Description
Observation tasks	These games privilege sight as a sense to investigate and explore the local environment. In general, these games tend to exploit the 'knowledge in the world' in order to develop cognitive activity (Dickey, 2003; Ducheneaut et al., 2006). They aim to stimulate spatial processing skills. Such skills are important in cognitive development since they allow an individual to create meaning by manipulating visual images (Pillay et al., 1999; Kahana et al., 1999).
Reflection tasks	These games tend to favour reflection, discussion among team members, analysis of questions and possible answers consideration of clues available in the neighbourhood and concepts learned previously during the game.
Arcade tasks	These games stimulate similar skills as observation games. Their specificity lies in the animated graphics and engaging interaction that helps to create a convincing and pleasant experience. They stimulate fantasy and evoke images and atmospheres that can be used to convey educational messages that are easily memorized by players.

Table 11.2 Description of task templates

Name	Description	Cognitive Aspects
Manuscript (Reflection)	Player has to find missing or wrong words in a text document.	Reasoning on text and language; evaluation of alternatives; retrieval of previous knowledge.
Image comprehension (Observation)	Player has to answer several questions related to an image, for example who are the people in the picture? What is the symbolic meaning of a detail/the whole picture? etc.	Observational skills; understanding of images; reflection; analysis of questions and search for possible answers; iconographic analysis (training of the player in the interpretation of a picture and its details).
Contextualized questions over a picture (Observation, Reflection)	The player has to explore an image with a special wand tool. In some areas the wand pop-ups a question related to underlying image details and the player has to answer in a brief time.	Observation skills; understanding of images; attention on details; critical reasoning; speed of reflex; iconological analysis.
Quiz, VisualQuiz (Reflection)	This is a simple multiple-choice list of questions. The question is generally tied with the Virtual World place where it is made. Sample quizzes include: historical quizzes, guessing games, local dialect/language. A version with images instead of written questions/answers is also available (VisualQuiz).	Reflection; analysis of questions and possible answers considering available clues and concepts previously learned; evaluation of alternatives; memory. Critical reasoning.
Wrong or missing details (Observation)	The player has to detect all the details that have been deleted or added to an image.	Analysis of the image; observation of and focus on the details; iconographic analysis.
RightPlace (Reflection, Observation)	The player has to move (by drag-and-dropping) several icons in their right places over a 2D (geographic or conceptual) map.	Observation; critical reasoning; matching; map comprehension.
Puzzle (Observation)	The player has to compose an image (e.g. a façade of a palace) whose elements appear randomly shuffled on the screen. The player may have seen the relevant item during her exploration or may be playing just in front of the 3D model.	Observation skills; memory; ability to identify geometrical patterns; attention on colours and shapes.
Couples (Reflection, Observation)	The player has to match the items in the right column with the ones in the left.	Observation; critical reasoning; matching; image comprehension.
Icon Tetris (Arcade)	Several 'cartooned' icons are subdivided into little squares. Like in the famous Tetris game, squares drop from the ceiling and the player has to rotate and move them in order to compose the original icons on the floor.	Promptness of reaction; observation; image comprehension.

of questions and answers, multimedia look, that is buttons, sounds, fonts, colours.

Important parameters concern the learning mechanisms and are used in the computation of the score, for example time elapsed, number of penalties, number of help requests, and the number of steps/moves to arrive at the solution. For instance, an author may reward precision (number of moves) rather than speed in accomplishing a task, in order to invite players to an accurate – rather than fast – analysis of the issue.

A last point concerns the interaction modalities of players with tasks. While exploring the Virtual World, the player encounters some virtual objects that are linked to tasks. Pointing and clicking on these objects, the player starts a task session. The user interacts with the task through a sort of virtual Smartphone (Figure 11.1). We investigated this solution also in test sessions with young people and teachers using early prototype versions (Bellotti et al., 2008). Results pinpointed that this interaction modality is appreciated by players. This solution has the advantage of maintaining players inside the Virtual World without distracting them with other interfaces.

Figure 11.1 An example of interface design. The player can interact with the task through a virtual smartphone

Dynamic delivery of tasks

Virtual Worlds are 3D settings that lend themselves to different uses by a player: free wandering, competition, training. Our approach proposes to enrich the environment with embedded tasks that can provide more information and that provides analysis/test opportunities for the player. Being instances of templates, tasks can be produced on a large-scale. Thus, authoring tools can be developed to support domain and pedagogical experts to visually create tasks. With a potentially large number of possible embeddable contents/tasks, it becomes important to define strategies for suggesting to the single users appropriate tasks during their exploration of the Virtual World. This requires defining a model of the task, a model of the user and a model of the target learning strategy. Models are implemented as XML files that we have described in detail in a companion paper (Bellotti et al., 2009c). A complete description of the algorithmic details of the teaching strategy model is provided in (Bellotti et al., 2009d).

Authoring support

The designed technological framework consisting of a Virtual World enriched with annotated tasks, generated as instances of software templates, is particularly useful for the efficient production of games and adventures that can be simply configured on top of the framework, for example by selecting 3D areas, instantiating task templates, defining learning strategy requirements. In order to make the authoring accessible to educational experts not familiar with programming, we have developed the Creative Toolkit (CT), which is a visual authoring tool that supports authors in configuring a Virtual World and creating instances of tasks. The Creative Toolkit allows the author to focus on the task itself (upon its annotation), without caring about how it will be used in a Virtual World. This also favours re-use of tasks in different Virtual Worlds.

The Creative Toolkit consists of two main modules, the Task Authoring Tool (TAT) and the World Configuration Tool (WCT), as depicted in Figure 11.2. The whole framework is implemented over the internet, in this way allowing remote authoring and sharing of tasks among different authors and Serious Games. The tool is described in detail in (Bellotti et al., 2010).

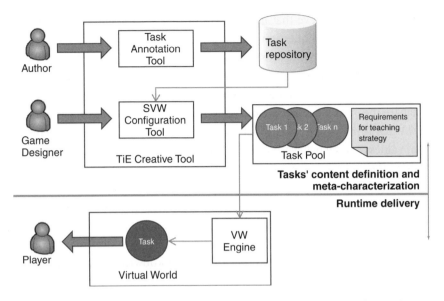

Figure 11.2 The TiE Creative toolkit architecture and overall system workflow from authoring to runtime VW management

Creating content for tasks in a cultural heritage serious game

In the proposed game structure, tasks are seen as a channel to provide content to the players and to test their knowledge. We have instantiated several types of tasks according to the user and task model, that is, different learning style of users and different skill requested in tasks. For instance, some tasks focus on the player's observation skills or critical reasoning, others on the promptness of reaction. The idea is to present content from different perspectives, also according to various authors' pedagogical views and objectives.

Every task is usually associated to a Point-of-Interest (PoI) in the Virtual World, where the task will be available for playing. For instance, contents could touch historical facts happened in that Point-of-Interest or present pieces of heritage preserved there. There is a variety of linking possibilities, but, in any case, a task's contents are usually related to the Virtual World area in which the task is placed, in order to support the player in building a properly geo-referenced mental map of the place.

In general, we believe that it is important that a game author can spur in the player meaningful questions about the city that is the core of the Serious Game, such as what are the most important historical periods and facts? What are the principal monuments and museum? Who are the most famous artists and personages that worked or lived here? What are the traditional customs? What are the opinions, attitudes or collective view of the people inhabiting the city? What is important for the local people? What is meaningful for them? In what values do they believe? What are the real motivations for their activities? How do they reveal them?

The tasks have to express these concepts, so that they become known to the players. Notions, for example dates, personages are important of course since they give concrete and clear structures upon which a player can build knowledge about the place. Some tasks have to support a smart investigation of the heritage and the territory, while other should test knowledge/skill acquisition. So, for every Point-of-Interest, we advocate that authors should develop some 'exploration' tasks, where players build their knowledge, and some test tasks, where acquisition is tested. Summative tests can also be performed in special checking points, such as the end of a game level, or the game's grand finale.

The Creative Toolkit supports authors in an easy visual configuration of Task Template instances. Task configuration involves on the one hand specifying the parameters of the Task Model that are useful for the runtime system to select and schedule the most appropriate tasks according to the current profile and the author's specifications. On the other hand Task configuration is also useful in creating the contents for the task. Some content are specific to the given task typology, for example image and levels for a Puzzle, questions and images for a VisualQuiz, etc. Others are generic and apply to all the typologies. These include: subject, title, description and general information about the task. This text may be used by the player to get more in-depth information; and automatically by the system to select tasks for a theme and/or identify links among the tasks. The text can include introduction, a statement (5–15 words) that appears before the start of the task to invite the player to play the task/game, for example why the featured item is important, why it is curious, and suchlike. The text has to be intriguing and create suspense and expectation: The text can also include a conclusion – 5–30 words to be shown at the end of the task. Here the idea is to complement the learning practice activity that a player has done within the task with plain text that should explain the key concept(s) that have been used in the task. Finally, text can include keywords (fixed and free) used by the system for selection of the task, historical period, stylistic/art school or author.

Top-down approach to content development

In the following, we provide an example of the procedure we suggest for developing content for a cultural context. We propose a Top-Down approach, starting from a city-level analysis where content developers define the main features of the area. The choice of the Points-of-Interest to be featured, and the tasks to be implemented comes as a consequence, and familiarizes players with the most important factors of the local culture.

The first step consists of preparing a table reporting the most important features of the city. Descriptions are structured along dimensions, such as geography, history, economy, popular traditions, art and literature and architecture. Once the major topics have been outlined, then it is necessary to identify what areas in the city are appropriate to convey the proposed content. By doing this, game authors focus the player experience in a limited set of relevant areas. For each area, a description is required, and the main reasons for interest that will have to be covered by its Points-of-Interest and relevant tasks.

For each area, the Points-of-Interest have to be selected. These may include interesting monuments such as churches, museums, parks, etc. for which descriptions are required, specifying reasons why the object is of interest. These will be guidelines for the definition of the tasks that will have to be developed for that Point-of-Interest. Finally, for every task, the author will have to specify its typology, also stating the reason why that typology is suited and prepare short introduction and conclusion texts that will be displayed to the player. The introduction serves to invite the player to the task, stimulating curiosity. The conclusion should help the player to focus on the most important aspects of the topics dealt with in the task.

Serious game example: Travel in Europe – a treasure hunt discovering the European heritage

The TiE platform has been designed as a flexible and extensible technological framework that can be used to implement a number of Serious Game applications with different types of contents. This architecture aims at supporting the project's long-term idea of having a European map with an ever-growing number of cities. The project has developed the following structure: Serious Game engine, Task templates, artificial intelligence for task-delivery strategy, the authoring tools (the Creative Toolkit) and deployed significant city examples from several participating European Union countries in the

Figure 11.3 Snapshots from the TiE 3D reconstruction of Genoa and Prague

project including Genoa, Strasbourg, Prague, Cluj, Maribor, Plovdiv, Tomar, Arousa Norte. After that, we aim at creating a community of users and educators that will be able to continuously increase the database of the system.

The first instantiation of the TiE environment is a game that takes the form of a cultural treasure hunt across Europe. Figure 11.3 shows two snapshots from the Genoa and Prague reconstructions.

In the basic game that we have implemented, the player has to visit a fixed number of cities, and in each town accomplish a mission. A mission is characterized by a number of general questions, which the player should consider while exploring the city. In order to answer these questions, the player's avatar explores the faithfully reconstructed urban environments in search of the places indicated in the mission. At each target place, the player looks for 3D icons linked to Points-of-Interest, such as important palaces and churches. These trigger task sessions in which the user can virtually manipulate pieces of the artistic heritage and face quizzes concerning the history, art and culture of that particular Point-of-Interest. Each task is selected by the Serious Game engine by matching the user model and the task models according to the defined pedagogical strategy. During the visit, the player freely chooses where to go, so orientation in the city and navigation are major challenges: the city really is a sort of labyrinth. Strategy has to be employed by the player in order to plan the path for all the destinations to be reached. Figure 11.4 shows two tasks about the façade of Palazzo Ducale played in front of the virtual reconstruction of the building. Accomplishment of a mission is verified at the end of the city exploration. There is a city-level final assessment with a sort of millionaire game on the city with quizzes that are related to the mission. Accomplishment of a mission rewards the player with a city-prize, for example a picture, a symbol, that can be conserved in the player's repository.

Figure 11.4 Snapshots of two tasks about Genoa's Palazzo Ducale

Figure 11.5 The reconstruction of two Pols

With regard to the 3D settings, we show the example of the Genoa historical city centre, which is one of the largest medieval urban centres in Europe. It consists of around 1,000m², with around 100 buildings. Buildings are thin and tall, separated by narrow pedestrian streets, namely 'Carruggi'. They show typically homogeneous features that we could efficiently model and process through the TiE likelihood algorithm. Inside the historical city, there is Strada Nuova, an area that contains outstanding palaces from the Renaissance and Baroque age, when Genoese bankers played a key role in the European financial scene. Strada Nuova was designed as the representative quarters for such families. Given their outstanding artistic and architectural value, these palaces are implemented as Points-of-Interest. Figure 11.5 represents the reconstruction of 'Palazzo Rosso', an important museum in Strada Nuova and 'Palazzo Tursi' the prestigious seat of the municipality of Genoa.

Evaluation

The structure of the TiE Serious Game is, in effect, a sequence of contextualized tasks performed in faithfully reconstructed 3D settings. The high-level plot we have built as a first option is a treasure hunt game, which is quite simple and schematic. But it represents a format that is scalable and flexible in terms of content that can be cost-effectively developed by third parties and also in a User Generated Content (UGC) perspective, for example with a software toolkit that supports easy visual creation of instances from task templates. Teachers/experts can have full control over it by simply specifying the tasks available in every city. This is easily supported by the Creative Toolkit. We have also built a simple, easy-to-understand structure coupled with mini-games created as instances of templates whose interaction modalities can be easily learned by a player and applied in several different content cases, and which poses little overload to the player, who can effectively focus his attention on the content and the context. Of course, it is important that the 3D settings, game mechanics and interactions modalities are similar to those of state-of-the-art games, in order to be appealing to players.

There is the risk that the player may experience this Serious Game as disjointed, since the author is not required to specify a complete narrative. However, SandBoxGames are successful on the market, where players build their own narrative experiences by interacting with contextualized situations and mini-adventures during a geographic exploration of a wide environment. The game author specifies such situations and specifies the game's general rewards/competition mechanisms, not the details of the plot. According to user tests, introducing tasks in *SeaGame* has led to player satisfaction levels not statistically different to those of state-of-the-art videogames (Bellotti et al., 2009a). We have not made tests to verify knowledge acquisition yet, as we would like to verify long-term effects as well. However, it is important that the developed games are able to attract users, in a way similar to commercial videogames, even if they deal with educational topics. This is an important target of educational games that aim at extending learning opportunities, particularly in attracting a demographic traditionally averse to pursuing cultural activities.

Conclusions

The dissemination of online virtual environments and related technologies is likely to open new important opportunities to enhance cultural tourism and new modalities of knowledge and interaction with virtual representations of the cultural heritage, given the possibility of creating compelling virtual adventures set in the context of artistic and natural places of interest. We are exploring these challenges and developing tools to build enriched virtual environments where the player can explore faithfully reconstructed places and live information-rich, contextualized experiences. The whole should be perceived as a compelling, exciting and culturally meaningful story/adventure in which the player can become familiar with items available to players in the territory of the game. Moreover, by embedding mini-games inside a 3D world exploration, we can realize something like the 'digital analogy' of a real visit to a city/region which is typically enhanced by visits to museums, galleries, churches and other important buildings and/or memory places, which is the traditional way through which a number of people, from general tourists to specialist scholars, have elevated their spirit by appreciating foreign artefacts, habits and people, and developing knowledge about history, art and geography – in other words, by discovering the world.

Discovery and appreciation of the cultural heritage has much to do with education and learning. Serious Games represent a great opportunity for learning and should embed high-quality contextualized information so that the players can benefit from explorations of the virtual environment. This requires defining new methodologies and tools for effective production. To this end, we have abstracted a conceptual framework relying on the Task-Based Learning theory. The model defines games set in realistic Virtual Worlds enriched with embedded educational tasks. The model involves pedagogical task annotation, which allows decoupling the tasks, which can then be re-used in different Serious Games, from the definition of their delivery strategy in the context of a specific Serious Game. This strategy is specified by the Serious Game designer and automatically managed by the runtime game engine. This approach simplifies the authoring work that can be easily supported by a visual authoring tool. The Creative Toolkit we have developed is being used by the fifteen TiE project partners for producing tasks for their reconstructed cities. We have collected early feedback from TiE partners through a questionnaire on their use of the Creative Toolkit. Results show a general appreciation of its effectiveness, efficiency and ease of use, that are the three dimensions of usability, according to ISO 9241 definition. Partners who are generally cultural experts without programming skills complained about technical problems, such as the stability of the program, in particular when doing the upload to the central database, inadequate feedback, for example on which Points-of-Interest/tasks are completed and which not, and lack of help and documentation. Video tutorials, for instance, were appreciated but considered as insufficient to deal with the variety of issues to be managed. However, they report that the structure allows clear organization of material, thanks to the exploitation of the Points-of-Interest as points of reference in the space of the resources. This way of collecting and structuring material around clearly defined, simple focus points is considered similar to the mind maps concept and can thus be applied to different domains other than cultural heritage. Partners also appreciated the structure and the standardization of the metadata for the multimedia objects. However some of them observed that they had difficulty in understanding structure and the, at times, lack of flexibility, for example in adding new categories/dimensions. Besides the TiE partnership membership, the Toolkit has been distributed to some high schools in the Genoa area, so that students and teachers are involved in the content production process as well. This is considered to have an important educational value, since it spurs students to study material and organize it in a way that is useful for peer-learning.

The experience and tools and methodologies developed in TiE have further opened important research questions and perspectives. Most important, we need extensive user testing in order to assess and analyse the support of the proposed framework for effective learning in an entertainment context. Next, we have to provide a standardized interface to support interoperability of the Serious Game framework with Learning Objects (Hodgins, 2000), that are widely used in current Learning Management Systems (LMSs). Finally, we intend to extend the simulation functionalities of the framework in the direction of a living world, with Non-Player Characters (NPCs) equipped with Artificial Intelligence capabilities and characterized by proper psychological features and cultural behaviours.

References

Anderson, C. (2006). *The Long Tail. How Endless Choice is Creating Unlimited Demand.* New York: Random House Business Books.

Atkinson R. C. and Shiffrin, R. M. (1968). Human memory: a proposed system and its control processes, in K. W. Spence and J. T. Spence, eds. *The Psychology of Learning and Motivation: Advances in Research and Theory* (vol. 2). pp. 89–195. New York: Academic Press.

Bell, F., Savin-Baden, M. and Ward, R. (2008). Editorial, learning and teaching in immersive virtual worlds, Special Issue. *ALT-J Research in Learning Technology*, Vol. 16, No. 3. pp 137–38.

Bellotti, F., Berta, R., De Gloria, A. and Zappi, V. (2008). Exploring gaming mechanisms to enhance knowledge acquisition in virtual worlds. *Proceedings of the 3rd International Conference on Digital Interactive Media in Entertainment and Arts (DIMEA 2008)*, Athens, Greece.

Bellotti, F., Berta, R., De Gloria, A. and Primavera, L. (2009). Adaptive experience engine for serious games. *IEEE Transactions on Computational Intelligence and AI in Games*, Vol. 1, No. 4, 2009, pp. 264–80.

Bellotti, F., Berta, R., De Gloria, A. and Primavera, L. (2009a). Enhancing the educational value of videogames. *ACM Computers in Entertainment*, Vol. 7, No. 2. pp. 23–41.

Bellotti, F., Berta, R., De Gloria, A.and Primavera, L. (2009b). A task annotation model for SandBox Serious Games. *Proceedings of IEEE Symposium on Computational Intelligence and Games (CIG 2009)*, pp. 233–240, 7–10 September 2009, Milano, Italy.

Bellotti, F., Berta, R., De Gloria, A. and Primavera, L. (2010). Travel in Europe: an online game environment to promote and divulgate European heritage. In N. Sharda, ed. *Visual Travel Recommender Systems, Social Communities and User Interface Design*. Hershey: IGI Global.

Bellotti F., Berta R., De Gloria A. and Primavera L. (2010). Supporting authors in the development of Task-Based Learning in Serious Virtual Worlds. *British Journal of Education and Technologies*, Vol. 41, No. 1, pp. 86–107.

Bennett, S., Maton, K. and Kervin, L. (2008). The 'Digital Natives' Debate: a critical review of the evidence. *British Journal of Educational Technology*, Vol. 39 No. 5, pp. 775–86.

Bille, W., Pellens, B., Kleinermann, F. and De Troyer, O. (2004). Intelligent modelling of virtual worlds using domain ontologies. *Proceedings of the Workshop of Intelligent Computing (WIC)*, pp. 272–79, Mexico City, Mexico.

Blizzard Entertainment – World of Warcraft: http://www.worldofwarcraft.com

Brown, E. and Hobbs, M. (2008). Second Life as a holistic learning environment for problem-based learning and transferable skills. Paper delivered at *ReLIVE08* Conference, The Open University, Milton Keynes, 20–21 November.

Brutzman D. and Daly L. (2007). *X3D: Extensible 3D Graphics for Web Authors*. New York: Morgan Kaufmann Publishers.

Burigat, S. and Chittaro, L. (2007). Navigation in 3D virtual environments: effects of user experience and location-pointing navigation aids. *International Journal of Human-Computer Studies*, Vol. 65, No. 11, pp. 945–58.

Cartelli, A. (2006). *Teaching in the Knowledge Society: New Skills and Instruments for Teachers*. Hershey: Idea Group Inc (IGI).

Christensen, C. M., Kjeldskov, J. and Rasmussen, K. K. (2007). GeoHealth: a location-based service for nomadic home healthcare workers. *Proceedings of OzCHI 2007*, pp. 273–81, Adelaide, Australia, 28–30 November 2007, ACM and CHISIG.

Conrady, R. (2007). Travel technology in the era of Web 2.0 in R. Conrady and M. Buck, eds. *Trends and Issues in Global Tourism*, New York: Springer, pp. 165–84.

de Freitas, S. (2008). *Serious Virtual Worlds: A Scoping Study*. Bristol: JISC.

de Freitas, S. and Neumann, T. (2009). The use of 'exploratory learning' for supporting immersive learning in virtual environments. *Computers & Education*, Vol. 52, No. 2, pp. 343–52.

de Freitas, S., Rebolledo-Mendez, G., Liarokapis, F., Magoulas, G. and Poulovassilis, A., (2009). Developing an evaluation methodology for immersive learning experiences in a virtual world. *Proceedings of Conference in Games and Virtual Worlds for Serious Applications*, pp. 43–50, Coventry, UK.

Dickey, M. D. (2003). Teaching in 3D: pedagogical affordances and constraints of 3D virtual worlds for synchronous distance learning. *Distance Education*, Vol. 24, pp. 105–21.

Ducheneaut, N., Yee, N., Nickell, E. and Moore, R. J. (2006). 'Alone together?': exploring the social dynamics of massively multiplayer online games. In *Proceedings of the SIGCHI Conference on Human Factors in Computing Systems (CHI 2006)*, 407–16 Montréal, Québec, Canada.

Ellis, R. (2003). *Task-based Language Learning and Teaching*. New York: Oxford University Press.

Frazer, A., Argles, D. and Wills, G. (2007). Is Less Actually More? The usefulness of educational mini-game. *Proceedings of the IEEE International Conference on Advanced Learning Technologies*, pp. 533–37.

Fullerton, T., Swain, C. and Hoffman, S. (2004). *Game Design Workshop. Designing, Prototyping and Playtesting Games*. CMP Books: San Francisco, CA.

Gee, J. P. (2003). *What Video Games Have to Teach Us about Learning and Literacy*. New York: Palgrave Macmillan.

Gee, J. P. (2005). How would a state of the art instructional video game look like? *Innovate Journal of Online Education*, Vol. 1, No. 6.

Greitzer, F. L., Kuchar, O. A. and Huston, K. (2007). Cognitive science implications for enhancing training effectiveness in a serious gaming context, *ACM J. Educational Resources in Computing*, Vol. 7, No. 3, pp. 2–18.

Hodgins, H. W. (2000). 'The future of learning objects', in D. A. Wiley, ed. *The Instructional Use of Learning Objects*. Bloomington: Agency for Instructional technology, pp. 281–98.

Johnson, W. L. (2005). Lessons learned from games for education. In *Proceedings of the ACM SIGGRAPH 2005 Educators Program*, Panel session, Los Angeles (Ca), USA.

Kahana, M., Sekuler, R., Caplan, J., Kirschen, M. and Madsen, J. (1999). Human theta oscillations exhibit task dependence during virtual maze navigation. *Nature*, Vol. 399, pp. 781–84.

Kelly, H., Howell, K., Glinert, E., Holding, L., Swain, C., Burrowbridge, A. and Roper, M. (2007). How to build serious games. *Communications of the ACM*, Vol. 50, Issue 7, pp. 44–49.

Kolb, A. J. and Kolb, D. A. (2005). Learning styles and learning spaces: enhancing experiential learning in higher education. *Academy of Management Learning & Education*. Vol. 4, No. 2, pp. 193–212.

Oblinger, D. and Oblinger, J. (2005). Is it age or IT: first steps toward understanding the net generation, in D. G. Oblinger and J. L. Oblinger, eds. *Educating the Net Generation*. Boulder, COL: EDUCAUSE, 2005. Available at http://www.educause.edu/educatingthenetgen

Papert, S. (1993). Situating constructionism, in Harel INITIAL and Papert, S. eds. *Constructionism.*: Norwood, NJ: Ablex Publishing Corporation.

Parker, J. R., Chan, S. and Howell, J. (2005). OceanQuest: a university-based serious game project. *Proceedings of the Digital Games Research Association Conference (DiGRA) Vancouver, BC*.

Pillay, H., Brownlee, J. and Wilss, L. (1999). Cognition and recreational computer games: implications for educational technology. *Journal of Research on Computing in Education*, Vol. 32, No. 1, pp. 203–216.

Prasolova-Førland, E. (2008). Analyzing place metaphors in 3D educational collaborative virtual environments. *Computers in Human Behavior*, Vol. 24, No. 2, pp. 185–204.

Prensky, M. (2003). Digital game-based learning. In *ACM Computers in Entertainment*, Vol. 1, No. 1, pp. 21–25.

Prensky, M. (2005). 'Engage me or enrage me': what today's learners demand. *EDUCAUSE Review*, Vol. 40, No. 5, pp. 60–65 Available at http://www.educause.edu/er/erm05/erm0553.asp. Last accessed 28.4.10.

Rowe, J. P., Mcquiggan, S. W., Mott, B. W. and Lester, J. C. (2007). Motivation in narrative-centered learning environments. *Proceedings of the Workshop on Narrative Learning Environments*, 13th AIED Conference, pp. 40–49, Marina del Rey, CA.

Salmon, G. and Hawkridge, D. (2009). Editorial: out of this world, *British Journal of Educational Technology*, Vol. 40, No. 3, pp. 401–13.

Slater, M., Khanna, P., Mortensen, J. and Yu, I. (2009). Visual realism enhances realistic response in an immersive virtual environment. *IEEE Computer Graphics and Applications*, Vol. 29, No. 3, pp. 76–84.

Sliney, A. and Murphy, D. (2005). JDoc: A Serious Game for Medical Learning. *Proceedings of the International Conference on Advances in Computer-Human Interaction*, pp. 131–36.

Squire, K. (2008). Open-ended video games: a model for developing learning for the interactive age. In *The Ecology of Games: Connecting Youth, Games, and Learning*, K. Salen, ed. Cambridge, MA: MIT Press, pp. 167–98.

Tulving, E. and Donaldson, W., eds. (1972), *Organization of Memory*. New York: Academic Press.

Tutenel, T., Bidarra, R., Smelik, R. M. and De Kraker, K. J. (2008). The role of semantics in games and simulations. *ACM Computers in Entertainment (CIE)*. Vol. 6. No. 4 http://portal.acm.org/citation.cfm?id=1462009&jmp=cit&coll=GUIDE&dl=GUIDE&CFID=100753121&CFTOKEN=2016130CIT. Last accessed 29/7/10. Vanacken, L., Raymaekers, C. and Coninx, K. (2007). Introducing semantic information during conceptual modelling of interaction for virtual environments. *In Proceedings of the 2007 Workshop on Multimodal Interfaces in Semantic Interaction*. Nagoya, Japan, November, pp. 15–15.

Van Eck, R. (2006). Digital Game-Based Learning: it's not just the digital natives who are restless. *EDUCAUSE Review*, v41 n2, pp. 16–30.

Whitelock, D. (1999). Investigating the role of task structure and interface support in virtual learning environments. *International Journal Continuing Engineering Education and Lifelong Learning*, Special Issue on Microworlds for Education and Learning. Guest Editors Darina Dicheva and Piet A. M. Kommers, Vol. 9, Nos. 3/4, pp. 291–301.

Whitelock, D. and Jelfs, A. (2005). Would you rather collect data in the rain or attend a virtual field trip? Findings from a series of virtual science field studies. In Constantinou, C. P, Zacharia, Z. C. and Kommers, P. A. M., eds. The Role of Information and Communication Technology in Science Teaching and Learning. Special Issue of the *International Journal of Continuing Engineering Education and LifeLong Learning*, Vol. 15, No.1/2, pp. 121–31.

Willis, J. (1996). *A Framework for Task-based Learning*. Harlow, U.K.: Longman Addison- Wesley.

Willis, J. and Willis, D. (1996). eds. *Challenge and Change in Language Teaching*. Oxford: Heinemann ELT.

Index

Page numbers in **bold** denote figures and tables.